Cultivating
Ecologies
for Digital
Media Work

CULTIVATING ECOLOGIES FOR DIGITAL MEDIA WORK

The Case of English Studies

Catherine C. Braun

Southern Illinois University Press | Carbondale

17   16   15   14   4   3   2   1

Library of Congress Cataloging-in-Publication Data
Braun, Catherine C.
Cultivating ecologies for digital media work : the case
of English studies / Catherine C. Braun.
  pages   cm
Includes bibliographical references and index.
  ISBN-13: 978-0-8093-3296-0 (pbk.)
  ISBN-10: 0-8093-3296-5 (paperback)
  ISBN-13: 978-0-8093-3297-7 (ebook)
1. English language—Rhetoric—Computer-assisted
instruction. 2. English language—Rhetoric—Study
and teaching. 3. Report writing—Computer-assisted
instruction. 4. Report writing—Study and teaching.
5. Electronic portfolios in education. 6. Scholarly electronic publishing. 7. Hypertext systems. I. Title.
PE1404.B696 2014
808'.0420785—dc23   201320378

For Chris

Contents

Tables

Acknowledgments

In English studies, we like to valorize the solitary scholar, but we all know that no author writes in isolation. My writing and thinking have been shaped by the institutions in which I work and by the communities of scholars with whom I am fortunate to work. This book would not have been possible without their continuing support and critique and without the generous participation of faculty and graduate students at my three research sites. Thank you to everybody for taking time out of your schedules to talk to me, for answering my questions candidly, and for allowing me into your classrooms. I will be forever grateful.

My deepest gratitude and thanks go to H. Lewis Ulman, whose mentoring has helped me immeasurably from the earliest stages of this project. Even after I was no longer a graduate student and his advisee, he was always willing to read anything, no matter how rough, and to provide extensive comments. He always seemed to know exactly the kind of feedback I needed to move my thinking and writing into the next stage, even when I didn't know myself. I am likewise thankful to the many friends and colleagues who read drafts (sometimes rereading chapters several times), helping me to shape and hone my arguments: Scott Lloyd DeWitt, Beverly J. Moss, Cynthia L. Selfe, Marcia Dickson, Cheryl E. Ball, Sara Webb-Sunderhaus, Jason Palmeri, Kristine Blair, and the anonymous peer reviewer. Thank you, Lynda Behan, for listening to me talk through ideas before they were fully formed and for asking lots of questions to help me figure out exactly what it was I was trying to say. Stuart Lishan, thank you for always encouraging me and fighting for me.

Besides the many individuals who have supported and encouraged me in the writing of this book, I have also received much institutional support. I am deeply grateful to the development office at the Ohio State University at Marion for a generous award for subvention funding. I would also like to thank the College of the Arts and Sciences at OSU, whose subvention program matched that funding. OSU also granted me several course releases and a quarter's research leave, which were invaluable in allowing me to make progress on the manuscript.

Throughout this process, my nonacademic friends and my Marion campus colleagues (many of whom have become good friends) have been like an oasis in the desert. When things seemed bleak, you made me laugh, you helped me to de-stress, you made me focus on something other than work, and you put things into perspective. Thank you.

Finally, I am grateful for my family, whose support and love keep me going. Chris Manion, in particular, deserves an award for reading the manuscript as many times as he did, for always encouraging me, for believing in me and picking me up when I thought I would never finish, and, most important, for keeping me fed with delicious meals. Oh, and for getting me to laugh, often and especially at myself. I believe he learned this delicate skill from his keen observation of my parents, who never let me take myself or anything else too seriously (unless it is something *really* important, such as analyzing the most recent episode of *Castle* or *Dancing with the Stars*, or lamenting the misquoting of a Cole Porter lyric or a bit of dialogue from a classic Hollywood movie). Thank you for keeping me grounded and for helping me remember what is truly important in life.

Cultivating
Ecologies
for Digital
Media Work

Introduction: Institutional Frameworks and "the Risky Thing" of Digital Scholarship and Teaching

> We are talking about a shift in the institutional structures of the profession. And, senior scholars, this is not something that is *happening to you*. You are, after all, the ones on the hiring and t&p committees. It is a thing you are making—through choices that you make, and through choices that you decline to make.
> —Natalia Cecire

In May 2012, the University of Missouri announced that it would be "phasing out" its university press and recovering the $400,000 per year subsidy. In July, amid criticism of the decision to close the press, the university announced plans to reinvent the press in a new form that would be

> exploring dramatically new models for scholarly communication, building on its strengths in journalism, library science, information technology, the libraries, and its broad emphasis on media of the future. . . . Much editorial work would be done by students who would work under supervision of faculty to prepare for careers in scholarly communication in the new media world. Utilizing a new business model, publications could include much more than text, such as simulations, audio, and other elements. ("UM System" n. pag.)

The closure and subsequent revamping of the press was merely one in a string of university press shutdowns over the past several years because of financial concerns, which some tie to diminishing state support for higher education. Several other presses had previously come close to closure but were saved (most notably Louisiana State University Press) or suspended for a time and reconstituted (such as Southern Methodist University Press). After a very public backlash from authors who had published with the University of Missouri Press and from the scholarly community, including a Facebook page protesting the changes, the university announced in August that it would not close the press after all but would continue it as a smaller operation administered by the Columbia campus rather than by the university system. In October, the press rehired its editor in chief, Clair Willcox, who then faced the daunting task of trying to woo back authors who had asked for the return of their publishing rights and taken their works elsewhere and also staff members who had found other jobs (Silvey n. pag.; Eligon n. pag.; Monaghan, "Clair Willcox" n. pag.).

The decision to close and then to revamp the press, not surprisingly, drew a great deal of criticism, some of which was leveled at the plan to recreate the press in a digital and multimedia format. As Frank Donoghue notes, citing several historical precedents, "digital publication is not a panacea for university presses" ("Consequences" n. pag.), though it often emerges as a potential solution to the monetary costs of operating them, given that most find it difficult to sustain themselves without subsidies from their respective universities or state governments. As several critics point out, it takes much human labor to publish a scholarly work, in print or digitally. Bruce Joshua Miller, a principal in Miller Trade Book Marketing and organizer of a Facebook page protesting the closure of the University of Missouri Press, calls arguments for technological fixes "seductive," saying, "People always like to think that problems can be solved with technology. One day you'll just press a button. But that doesn't work. People are going to find out with respect to scholarly publishing that you have to have a scholarly process that costs money" (qtd. in Monaghan, "Critics Attack" n. pag.). Certainly, this is true. The construction of digital media methods as efficiencies and money-saving strategies is problematic; yet, it does not mean that the profession should altogether eschew digital media models for reimagining a sustainable future for scholarly publishing.

What intrigues me most in the debate over the closing of the presses is that the subtext of many of these arguments pits digital and print forms of scholarship as opposing forces in a war of textuality. For instance, Douglas Armato, director of the University of Minnesota Press, who has often worked with the Association of American University Presses to help figure out how to save threatened presses, says, "The digital environment is not the first challenge university presses have faced and emerged from stronger than when we went in. . . . Missouri is an awfully significant university, and an awfully large state, to be without a press" (qtd. in Howard n. pag.). He and many others see digital publishing as a challenge to traditional publishing. I suppose in a certain sense it is; fewer university presses means fewer books—especially scholarly monographs—printed on paper. However, digital media work is not necessarily a challenge to scholarly publication and communication broadly conceived.

For better or worse, we are faced with a rhetorical context in which money is the bottom line. Those who make budgeting decisions want university presses to recover their costs, which is often difficult, partly because so many of the monographs published by these presses are written by untenured faculty in incredibly specialized fields in order to get tenure. Donoghue addressed this reality in a recent blog post:

> University presses have been an essential component of research institutions since the founding of Johns Hopkins, venues where scholarly knowledge could be dispersed to an admittedly small but . . . intellectually interested community. It is, I admit, hard to imagine major universities without presses. But one has to at least consider: Have those various intellectual communities become too splintered, specialized and small? Have the monographs that university presses produce become so costly that individual scholars can't purchase them? And, thus, have university presses outlived their time? ("Consequences" n. pag.)

If the answer to that question is yes, then digital solutions emerge not so much as a problematic efficiency but as a rethinking of humanities-based scholarly communication in order to keep it vital and to advance knowledge in the face of our new rhetorical and media context. As Peter Brantley writes, "While closing UPs might, on one hand, mean a diminution of the number of outlets for scholarly work, it could just as easily be a more positive bellwether for a healthy shift in emphasis from one model of scholarly publishing to another" (n. pag.). With so much of the focus on the medium and form of publication, the values undergirding scholarly communication often seem to get lost. Several presses, however, are exploring new approaches to scholarly access and publication, shifting the medium in which they distribute works but not stopping scholarly output.

Utah State University Press (in collaboration with the University of Illinois at Urbana-Champaign, the Ohio State University, Miami University, Illinois Institute of Technology, and the Institute for the Future of the Book), for instance, now has an online, open-access, peer-reviewed digital imprint, the Computers and Composition Digital Press, which publishes book-scope projects in a variety of media and makes them available at no charge. According to the CCDP's mission statement,

> The goal of the Press is to honor the traditional academic values of rigorous peer review and intellectual excellence, but also to combine such work with a commitment to innovative digital scholarship and expression. For the Editors, the Press represents an important kind of scholarly activism—an effort to circulate the best work of digital media scholars in a timely fashion and on the global scale made possible by digital distribution. (*Computers and Composition Digital Press* n. pag.)

In addition, the press has several digital initiatives, including Digital Commons@USU, an institutional repository that is coordinated by the campus's library that "provides open access to scholarly works, research, reports, publications, and courses produced by Utah State University faculty, staff, students, and others" (*Digital Commons@USU* n. pag.). Many of these initiatives represent a collaboration between the press and the library, a new trend in thinking about how scholarly communication can be sustained using new administrative and cost-sharing models, not to mention digital technologies.

A similar collaboration can be seen at the University of Michigan, where the university's press and MPublishing have partnered with the Sweetland Center for Writing on the Digital Rhetoric Collaborative. MPublishing is the primary publishing operation at the university and is housed in the university's library (the traditional press morphed into MPublishing in 2009 when it combined with the library and shifted most monograph publishing to digital formats). According to Naomi Silver, the first dimension of the collaborative is "a book series that will publish born-digital and digitally enhanced texts focused on the intersections between technologies and communications (teaching, writing, reading) and the social, aesthetic and political contexts where these occur" (n. pag.). There is a second dimension to the collaborative, as well, which is "a community Web space by and for scholars and teachers working in computers and writing and digital rhetoric" (Silver n. pag.).

All of these innovative publishing initiatives have clearly articulated goals and missions that honor the values of traditional scholarly publication in the humanities (such as peer review, intellectual excellence, and knowledge making) and the function of publishing (to disseminate scholarship to as broad an audience as possible) while also responding to new digital contexts and new means of advancing knowledge. It is these questions about the values we share and the functions of producing and disseminating scholarship that should guide our discussions and decisions, rather than arguments about which medium is best. Addressing such questions will likely be difficult and take many faculty out of their comfort zones, but it is imperative that we proactively address such questions lest the top-down power structure that is emerging ever stronger at many universities foist its model of scholarly production onto us. Such models often have efficiency and cost-savings at their core. The pushing of such "efficiencies" (that is, the corporatization of the university) is changing the nature of the work professors do, and many are having a hard time either reconceptualizing or rearticulating their work to fit with the ways different institutions define their work. At the same time, these institutions that they hold dear (such as university presses, peer review, 2–2 teaching loads) are changing radically beneath them, often from the top down with minimal faculty input and often because of economic conditions.

Digital media work often emerges as a solution to the problem or as an efficiency that is problematic, when it can be better conceived as a site to reconceptualize the work of scholarship and teaching. In this book, I seek to demonstrate the ways that digital media teaching and scholarship afford the discipline the opportunity to fundamentally reevaluate central questions about texts, reading, and composing in ways that help keep the field vital. We should be constantly probing these questions anyway, whether or not the "digital media turn" asks us to reevaluate them. Although some departments have begun trying to accommodate digital media work, they often do so in a haphazard manner, either making minor tweaks to tenure and promotion policies or paying lip service to digital media work rather than addressing difficult questions about the relationships between our core disciplinary values, our institutionalized reward structures, and the media of our work. As a result, individuals who are invested in digital media teaching and scholarship must negotiate complex waters, often having to make a choice between doing the innovative work that is their passion (and for which they were ostensibly hired) and doing more traditional work that has more potential to advance their careers at a particular institution.

Likewise, a failure to address these questions departmentally within local contexts leaves the profession in a kind of antagonistic relationship with digital media work, unable or unwilling to deal with the ways that it is changing "business as usual." Pushing this question aside, trying to ignore digital media, or wringing hands over the changes that it is bringing reduces our agency in responding to the contextual situation in which we find ourselves. As Natalia Cecire writes, "[Digital humanities] has the potential to do something great to this profession, but realizing that potential is all of our jobs, whether or not we identify with the label 'digital humanist.' One way or another, it's already doing *something*" (n. pag.). If we want to have a hand in what digital media work does to our profession, we need to tackle the tough questions this book raises and "get agile and nuanced about describing the myriad ways that [digital media] has, and will, alter" our work (Cecire n. pag.).

Institutional Frameworks as Technological Ecologies

The metaphor of the technological ecology is one way to frame discussions of the ways that digital media work is influencing and changing teaching and scholarship. In their edited collection, *Technological Ecologies and Sustainability*, Dànielle DeVoss, Heidi McKee, and Richard (Dickie) Selfe use the concepts of ecology and sustainability "to suggest the important task of maintaining the richly textured technological environments in which composition teachers and students learn, study, and communicate" (Selfe, DeVoss, and McKee 1). Drawing on previous scholarship, they assert that "these environments—which include both human and technological actors—are akin, as many scholars have suggested, to ecological systems" and that they "deserve to be studied in all their layered, interconnected complexity" (1). This book participates in such a project. While their project focused specifically on teachers of writing (many, but not all, of whom reside in departments of English), this project focuses more broadly on English studies as a discipline, of which writing studies (or rhetoric and composition) is one large field.

Analyses of my data in the following chapters reveal the following elements to be essential in creating and sustaining a technological ecology for digital media teaching and scholarship: official policies supporting such work, the chair's leadership in speaking on behalf of and advocating for such work, similar advocacy from other digital media leaders in the department, public forums for digital scholarship and teaching, curricula and course requirements, appropriate facilities and opportunities/spaces for talking about digital media work, and mentoring. This metaphor and these elements are used heuristically throughout the book to help organize and make sense of the data and to make comparisons among the sites studied.

Reflections on (Not) Doing "the Risky Thing"

My own affiliations have profoundly influenced this project. I am lucky that my campus has a strong culture of support for digital media teaching. There are multiple computer lab classrooms on campus, and English is able to schedule all writing classes as well as many other classes in the labs. So I have not had to struggle with scheduling issues or justifying the use of teaching methods that, while perhaps not conventional, do not raise eyebrows in my subfield. Thanks to the work of colleagues who preceded me—namely Marcia Dickson and Scott Lloyd DeWitt—digital composing is accepted as desirable and even necessary in writing classes, which represent the majority of the classes I teach. While some students often have preconceived notions of what an English composition class "should be" based upon their experiences in high school, many of them become persuaded that the digital composing we do in class will be beneficial to them and will help them to develop the same underlying critical thinking skills as the traditional writing assignments I require. Even so, there is always one student who writes something on the evaluation form along the lines of "The class was fun, but we didn't do much writing" or "We spent too much time on the computers and not enough time writing," to which I must respond in annual evaluation meetings. However, the evaluation committee understands my pedagogical framework and values the work I do, so incorporating digital media and emerging forms of writing into my classes is not that risky an endeavor. I can imagine, however, that a faculty member in my position at an institution with a less supportive culture might do this work under increased scrutiny and with far more risk involved, particularly if that person is one of the first to do such work in the department or in his or her subfield.

My investment in digital scholarship has illuminated these issues of textuality, reading/interpretation methods, and textual production in more complicated/conflicted ways than my teaching has. Early on in the process of writing this book, I was talking with two tenured professors in my department (neither of whom works in the field of digital media studies) who asked me about potential venues for my work. I listed a couple of journals, and they asked why I wasn't considering digital publications. The question truly took me by surprise, and I mumbled something I don't remember. It got me thinking, though, about how strongly my own graduate program had trained me to value the printed product even though the focus of my research was digital media, the methods of my research lent themselves to digital production, and the focus of my teaching had been (and continues to be) digital composing. Although I used digital media to code and analyze my interviews (which had been recorded digitally) for this project, I had never thought about producing anything other than a printed document. I recognize an irony, as well, in producing a printed treatise about the importance and relevance of digital media work and arguing specifically for the valuation of nonprinted, nontraditional digital works. Yet I also agree with the editors of *Hacking the Academy*, Dan Cohen and Tom Scheinfeldt, who write that "scholarly and educational content can exist in multiple forms for multiple audiences" (n. pag.). They argue that the different forms of their project have different purposes and will reach different audiences, suggesting that the web version "will continue [to] host a much larger and more diverse version of the work, including themes and genres missing from the print edition. If this book is static, the overall project is anything but" (n. pag.). And so I see the printed book as the best vehicle at this moment in time to reach my intended target audience.

But I would be lying if I said that professional/institutional considerations did not also strongly influence my decision. It is still understood in my current department that the currency for tenure and promotion is the single-authored scholarly monograph. It is local constraints such as this that have a great influence on the work that faculty and graduate students are able to do and on the amount of risk involved in such work.

Recently, Kathleen Fitzpatrick wrote about fielding a question at a talk from a graduate student who wanted to know if it would be better for her to be conservative and do a traditional dissertation or to take a risk and do a digital dissertation in an innovative form. Fitzpatrick responded, "Do the risky thing," but then quickly added, "Make sure that someone's got your back." She verbalized several concerns with her initial piece of advice: "I'm not her dissertation director; I don't want to create conflict in her progress toward her degree; I don't want to set up unreasonable expectations about what her department will actually support." She recognized that local contingencies will make or break such digital work. However, she also recognized that it is important for senior faculty to support and advocate for such work, to help their younger colleagues do "the risky thing." She notes, "Too many young digital humanists find themselves cautioned away from the very work that got them hired by well-meaning senior colleagues, who now tell them that wacky digital projects are fine on the side, or once the work necessary for tenure is complete." And she argues that such advice risks either stifling innovation or leading younger scholars to burn out because they have to produce twice as much work: traditional work for tenure and the innovative digital work that is their passion and that they were hired to do. And so she stands by her advice: "Junior scholars with truly innovative projects need to do the risky thing. But they need to know that someone's got their backs, and that their senior colleagues will learn to evaluate new kinds of work on its own merits and will insist upon the value of such innovation for the field and for the institution" ("Do 'the Risky Thing'" n. pag.).

There are junior scholars in English studies who are doing "the risky thing." Although I am fulfilling my department's requirement of a book, most of my other published work is in digital forms (including one scholarly movie), and all of it is collaboratively authored, both of which are often risky propositions for scholars in English departments. However, one of my colleagues is truly doing the risky thing by going up for tenure with a digital book project that is under contract by Computers and Composition Digital Press, an online, open-access imprint of Utah State University Press. Senior faculty in her field definitely "have her back," and the rest of the department has accepted this project as "equivalent to" a printed book. This is an important step forward for scholars doing digital media work in fairly traditional departments; it sets a precedent for the valuing of such work for future scholars in this particular department, but it also demonstrates that new kinds and forms of scholarship are not alien to the discipline and do have a place in English studies.

While they are risky, such projects are important because they force departmental communities to discuss the issues and questions raised by this book.[1]

It is these conversations that have the potential to create change.

It is these conversations that this book seeks to spark in local contexts, to help lessen the risk of doing digital media work for faculty and graduate students in humanities departments. Though this book focuses on English studies, the questions that are posed provide a method for other humanities-based disciplines to use to spark conversations about the integration of digital media scholarship and teaching into those fields.

Chapter 1, "Cultivating Digital Media Work in English Studies: Negotiating Disciplinary Questions," lays the groundwork for these conversations by reframing the discussion of digital media teaching and scholarship (which is often cast in binary terms) around three "big questions" that digital media use occasions for English studies: what counts as a text, how should we approach the reading of texts, and how should we approach the production of texts? At the end of the chapter, I introduce a matrix that plots these three big questions against the different contexts in which digital media work occurs. This matrix of questions frames analyses in the following chapters, helping to demonstrate the role of technological ecologies in each local context and revealing how participants address (or don't address) these questions within their departments' contexts.

Chapter 2, "Situating Digital Media Teaching: Challenging the 'Hierarchy of Signs,'" explores the technological ecologies for digital media teaching in the three departments I visited and studied for this book and suggests a set of questions for the matrix that can spark an open discussion of issues related to digital media and teaching within departments. Drawing on Ellen Cushman's critical framework of the "hierarchy of signs" in English studies and Robert Scholes's characterization of English as a binarized discipline, the chapter also analyzes the ways that individuals within their local contexts address or elide (deliberately or not) these questions and the effects of those choices on departmental cultures of support for digital media pedagogies.

Chapter 3, "Scholarship Through a New Lens: Digital Production and New Models of Evaluation," explores the departments' technological ecologies for digital media scholarship, focusing on what their policies—both explicit (that is, written) and implicit (that is, followed in practice—reveal about what departments value most about scholarship and how individuals position their work within such value frameworks. I extend the matrix with sets of questions for two different groups: individuals creating digital scholarship and departments seeking to update their policies toward digital scholarship. The questions for individuals encourage deep thinking about the scholarly value of specific projects and ways to describe those projects to colleagues, while the questions for departments are prompts for localized discussions about what is valuable about different types and forms of scholarship.

Chapter 4, "Professional Development in/with Digital Media: Sustaining a Technological Ecology," explores the issues associated with supporting faculty and graduate student efforts to learn new pedagogical and scholarly forms/methods. Responding to Debra Journet's call for thinking about how best to provide such professionalization, the chapter looks at some of the ways departments are responding to questions surrounding professional development in digital media. Furthermore, the chapter continues to build the matrix with questions that are important for a department to consider in order to create an intentional technological ecology or culture of support for professionalization in digital media.

Finally, the conclusion, "The Future of Digital Media and/in English Studies—Models of Practice," uses the matrix of questions as a critical frame to read a variety of examples drawn from published scholarship (with screen captures of some of the work) to help those who are not very familiar with digital media scholarship and teaching better visualize the kind of work that is happening now and to model the kinds of conversations that departments can have about such work. Reading this work within the context of calls by university presidents and other groups, such as the Modern Language Association, for broader evaluation criteria for work in the profession, the chapter argues for the necessity of creating cultures of support for new forms of work within English departments.

The media and literacy landscape we find ourselves in is increasingly digital and rapidly changing. With diminishing financial support for the humanities, more top-down decision making about budgets and curricula, and a drive toward e-learning, the discipline needs to do some soul searching to determine—lest someone else determines for us—how we fit into this new landscape. Instead of letting digital media *happen to us*, we need to proactively resee and reshape our discipline to respond to and incorporate the new forms of textuality coming into being around us while maintaining our core disciplinary values within this context of the "turn to the digital."

1

Cultivating Digital Media Work in English Studies:
Negotiating Disciplinary Questions

> The web is a fabulous—& dangerous—resource.
> —Anonymous survey respondent

Imagine an assistant professor in a literary field who works in an English department; we'll call her Polly. She is creating a scholarly hypertext edition of one of the texts of a somewhat unknown female author and wants to bring this type of work into her introductory literature class, having students create annotated online editions of literary texts. The biggest challenge she sees in teaching students literature is that they struggle with critical/analytical reading. She read a white paper published online by David Barndollar arguing that in learning to read literature, students are learning to "make different distinctions in texts from those they are accustomed to making; and making distinctions in texts is the very definition of reading" (n. pag.). He further asserts that by "marking the text" (using hypertext markup language—html—to make the text look a particular way on the screen and to annotate the text), those distinctions are made visible for students in concrete ways. In other words, creating hypertexts helps students attend to textuality and attend to reading and interpretation in a more active and self-conscious way by forcing them to make decisions about the presentation of a text based upon their interpretations of its meaning. Hypertext annotation requires students to interrogate a text in order to understand both the meaning of the text and how the text creates that meaning, then to communicate that knowledge to others in the form of hypertext markup language. Additionally, because students have familiarity with hypertext from the standpoint of reading/interacting with websites, Polly feels that they may perceive a greater connection between the course content and their own lives and will thereby attend to the work with more enthusiasm and focus.

When Polly asks the university's scheduler to schedule her class into a particular computer classroom (one that has web composing software installed on the computers), the scheduler responds that it is not possible. Polly was prepared for this response. Space is at a premium at the university, and most special requests for particular spaces cannot be accommodated. Although the composition program has made special arrangements for first-year writing classes to meet regularly in computer labs, literature classes are much more difficult to schedule in the computer classrooms. Polly talks to a colleague in creative writing who had similar difficulties in a previous semester scheduling a creative nonfiction course focusing on digital storytelling in a computer lab but eventually prevailed. He says he merely went to talk to the department chair and explained what he was doing in the class and why he needed the space, and the chair cut through the bureaucracy to get the course scheduled in a computer classroom.

Polly emails her syllabus to the chair and makes an appointment to talk about scheduling. In the meeting, she explains in more detail what she wants to do in her class and why this plan necessitates that the class meet for at least several weeks in a computer classroom; Polly would prefer to be there the entire semester but recognizes the reality that there are fewer computer classrooms than faculty who wish to use them. Polly expects her chair to ask a few questions about her assignment before committing to help her get her class into a computer lab. However, she is caught off guard when her chair says something to the effect of "You teach literature, not creative writing. You don't need a computer classroom."

Polly responds that her hypertext project requires computers; the students can't be expected to create hypertexts completely outside of class without any hands-on instruction. To this, her chair replies, "You're paid to teach literature, not technology. This project sounds like it's going to take a lot of time, and this is a survey course. How are you going to achieve historical coverage when you're wasting so much time teaching students to make websites?"

Polly tries to explain that making websites will help students find meaning in the literature and make connections between the course texts and their own lives, which are increasingly digitally mediated. But the chair is not convinced and responds that students already know about websites but need to learn how to read literature and write about it coherently and critically.

Disheartened, Polly puts her idea on the back burner until she can discover the arguments that will convince her chair that this is a worthwhile plan for a survey course in literature.

***

Now imagine an associate professor specializing in the history of rhetoric whose department (a different English department than Polly's) maintains several computer classrooms and has a center devoted to helping faculty and graduate students incorporate digital media into the courses they teach. Most faculty in the department who want to use the computer classrooms can be accommodated because scheduling is based on faculty interest, and only a few tenured faculty request the space. This associate professor—we'll call him Perry—has been teaching upper-level courses and graduate seminars in his field in the computer classrooms for several years.

Because of a lack of physical access to many of the texts Perry sees as most useful for his classes, he and a colleague at another institution have been collaborating on the development of digital materials that can be used for a variety of courses in the field, sort of a digital textbook with a scholarly scaffolding and scholarly applications beyond teaching. They applied for and received grant money to build an online repository of materials, including

- images of original texts
- annotated versions of the texts
- scholarly analyses of the texts
- a database that allows users to search the primary texts for rhetorical tropes and schemes used; for rhetorical aspects such as context, audience, and purpose; for aspects of content such as themes, motifs, and keywords; and the like
- a database that allows users to search the scholarly analyses using parameters such as author, theoretical approach, date of publication, and so on
- a pedagogical scaffolding that allows other teachers to use the resources in a variety of different ways for different levels of courses, from introductory to graduate
- a scholarly introduction

Perry has devoted considerable time and intellectual energy to this project, which he sees as a major contribution to both scholarly and pedagogical inquiry in his field. Not only did he and his colleague use some of the grant money to travel to libraries and archives and, with permission, to make high-resolution digital images of the texts, but they also spent time learning how to code the images and annotations and build the resource. Furthermore, he and his colleague have each piloted the resource in three classes and presented the findings at several conferences; they have also published several articles about the project in peer-reviewed venues.

His is a "book department" that expects a second book for promotion to full professor. Perry deems the amount of work put into this project and its potential impact as at least equivalent to a scholarly monograph, but some of his colleagues in the department have reservations. Faculty in Perry's department have typically been promoted based on a scholarly monograph; furthermore, nobody has been promoted based upon any kind of digital work, so the department is unsure of how to evaluate his project. Adding another wrinkle to the case is the collaborative nature of the work. While many of his rhetoric and composition colleagues have presented collaboratively written articles and coedited collections in their dossiers, nobody has been tenured or promoted based solely on such collaborative efforts. The department is thus struggling to evaluate his work. Department members believe he has put a great deal of work into the project and that the project is valuable, but they are not sure that it satisfies the department's criteria for promotion to full professor.

***

These scenarios illustrate several of the issues that faculty encounter when they attempt to integrate digital media into their scholarship and teaching: the nature of textuality (what English departments count as a "text" and the hierarchies that influence their decisions), the nature of reading (what methods or lenses we bring to texts), and the nature of production (the kinds of texts/composing that result from encounters with reading/analysis). To say that Polly and Perry confront the question "What is a text?" might sound silly. Because of the influence of Barthes's theories about text, English scholars acknowledge an expansive vision of the kinds of texts that can be analyzed (including films, television shows, advertising, music, photographs, magazines, video games, and so on), although there is still a fairly clear hierarchy determining which texts are central and which are marginal. It is common to find courses focusing on film, popular culture, and other nonliterary texts within English departments, and it is likely that one of these classes might even be required of English majors; at my university, for instance, students must take one nonliterary course of their choosing. However, it's safe to say that the English major in most departments is still built around literary periods and literary works. To suggest that the study of nonliterary texts should occupy a space in the curriculum equal to that of literary texts would probably be a radical position in most English departments. And so Polly does have to face the question "What is a text?" when her chair asks her how she will achieve historical coverage in her seminar because departments and faculty still place canonical literary works at the top of a hierarchy of textual forms. Perry, though he does not have to justify teaching digital texts, also has to contend with this issue of textuality in the question of what counts as a scholarly text. This question has certainly become more salient as more faculty produce digitally mediated scholarship, but it is not a new question, as Perry's case attests. The digital nature of his work might raise eyebrows, but so does his assertion that a textbook is a piece of scholarship.

Defining what counts as a text is not the only issue Polly's and Perry's digital work emphasizes. They both also confront the question of the reading/interpretation of texts, although in different ways. For Polly, the issue is how to best teach textual analysis, relying on traditional methods or using digital media annotation. For Perry, it is the definition of scholarly methods that is at stake, as his analysis of texts ultimately serves a pedagogical purpose, though he certainly engages in scholarly inquiry in order to prepare those texts for further inquiry by students. For both, the question of reading/interpretation thus becomes a question of methods, whether teaching or scholarly, and of *how* the discipline approaches literary and other kinds of texts.

Intimately related to the ways that faculty approach reading/interpretation/research are the ways that they approach sharing the results of such inquiry with others, or in other words, the ways that the discipline approaches the production of texts. While the discipline seems to be relatively open to the broadening of what counts as a text worthy of analysis, the same cannot be said about the production and dissemination of scholarly texts; English departments still typically expect much of a scholar's output to be in print or print-like forms. Even if they are open to accepting alternative forms of output, many individuals simply have no experience assessing such work, as Perry's scenario illustrates, which can be devastating for untenured faculty, in particular. Similarly, the incorporation of digital production by students is often seen as outside the purview of the discipline, as in Polly's scenario.

Though these questions about textuality, methods, and scholarly production have been discussed frequently in the past, the discipline needs to revisit these questions in the context of digital media, and in this book I seek to frame that discussion. The values that have surrounded and supported issues of textuality in English departments are being challenged by emerging forms of digital scholarship and teaching, and as Perry's and Polly's scenarios suggest, these issues are ripe for discussion within local contexts. However, as my data indicate, those who are often in charge of framing and leading such discussions in English departments might have little experience with digital teaching and scholarship and therefore might not know where to begin to discuss the issues. Like Perry's colleagues, they might be more than willing to accept alternative forms but unsure of how to best understand and evaluate them. Likewise, untenured faculty for whom these issues are particularly salient, like Polly, might need help articulating their work in terms that senior faculty who have less experience with digital forms can relate to. It is to these audiences—tenured faculty and administrators in all areas of English studies who want to support both traditional and emerging forms of scholarship and teaching, untenured faculty in all areas of English studies who want to articulate their digital work in terms that highlight the overlaps between their work and traditional work, and tenured faculty new to digital scholarship and teaching who are struggling to find the support they need for professional development—that this book is aimed.

Cynthia L. Selfe, Gail E. Hawisher, and Patrick W. Berry argue that "change, we are convinced, produces less anxiety and less resistance when individuals and groups—both those who *support* change and those who are *resistant* to change—can focus on shared values" (5, emphasis in original). The importance of having such conversations from shared values is also emphasized by Debra Journet. In her narrative of learning how to incorporate digital media assignments into her teaching, she argues that her experiences at Digital Media and Composition (DMAC), an intensive workshop in which she read scholarship in the field, engaged in conversations with colleagues, and gained hands-on experience creating digital texts, were foundational to her success and "conversion" to using digital media in her teaching: "DMAC and the conversations it fostered not only provided essential how-to advice; it also stimulated me to think about digital media from broader perspectives. Of course, these represented unusual opportunities. But it's essential to foster such intellectual conversations if senior faculty are to get on board" (117).

In order to help foster such conversations among my target audiences, I have created a matrix of questions that will help to frame discussions of the data I analyze throughout the book; I also suggest a range of questions for both individuals and departments to consider as they negotiate how to maintain shared values while recognizing new forms of teaching and research that are increasingly common in English departments. The matrix of questions is organized by the three questions of textuality that framed my discussion of Perry's and Polly's scenarios: What counts as a text? How should we approach the reading of texts? How should we approach the production of texts? (See table 1.1.)

Table 1.1. Matrix of questions

	What counts as a text?	How should we approach the reading of texts?	How should we approach the production of texts?
Teaching	*Questions for individuals*	*Questions for individuals*	*Questions for individuals*
	Questions for departments	*Questions for departments*	*Questions for departments*
Scholarship	*Questions for individuals*	*Questions for individuals*	*Questions for individuals*
	Questions for departments	*Questions for departments*	*Questions for departments*
Professional development	*Questions for individuals*	*Questions for individuals*	*Questions for individuals*
	Questions for departments	*Questions for departments*	*Questions for departments*

Through a series of case studies, this book describes three very different departments and the ways in which they have responded to these three "big questions" of textuality in the face of digital media. The perspective that this analysis provides can help faculty and administrators locate the positions their departments take regarding these questions as well as identify the impact of digital and other emerging forms of teaching and scholarship on their faculty, curricula, and students. Furthermore, faculty and administrators can use the matrix of questions to facilitate discussions of how best to maintain a strong value on humanistic, creative, literary, and rhetorical studies in a time of rapid technological change.

Studying Digital Media Work in Context:
Disciplinary Values, Traditions, and Debates

Many scholars have called for a digital turn in literacy studies and rhetoric and composition.[1] Cynthia L. Selfe, for instance, argues in *Technology and Literacy in the Twenty-First Century: The Importance of Paying Attention* that we must resist one narrow definition or official version of literacy, value multiple literacies (technical and nontechnical), and recognize that technology and critical technological literacy are part of our work as humanists. Additionally, she maintains that we must teach students to think critically about technology, help teachers develop new classroom activities, and train teaching assistants in technology use and critical technological literacy. Stuart Selber argues that a rhetorical digital literacy is also necessary, in addition to functional and critical technological literacies, so that students and teachers are able to not only use technology and critically evaluate it but also reshape it to their own needs.

Broadening the focus from rhetoric and composition, Gunther Kress asserts that English curricula in general need to move from critique to design, where writers are remakers rather than simply users/readers of technology and/or texts who create "complex orchestrations" in multimedia, not simply compose traditional papers. He argues that the current visual and electronic nature of mediation necessitates such a rethinking of English curricula at all levels. Furthermore, he sees emerging forms of reading and writing as an argument for reshaping English curricula to focus on the future and on the skills that students will need for participation in society, which are skills with visual and digital texts ("'English' at the Crossroads").

In redefining curricular goals for the fields that teach the literate skills of reading, writing, and critical thinking and arguing for the incorporation of digital media, these scholars implicitly challenge the identity of "teacher," that is, how the discipline defines what is involved in teaching those literate skills. If digital media challenge traditional "teacher" identities, then in order for digital media to be fully integrated throughout English curricula, it follows that individuals must learn to resee their professional identities in a way that includes digital media teaching. In other words, "teacher" must come to have some sort of implicit digital component to it.

Besides challenging traditional teacher identities, digital media work also challenges traditional scholarly identities. Many scholars in the discipline are producing digital scholarship, which often does not look like traditional literary or rhetorical analysis. This scholarship frequently pushes the boundaries of what many perceive to be core disciplinary values; for instance, much digital scholarship eschews the linear expression of an analytical argument about a text or set of texts in favor of a more associative presentation of claims, and the texts that are analyzed are often noncanonical and in some cases new media texts themselves. In other words, such scholarship confronts what it means to be a scholar in our discipline. Although new online venues and nonlinear, multimedia-based forms of composing proliferate, they confound many tenure and promotion committees. This is likely because the monograph is still the gold standard for getting tenure at doctorate-granting institutions and, according to the 2006 report from the MLA Task Force on Evaluating Scholarship for Tenure and Promotion, "65.7% report no experience evaluating monographs in electronic format." Additionally, "40.8% of departments in doctorate-granting institutions report no experience evaluating refereed articles in electronic format," indicating that digital scholarship goes against the grain at many institutions (11). Furthermore, the print article remains the standard at many non-doctorate-granting institutions, as well. Consequently, just as individuals must negotiate a reseeing of their teacherly identity to include digital media, they must also negotiate a reseeing of their scholarly identity so that "scholar" comes to include some sort of digital component.

Selfe, Hawisher, and Berry have recognized that although the digital turn has greatly influenced work in other sectors—public, business, government—it has yet "to fully permeate the humanities, or, more specifically, departments of English." They explain:

> Many of these academic units retain long-standing historical and cultural values that seem highly resistant to new forms of knowledge production, especially those situated within digital environments— among these, a value on the scholarly and research performance of individuals rather than teams; a value on conventional forms of information exchange, particularly printed books and journal articles; and a value on models of scholarly production tied to institutional capital in university presses and professional journals. (1)

Because of the focus on these values, they argue that "for scholars who recognize the strengths of both *conventional* and *emerging* forms of knowledge production, this situation is becoming increasingly problematic to negotiate, especially for junior scholars working toward tenure." As such, they call upon senior scholars "to establish an increasingly sustainable system of scholarly production in English departments—one that works both for scholars who want to retain traditional values of humanist scholarship and those who see needed changes in such values" (1). They then define four principles that represent "a productive middle ground" between the values of traditional humanistic scholarly production and emerging environments for digital scholarly production that have allowed them to create sustainable projects and venues for emerging forms of scholarship and collaborative research over the course of their careers. They argue that English studies "can retain its traditional value on scholarship that is original, innovative, intellectual, and sustained, peer-reviewed and published, while acknowledging that scholarly fields, forms, and values change," and they stress that the profession must recognize that "scholarly modes of production and form are not fixed," that scholarship increasingly uses "multiple semiotic modalities . . . to convey meaning in increasingly effective and robust ways," and that it is important to recognize and value collaborative scholarship (2). As evidence of their assertions, they describe multiple projects and initiatives they have been involved with that have been guided by these principles and that have allowed scholars in emerging areas of English to publish innovative work—journals such as *Computers and Composition* and *Computers and Composition Online*, the establishment of several awards and prizes for digital scholarship, and the development of the Digital Archive of Literacy Narratives and the Computers and Composition Digital Press.

Although Selfe, Hawisher, and Berry focus on scholarly values, it is also true that the digital turn has influenced teaching in the discipline in ways that might sometimes seem antithetical to the traditional values embraced by English departments. However, increasingly, many instructors of English (in general) and writing (in particular) are incorporating digital technologies into their classes and asking students to produce texts that, like current scholarship referenced by Selfe, Hawisher, and Berry, use multiple semiotic channels or modalities (sound, video, image, word, and so on) to convey meaning. Their methods are not always understood or embraced by colleagues evaluating their teaching, just as new forms of scholarly production are not always understood or deemed appropriate by colleagues evaluating such work for tenure and promotion.

Consequently, faculty who incorporate digital media into their teaching and scholarship often do so at considerable risk. While scholars like Selfe and Hawisher have laid the groundwork for faculty in rhetoric and composition by creating venues for publishing emerging work and by helping set precedents for valuing not only emerging forms of scholarship but also collaborative work and digitally enhanced teaching, these faculty still often face an uphill battle to have their digital work "count," and such work is often even riskier for literature faculty because there are so few venues for emerging forms of scholarship in literary fields and much less of a culture of pedagogical scholarship. These are some of the issues I hope to illuminate through this study.

A bit of background about the study is in order at this point. I visited three departments, all in different universities, and interviewed key administrators: the department chair, the chair of the committee on promotion and tenure, and the technology advisor (if such a position existed). I also conducted semi-ethnographic[2] case studies in order to paint a rich portrait of participants' uses of digital media in their classes and to investigate the effects of departmental culture on pedagogical and scholarly uses of new media. Case study participants were PhD students and tenure-track assistant professors who were engaging in either digital media teaching or scholarship. I interviewed participants about their work with digital media and collected course materials—such as syllabi, writing prompts, discussion board transcripts, and the like—for analysis and to use as the basis for discourse-based interviews, in which I asked participants to reflect upon the class session(s) that I observed.

In addition to the semi-ethnographic case studies and key administrator interviews, I also conducted a paper-based survey of all PhD students and assistant professors (tenure track as well as non-tenure track) in the three departments. The survey asked participants to rate their attitudes toward digital media and to describe their pedagogical philosophies regarding digital media, their uses of new media (to teach, for research/scholarship, for administrative tasks), and available support for pedagogical and scholarly uses of new media. A total of 105 individuals responded to the survey: 78 PhD students and 27 assistant professors.

The three institutions I visited, though in different states, have much in common. They are all major research universities in the Midwest; all are public institutions. Each enrolls 35,000–40,000 undergraduates and at least 10,000 graduate students. The departments, however, are very different, and each department is positioned somewhat differently regarding other departments in its institution. The department I will refer to as the "print-centric department" is situated within a college of arts and sciences. The department offers a PhD in English, an MFA in creative writing, an MA in English, and a BA in English. The department I will refer to as the "parallel cultures department" is situated within a college of humanities, itself situated within a larger managerial entity, a collection of colleges of arts and sciences. The department offers a PhD in English, an MFA in creative writing, an MA in English, a BA in English, and coursework contributing to several university interdisciplinary minors and focus areas. The department I will refer to as the "integrated literacies department" is situated within a college of arts and letters and offers undergraduate majors in rhetoric and writing. The affiliated graduate program (an interdisciplinary program housed at the college level) offers an MA in rhetoric and professional writing and a PhD in rhetoric and writing with several different concentrations.

Each of these three departments has a mixture of scholars in fields traditionally concerned with the printed text (such as literature, composition, and/or creative writing) and in fields concerned with alternative texts and literacies (such as folklore, literacy studies, rhetoric, and/or cultural studies). In addition, each of these three departments administers its university's first-year writing course, a required "gateway" course at each institution, a gateway not only to the academy but also, often, a gateway to the department and, as a result, to the discipline.

"Discipline" is a fluid term, and departmental structure does not necessarily completely determine disciplinary identifications of individuals within a given department. In other words, all individuals in a department might not identify with quite the same discipline. For instance, the study of rhetoric and composition often, but not always, resides in an English department. Is the field of rhetoric and composition, then, a subfield of "English studies," or is it a separate discipline? The same could be asked of many areas of study often found in English departments, including film, linguistics, cultural studies, and so on. I am not concerned in this book with positing a firm definition of the discipline of "English studies." Rather, I am using that term to refer to a set of fields, or "inter-disciplines,"[3] that espouse similar values and focus on the study of texts, textuality, reading, writing, and the circulation of discourse. So, although two of the departments in this study are English departments and one is a writing department, they all share some similar goals and values. In this book, I seek to understand how digital media work either embodies or challenges the values of the discipline, and I contend that individuals' disciplinary identities[4] influence how they approach integrating digital media into teaching and scholarship. In other words, I consider how participants' disciplinary identities influence the ways they think about and use digital media. So, I analyze the ways that disciplinary language, values, traditions, and debates shape participants' understandings of the nature of pedagogy, of the nature of scholarship, and of digital media's role in each. Conversely, the ways that individuals work with digital media have an influence on those disciplinary debates and values and could eventually lead to new traditions and new language about the nature of pedagogy and scholarship.

Several scholars have written about the discipline of English and its values and in a sense have defined its identity. In his book *What Is English?*, for instance, Peter Elbow demonstrates that college English has long been characterized by a split between literary studies on the one hand (representing reading) and rhetoric and composition (and some-times creative writing) on the other hand (representing writing), with literary studies often more highly valued. He further notes that such a split does not exist at the primary and secondary levels, where English is more often conceptualized as language arts. Along the same lines, Ellen Cushman argues that English is characterized by a "hierarchy of signs" that places printed forms and "the word and the letter" above all other forms of textuality and knowledge production. Similarly, Robert Scholes asserts that English is characterized by two binary oppositions: that be-tween literature and composition and that between theory and teaching, with the discipline placing more value on literature and theory/theory building than on writing and teaching. He seeks to break down these binaries and remake English as the study of textuality. Digital media integration is often viewed by English studies as a threat to the printed word, particularly books. But if we see English as Scholes does, as the study of textuality in all its forms, then this is not necessarily the case. Digital media forms fit easily and naturally into a study of textuality, as do books and a variety of textual forms.

Other scholars maintain that the discipline must change along the lines that Scholes suggests or risk obsolescence in the face of the cur-rent media and literacy landscape. In "Obsolescence," Kathleen Fitz-patrick suggests that the profession needs to rethink the entire system of scholarly publication because traditional models are unsustainable. Similarly, Cathy N. Davidson argues for a paradigm shift and for seeing "technology and the humanities not as a binary but as two sides of a necessarily interdependent, conjoined, and mutually constitutive set of intellectual, educational, social, political, and economic practices." She further asserts that the technological changes that have influenced other disciplines have also influenced ours and "hold possibilities for far greater transformation in the three areas—research, writing, and teaching—that matter most" (708).

Such calls, however, threaten some English faculty at the level of professional identity. For Cushman and Scholes, the identity of the English faculty member is almost inseparable from print forms and print culture, and so changing that creates anxiety. It is in this context of conversations about what English studies is and what it values and about the calls for reshaping it that I discuss the concept of professional identity for faculty and graduate students in English studies. In *Engaged Writers Dynamic Disciplines*, Chris Thaiss and Terry Myers Zawacki review major works on the concept of identity as it relates to disci-plinary change and theorize a process by which alternative discourses become mainstreamed. Interviewing faculty from disciplines outside English, Thaiss and Zawacki note that their interviewees had carved out a unique, individual place for themselves by challenging established genres and forms of research in the discipline and over time had found that their cutting-edge work became standard practice as their careers progressed—as their once transgressive books, for example, became standard texts for graduate classes.

They also describe the ways that tensions between alternative genres are negotiated within the academy. For example, they explore the digital media work of a colleague in history and the tensions she faced between her academic training and her new field. Thaiss and Zawacki call her digital work "intergeneric," explaining that in her work, she "crosses many genres and invokes multiple audiences" in ways that fundamentally challenge common academic discourse and practice. In particular, she must negotiate a significant tension between the values of her training as an academic historian and the "dynamism" of her field of new media and hypermedia, which, Thaiss and Zawacki note, "doesn't sit still for the kind of disciplined analysis and reflection characteristic of academic writing." They further suggest that her "intergeneric" multimedia work is vastly different from other "alternative" forms of academic discourse that their other informants across a variety of disciplines discussed and that it pushes more radically against prevailing academic conventions (55). In this book, I consider the ways that scholars in English studies use the language of professional identity to position themselves in relation to digital media work and to negotiate some similar tensions. I also suggest ways for scholars from a variety of positions to enter the conversation about textuality in order to minimize these anxieties and focus on shared values.

Individuals' negotiations of such disciplinary issues can be seen in responses to open-ended questions on the survey I conducted. The responses varied widely—some were enthusiastic about technology, some were concerned or ambivalent, and some were opposed. Such a distribution of attitudes makes sense if we accept Jay David Bolter's argument that we live in the late age of print, a time characterized by tension between print and digital forms of writing. According to Bolter, during the late age of print we will see a "transformation of our social and cultural attitudes toward and uses of" the technology of print (3). As that transformation occurs, it will also bring a transformation of attitudes toward writing, rhetoric, pedagogy, and scholarship. The spread of responses, at first glance, seems to indicate individuals' taking sides in the opposition of print and digital media. Those who side with print worry that digital media will change the processes of teaching and scholarship, objects of study, and central goals/questions of their profession. Those who side with digital media use digital tools to enable processes of teaching and scholarship, to study different objects, and to achieve new goals/answer new questions, exactly what the others express concern about.

Two responses in particular represent the extremes of this binary opposition yet also indicate an awareness of the binary and an attempt to navigate their professional identities in relation to it. One graduate student in the parallel cultures department writes, "Really, I'm just not interested in digital media at all. Also, I am (at least to an extent) old-school, and I believe that English Departments are some of the last places where BOOKS are valued over technology, and I guess I'd like to see it remain that way" (emphasis in original). This respondent identifies as "old-school" yet is keenly aware of the presence of digital media in the discipline. If digital media were not an oppositional force and did not threaten this person's professional identity, she would not have emphasized the word "books" by capitalizing it. Digital media threaten the object of study central to her professional identity as teacher and scholar; therefore, she navigates the binary opposition by emphasizing the book and distancing herself, as much as possible, from digital media. An assistant professor in the integrated literacies department expresses the polar opposite position, writing, "Everything I do is mediated by the Web, Adobe Photoshop, MS Word and Corel WordPerfect, PowerPoint, etc. *Everything*" (emphasis in original). She expresses a professional identity that is completely saturated with digital media. This person focuses on the ubiquity of digital, rather than print, mediation in her professional life. Her insistence that *everything* she does is mediated digitally seems to be an intentional overstatement. She identifies herself in this way with one extreme of the digital/print binary, just as the graduate student identifies herself with the other extreme.

Other responses, however, reveal more complex stories about the tension between print and digital media in the professional lives of these individuals and remap these binary terms in interesting ways. One graduate student writes, "I'm stuck in a culture of human face-to-face interaction & I believe that is how teaching must be done." Digital media threaten this person's sense of what it means to teach—to communicate face-to-face with students—yet also makes the person feel "stuck," indicating an awareness that digital media open up new opportunities but an unwillingness or, perhaps, fear of re-identifying as a teacher in order to take advantage of those opportunities. The binary terms here are remapped onto pedagogical methods: face-to-face interaction/online interaction. There is a tradition in rhetoric and composition, in addition to valuing the printed word as an object of study, of valuing oral performance and interaction in the classroom. Digital media, in this person's view of teaching, disable that process, suggesting that individuals also need to make choices about the methods that define their teaching (and, by extension, the methods/processes that define their research) and the ways that different media enable or hinder those methods.

For others, the issue at stake is the question of shifting pedagogical goals. One assistant professor frames the print/digital binary as teaching writing/teaching technology, noting, "Technology is becoming an important part of my department, which has recently changed its name to reflect this new emphasis. Although I am sure technology helps us be better teachers, I am concerned that the priority of teaching coherent writing is being undermined." For this assistant professor, writing should be mediated by print, and teaching students to create other types of texts mediated digitally undermines the teaching of writing. A graduate student in the parallel cultures department, on the other hand, does not see the terms existing in a binary opposition at all. He writes, "I'd like to use technology to create an environment that is fully accessible to students with disabilities and different learning styles. Also, I'd like to use digital media to challenge students to build on their traditional writing skills." Instead of a binary, he constructs a continuum—students will write traditionally *and* use digital media to build upon traditional writing skills, perhaps by producing nontraditional, digital texts.

The struggle voiced in these responses—the certainty that "technology helps us be better teachers" even as our central pedagogical goal of "teaching coherent writing is being undermined"—indicates the complexity of the issues at stake. Digital media work, for many of the people in this study, is a mixed bag. As another survey respondent writes, "The web is a fabulous—& dangerous—resource." Digital media work is alternately constructed by the participants in this study as both fabulous and dangerous, representing a struggle to navigate the tensions of the late age of print. These five survey quotations illustrate broad disciplinary tensions about digital media work and its ability to enable and hinder central methods and processes of teaching and research, provide new or alternative objects of study for ourselves and our students, and transform the central goals of teaching and the central research questions of the discipline.

These quotations only hint at the role individuals' disciplinary identities play in the decision-making process as they navigate these tensions.

Though the responses quoted here frame this tension as it affects teaching, this is also a tension that affects scholarly production. "What form should student texts take and in what media should they be produced?" and "What form should scholarly texts take and in what media should they be produced and disseminated?" are two related questions whose "answers" rely upon the disciplinary identities individuals and departments forge.

Intersecting Dimensions of Digital Media Integration

Although the discipline provides a common language to talk about teaching and scholarship and constructs a set of values, each department is left to interpret and put those values into practice. This practice is different at each location because of local values, institutional contingencies, and other conditions that affect how digital media can be used. I see these elements as part of what Richard Selfe calls a department's "culture of support" for digital media. Selfe argues that "sustainable practices (not short-term solutions) are essential to the successful integration of technologies into English, language arts, and literacy instruction" (*Sustainable Computer Environments*, xi) and that departments need to work toward creating supportive environments that put teachers first, then pedagogy, then technologies. What I understand him to mean is that the technology should not drive the decision making; rather, the stakeholders (that is, teachers as well as students) and good pedagogy should drive decisions about technology. In other words, teachers, pedagogies, and technologies shape each other in an ecology, and we should maintain a focus on the teachers' shared values about pedagogy and on the ways those values can find expression through various media and technologies. He further argues that within local contexts, "stakeholders can act collectively to leverage pedagogical and institutional change that support[s] appropriate critical approaches to technology-rich learning environments" (11). Although he focuses primarily on teaching and learning environments and undergraduate instruction, his concept of a culture of support is just as important in the context of graduate education and scholarship, in which people can work together to create environments and structures that support a variety of work, including digital media teaching and scholarship. In other work, Selfe and collaborators Dànielle Nicole DeVoss and Heidi A. McKee refer to technological ecologies, a term which suggests cultures of support that engage in "the important task of maintaining the richly textured technological environments in which composition teachers and students learn, study, and communicate" (1).

The concepts of culture of support and technological ecology draw upon the work of Bonnie Nardi and Vicki L. O'Day, who developed the metaphor of the information ecology: a system of people, practices, values, and technologies where the spotlight is on human activities served by technology rather than on the technology itself. Information ecologies are sustained by active, intelligent participation, and Nardi and O'Day assert that it is especially important to negotiate values in information ecologies and to integrate values with the technology. This gives members of information ecologies freedom because they don't have to accept the rhetoric of inevitability, which offers extremes—technophilia and dystopia—and encourages people to accept technology as inevitable. Instead, they are able to make deliberate, conscious choices about how their values will influence their use of technology. To "evolve" an information ecology, they argue that individuals must notice the "spaces between," work from core values, pay attention, and ask strategic questions, including deliberately evaluating whether a practice has merit, rather than uncritically accepting the practice as the way it has always been or as simply the way things are done.

Nardi and O'Day's work has influenced my thinking about the ways that departments and institutions work and about the importance of departments of English deliberately attending to questions raised by digital media in order to create intentional technological ecologies or cultures of support for digital media work. I see departments and institutions as information ecologies that are constantly shifting and changing based upon the work of individual stakeholders within the constraints of local contexts. Moreover, I see the role of local conversations as crucial to the sustainability of local ecologies, and I agree with Nardi and O'Day that even long-held practices must be critically examined occasionally to make sure they continue to suit the needs of the community and reflect the values that the community holds most dear. It is in this spirit of self-reflection within communities of practice that I offer my matrix of questions. Throughout the book, I use these terms—culture of support and technological ecologies—interchangeably.

These concepts also inform my construction of digital media integration as something that occurs along three intersecting dimensions: scholarly values, curricular values, and institutional or cultural climate (technological ecologies). The vertical axis represents curricular values, with traditional/conventional values at one end and emerging/digital values at the other. The horizontal axis represents scholarly values, with traditional/conventional values at one end and emerging/digital values at the other. These axes intersect in the middle, which marks the "sweet spot" of digital media integration into English studies and a perfect balance of shared values that enables both traditional/conventional and emerging/digital work. The axis for plotting the richness of each department's technological ecology represents the "z-axis," making the model three-dimensional.

The departments' pseudonyms thus represent their center of gravity in this three-dimensional space of intersecting dimensions of technology integration, which is not fixed but constantly shifting based upon the work that individuals do within their departments and institutions.

The pseudonyms should not be interpreted as representing an assessment of each department; they are instead intended to be descriptive of the values that seem to be most at play in each department's culture and practice. Rather than trying to represent this three-dimensional space in the two dimensions of the page, I have created three figures that represent the departments' different values plotted against each other and the way that the view changes when the axes change. Figure 1.1 plots each department's curricular values against its scholarly values; figure 1.2 plots each department's curricular values against its technological ecology for digital teaching; and figure 1.3 plots each department's technological ecology for digital scholarship against its scholarly values. As the figures demonstrate, although the integrated literacies department is more integrated in terms of curricular and scholarly values, it has less of a technologically rich environment for teaching and providing professional development opportunities than the parallel cultures department, which will be demonstrated as the book unfolds.

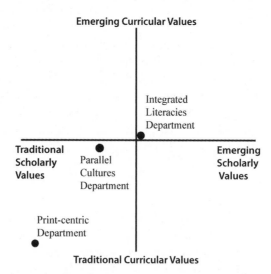

Figure 1.1. Each department's curricular values plotted against its scholarly values

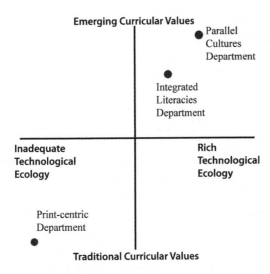

Figure 1.2. Each department's curricular values plotted against its technological ecology for digital teaching

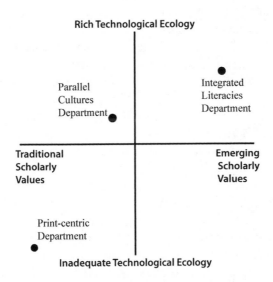

Figure 1.3. Each department's technological ecology for digital scholarship plotted against its scholarly values

While members of all departments use digital media, the print-centric department is heavily invested in print culture and the literacies and values associated with it, placing print at the top of a media hierarchy. The parallel cultures department also sees print literacy as its business yet has invested tremendous resources in digital media and the teaching of literacies associated with technology; in spite of such investment, digital media have not been integrated into the curriculum. This department is trying to break down the media hierarchy that privileges print and to value a plurality of media; however, it has not quite effected this change. Instead, is has created two parallel paths: one that highly values print and one that highly values digital media. The integrated literacies department, however, does have an integrated curriculum and does not require its members to "take sides" in what is often constructed as a battle between print and digital forms. This department is actively encouraging a culture that resists creating a hierarchy of media. A department's culture influences not only what individuals do with digital media but also how they perceive the value of what they do and how they construct their identities in the classroom, department, and discipline. In other words, these cultures encourage individuals to see their work in particular ways and thus make certain professional identities, and not others, available and/or desirable.

The survey responses quoted in the previous section can also be analyzed in relation to each department's culture of support. The graduate student who calls herself "old-school," for instance, is a member of the parallel cultures department. Because the department is increasing its investment in digital media and making digital media a more visible presence in the department, she names her disciplinary identity as "old-school," even though in a different department her identity might be more mainstream and not necessarily seen as "old-fashioned." Her lack of interest in digital media goes somewhat against her department's culture, but the department's culture does not completely influence her disciplinary identity. She still rejects digital media, but she labels herself in a way that is clearly influenced not only by her own conception of the discipline but by her department's culture, as well. Similarly, the first assistant professor quoted, a member of the integrated literacies department, is in a position to claim that *all* of her academic work is digitally mediated because of the department's heavy investment, materially as well as philosophically, in digital media. She doesn't have to qualify or defend her interest in digital media in the ways that individuals in other departments do because of her department's culture (which will be explored in more depth throughout the book).

In addition to creating varying cultures of support for different media, these departments also take stances on how to define the central concerns of the discipline and to enact the discipline in their departments through curricula and tenure and promotion standards. The three areas in particular on which departments take a stance are the three "big questions" occasioned by digital media work: how to define what counts as a text, how to approach the reading of texts, and how to approach the production of texts. These three issues, in turn, have direct implications for three realms of academic work: teaching practices, the professional development opportunities that are provided for graduate students and faculty, and the valuing of different kinds of scholarship in each department.[5] Throughout this book, I describe the stances or cultures of support of the three departments as a means of showing the range of approaches to digital media work that exists across the various fields within or connected to "English studies," as well as of demonstrating the ways that different technological ecologies can cultivate or shut down not only particular practices but also community-based discussions of digital media issues.

Terminology: Categorizing Digital Media Work

In order for discussions of digital media issues to proceed smoothly, it is important to have a common vocabulary for naming different types of digital media work. Cheryl E. Ball has posited a taxonomy for understanding different types of online scholarship, based upon the extent of their multimodality, or how many different communicative modes (visual, aural, verbal, and so on) they utilize. She distinguishes online scholarship and scholarship about new media—which usually take more traditional forms and rely mostly on text to make an argument—from new media scholarship, which uses modes other than text to make an argument (such as images, animation, sound, motion, and the like). Her goal is to help readers make meaning from new media texts and to understand the difference between scholarship that is relatively traditional in form but appears in an online venue and scholarship that uses semiotic modes other than text in aesthetically pleasing ways to make an argument ("Show, Not Tell").

There is a similar spectrum for other uses of digital media, particularly teaching applications, and having a similar taxonomy that can be applied to other types of work with digital media provides insight into the ways that digital media support our work as teachers, scholars, and administrators. Digital media not only can support the processes central to our work but also can transform the products of that work. In other words, digital technologies (such as word processing) can be used to create a text that is traditional in form and distributed in print, they can be used to create a text that is traditional in form but distributed through a digital medium (such as an online journal), or they can be an integral part of both the creation and examination of the text, not to mention the dissemination of it (such as a Flash movie). These nuanced distinctions are important because the materialities surrounding different ways of using digital media are different; in other words, different ways of composing with digital media require different types of support.

Additionally, some types of media used for composing are naturalized. Word processing, although technically a digital means of composing a text, most often leads to a text composed primarily of words and meant for print. Most scholars use word processing, rather than pencil and paper, for composing their texts. Similarly, most of us probably use email and online databases regularly in our day-to-day teaching and research activities. These are scholarly uses of digital media, yes, but not in the same vein as using image creation tools and an animation program like Flash to create a text that makes a scholarly argument using images and motion rather than or in addition to words. Likewise, there is a qualitative difference between having students access texts online or turn in texts through an online course management tool and having them create a new media text for a course. It is this distinction that is important for classifying digital media use and for understanding why some uses are almost taken for granted while others are hotly debated.

I thus propose a taxonomy similar to Ball's for classifying digital media work more generally and for understanding the different ways that we can use digital media as professionals: digital management, analysis of digital media, and digital media production. *Digital management* focuses on the processes that are enabled and disabled by digital media. It describes uses of digital media that involve management of professional activities but do not necessarily change, fundamentally, the tasks being performed. Some examples are using a word processor for writing papers/articles, using online databases to search for primary or secondary texts, using the web to post course updates for students, and using an online discussion board to facilitate class discussion of texts. Though they don't necessarily require altering the fundamental nature of research, writing, or teaching, they can; moreover, these uses raise concerns about disciplinary identity for some of the study participants. *Analysis of digital media* describes uses of digital media that involve the analysis of alternative texts—including visual images, films, websites, and other digital texts—as well as the analysis of technologies as cultural artifacts and/or analysis of the uses of those technologies in various contexts (classroom, workplace, personal, and so on). It can describe the texts that faculty and/or graduate students analyze as part of their scholarly research agendas or the texts they ask their students to analyze. For some study participants, these uses raise questions about disciplinary identity because they often challenge central questions and texts of the discipline. *Digital media production* describes uses of digital media involving the production of alternative texts, such as websites, digital videos, visual arguments, and the like. It can describe the texts that faculty and/or graduate students create as part of their scholarly activities or the texts they ask their students to create. This category is fundamentally concerned with uses of digital media that challenge traditional disciplinary constructions of teaching goals and/ or the purposes and central questions of scholarship.

These three categories of digital media work are similar in structure to the three computer literacies that Stuart Selber lays out: functional, critical, and rhetorical. In addition to a functional literacy in which students become effective users of technology, he adds a critical literacy in which students become informed questioners of technology and a rhetorical literacy in which students become reflective producers of technology. Selber's construction is primarily pedagogical; he defines three relationships students should be taught to forge with digital media work: the ability to use it to manage their digital lives, the ability to question and critique it in order to understand it in broader social and political contexts, and the ability to reshape it through the design of interfaces. Digital management, analysis of digital media, and digital media production, on the other hand, describe the ways in which faculty and graduate students integrate digital media into their teaching and research activities.

Each category can involve all three of Selber's literacies, though it need not necessarily. For instance, many teachers use a course management program (like WebCT or Blackboard) to disseminate texts to students, as a dropbox for assignments, and to make communication with and among students more accessible. In using digital media in these ways, the goal is digital management—of class materials, of class time, and of students' work. However, in order to accomplish this management, teachers must employ functional, critical, and rhetorical computer literacies. They have to know how to use the course management tool and possibly a word processor or slideshow program in order for this digital management strategy to be effective; they also need to understand the social and rhetorical contexts (particularly academic contexts) in which those tools are embedded in order to use them to most effectively reach their goals (functional digital literacy). Although they do not *need* to question and critique the media they use in order to use them as they do, in chapter 2 I examine the ways many teachers do question and critique digital media's role in pedagogy and in the discipline and how this questioning influences their uses of digital media (critical digital literacy). Teachers in this situation also need to be able to understand the course management system rhetorically, as an interface, in order to reshape that interface to best guide their students through the course materials contained in the site (rhetorical digital literacy). However, their actual teaching might not encourage students to develop all three literacies, even though they draw upon all three to manage the course.

Understanding these different categories helps us to better understand specifically *how* individuals are integrating digital media into their academic work and the types of support (disciplinary, departmental, curricular, and institutional) needed to facilitate their work. This taxonomy also provides language used throughout the book to describe participants' work with digital media. In the next chapter, I look at how individuals are integrating digital media into their teaching and the types of support needed to facilitate that work.

2

Situating Digital Media Teaching:
Challenging the "Hierarchy of Signs"

"I Can Haz Writin Skillz?" is the title of the writing workshop section of Robert Lanham's parody of a writing course, "Internet-Age Writing Syllabus and Course Overview." This middle segment of the course "is a workshop where students will work to perfect their tweeting, blogging, and short-form writing skills." It follows a lecture and discussion segment of the course titled "The Writing Is on the Wall: Why Print/ Reading Will Go the Way of the Pictograph," with discussion topics such as "Reading is stoopid," "Printing words isn't good for the environment," "Curling up with a good book/newspaper is dangerous," and "The Kindle Question." In the third and final section of the course, "students will learn inside knowledge about the industry—getting published, getting paid, dealing with agents and editors—and assess why all the aforementioned are no longer applicable in the post print post-reading age" (n. pag.). As much a send-up of teaching as of online writing, this course exhibits some uneasy assumptions about writing pedagogy, the student-teacher relationship, and the role of digital media in teaching and literate practice.

The pedagogy of this class assumes Paulo Freire's "banking model" of education, in which the teacher has all the knowledge that is passed on to students, whose "blank slates" are filled up with information the teacher deems important. The "lecture and discussion" section pays lip service to the importance of discussion and problem solving as pedagogical methods; for instance, in the session "Curling up with a good book/newspaper is dangerous," the syllabus states, "Students will explore the dangers of curling up by the fires with books and newspapers." And in the session "Reading is stoopid," "students will examine why former generations carried around heavy clumps of bound paper and why they chose to read instead of watching TV or playing Guitar

Hero" (Lanham n. pag.). However, although students are "examining/ exploring" issues and asking "why," the conclusions are already determined by the teacher; the sessions are more about coming to the right conclusions (the teacher's conclusions) than they are about exploration of the issues by students. In its irony, the syllabus presumes the inherent value of teacher-centered pedagogy, not to mention printed texts. Not only does it make fun of active learning and show an extreme disdain for student-centered pedagogy, but it is also obsessed with portraying digital writing as a completely empty sign—it stands in for all types of technology-enhanced teaching and digitally mediated forms of communication while being portrayed as devoid of anything substantial, in stark contrast to "dying" printed media.

At the same time the course disdains the emptiness of digital writing (stating that students in the writing workshop segment of the course "will be encouraged to nurture their craft, free of the restraints of punctuation, syntax, and grammar"), it nonetheless recognizes that there *is* a grammar of online writing that needs to be studied in order to be used well. Week 5, for instance, focuses on "Grammar and Technique." Students will focus on using "Internet slang and chatspeak" to craft "effective tweets, instant messages, and text messages." They "will practice using emoticons to create powerful dialogue and to establish dramatic irony" and

> learn to gracefully integrate complex expressions into their IM writing, substituting the trite LOL ("laughing out loud") and "meh" (the written equivalent of a shrug) with more-advanced expressions like BOSMKL ("bending over smacking my knee laughing") and HFACTDEWARIUCSMNUWKIASLAMB ("holy flipping animal crackers, that doesn't even warrant a response; if you could see me now, you would know that I am shrugging like a mofu, biotch"). (Lanham n. pag.)

The syllabus effectively reduces all types of digital media composing to "chatspeak" and dismisses any way of making meaning that is not based on the stringing together of complete sentences to form literary-styled prose. The "visual turn" in English studies and the rise of visual rhetoric in composition, not to mention the rise of multimodal composition pedagogy, are effectively ignored.

The syllabus's view of digital media's role in teaching is that digital media have no role in teaching; digital media are not/should not be transformative to pedagogy. The subject matter may change, but the methods shouldn't change. It is ironic, of course, that a course making fun of new media writing would be so traditional in its pedagogy and not try to incorporate the new medium itself as a component of the course. The only nod to the methods of distance education in particular and new media pedagogy in general is in the attendance section, which notes that attendance is "unnecessary, but students should be signed onto IM and/or have their phones turned on." In its final assault on new media pedagogy, the course purports to evaluate students by the "RBBEAW system" ("Raised by Boomers, Everyone's a Winner"), "developed to assess and score students based on their own relative merit" (Lanham n. pag.). The grading scale goes from an A+ (100–90) down to an A minus-minus-minus-minus (49–0). Such a grading scale implies not only that writing pedagogy is "soft" but also that multimodal texts can't be evaluated by any substantial textual criteria; only the "effort" can be evaluated.

Although it is meant to make us laugh, this fictitious course nonetheless raises some of the same questions that this study addresses:

- How do we define what is a text, and how do we approach reading those texts? Which texts are appropriate to teach?
- How do we approach the production of texts, and in what forms/genres should students be asked to write?
- What should we be teaching, and how should we be teaching it?

After bringing up these questions, though, Lanham's course uses irony to dismiss them and concludes that the way we've always done things is the way we should continue to do things. Lanham raises many of the same issues that participants in this study raise, while ridiculing many of the underlying assumptions of faculty and graduate students in the study who try to incorporate digital media into their pedagogies.

This chapter looks at these questions in detail as they are being negotiated by individuals in particular contexts. However, for the purposes of analyzing digital media teaching, the "big questions" laid out in chapter 1 need to be slightly reframed. The question of what counts as a text, while certainly an item of theoretical interest (and fodder for classroom discussion), also has a practical side to it: which texts do we assign for students to read—that is, which texts make appropriate primary "readings" in our classes? The question of how we should read texts translates easily to the question of what methods of reading/research are appropriate to teach students. Finally, the question of how to approach production becomes a question of which kinds of texts/genres (and in which media) do we teach/expect students to produce (see table 2.1).

Table 2.1. Organizing questions reframed in the context of teaching

Organizing questions	Questions reframed for teaching
How do we define what counts as a text?	What kinds of texts do we assign as primary "readings"?
How do we approach reading texts?	What methods of reading/ research do we teach students?
How do we approach the production of texts?	What types of texts/genres do we teach/expect students to produce?

We are experiencing a potentially transformational moment, one brought about by the influence of digital media, which provides an opportunity to revisit the assumptions that underlie our ideas about what constitutes good teaching. The negotiation of these questions is as much about the discipline and what it should be in the twenty-first century as it is about digital media's usefulness to teaching or how people are using it in their teaching. In "New Media Scholarship and Teaching," Ellen Cushman argues that English upholds a "hierarchy of signs" with the language of print/the letter and its consumption at the top and other forms, such as image and sound, and their production below. She contends that this hierarchy could be balanced if English faculty created more multimodal scholarship and production assignments in their undergraduate courses and asserts that "new media compositions privilege all sign systems equally to the alphabet; thus, new media composition potentially can change the cultural practices of knowledge production and teaching in English studies" (66).

Cushman's argument extends Robert Scholes's case that English needs to move away from a canon of texts to a canon of methods for studying textuality. He states that in order to maintain relevance and better teach students the knowledge and skills (which, he argues, are not in opposition to each other) they need, English should shift from focusing primarily on reading and interpreting a canon of literary texts toward a more balanced focus on reading and writing a variety of texts. More specifically, he describes four intellectual activities that already occur in English that must, he believes, become equally balanced—theory (the core canon of methods used to study the other three elements of textuality), history (how to situate a text), production (how to compose a text), and consumption (how to read a text). He specifically includes digital media texts in his argument: "Production, in this age, must also mean film, video, and digital composition, for all of these use the verbal language as well as the languages of images and tones. An English department cannot do everything, of course, but literary study that cuts itself off from the performing and media arts risks going the way of classics" (161). He and Cushman both maintain that we need to start where the students are, otherwise we risk irrelevance. Cushman argues further that

> the hierarchy of signs hinders knowledge making and teaching practices with multimodal discourses. Even though multimodal discourses and the sign technologies that allow their production are increasingly important to everyday acts of meaning making in schools, workplaces, and communities, the cultural practices of knowledge production in English still largely rely on the letter and print. (66)

She reasons convincingly that digital media teaching could effectively challenge the hierarchy of signs, and my data indicate that the hierarchy of signs influences what individuals choose to do in their classes. At the same time, my data also reveal some of the ways that individuals challenge the hierarchy of signs through their teaching and the extent to which they and their departments are actively attending to the questions occasioned by digital media teaching.

And yet, because of the prevalence of the hierarchy of signs, some individuals who decide to incorporate digital media into their teaching are at odds with their department's construction of the discipline, causing tension. Participants in this study tend to frame their discomfort with changing teaching methods as a digital media problem (as does Lanham), but their discomfort also stems from disagreements about disciplinary definitions. Within the large departments in this study, where many field identities are represented, not all individuals see themselves as belonging, necessarily, to the same "umbrella" discipline of English studies. Who gets to define the department's disciplinary connections and how various disciplinary values are enacted in the department's curricula and other structures thus become very important to questions of digital media pedagogy, particularly the types of digital media work that are possible within individual classrooms. Individual teachers must negotiate not only their own professional identities but also the disciplinary identity of the department when they make decisions regarding teaching; this includes examining the assumptions that underlie their teaching methods, whether those assumptions match up with the department's take on the discipline, and how digital media fit in. Throughout this chapter, the framing questions from table 2.1 will help to organize my analysis of the ways that individuals within their local context address or elide (deliberately or not) these questions and of the effects of those choices on the departmental culture of support for digital media pedagogies. First I will discuss these questions in the context of the department chairs' leadership; then I will discuss examples of how individuals negotiate these questions within the local contexts that are shaped by their respective chair's leadership and their department's technological ecology.

Digital Media and Teaching: Three Departmental Stances

Individuals' negotiations play out in practice differently in different departments because each department has a different stance toward digital media work and its role in teaching. This section explores in detail the importance of the department chair's leadership in defining the disciplinary home of the department, setting the tone for support for digital media pedagogies in the department, and considering how digital media intersect with the discipline's and the department's missions. Additionally, this section looks at the role of local agents in advocating digital media agendas and at the power they have to influence the department chair's thinking on the issue of the intersections between the discipline and digital media, thus shaping the forces that individual instructors must negotiate as they decide how to incorporate digital media into their teaching. Finally, this section addresses the extent to which departments create a culture that is open to discussing some important questions about digital media pedagogy and its role in the discipline.

Table 2.2 lays out the questions that are important for a department to consider, and the reason for their significance will become apparent as I analyze how each department in my study sets the stage either to allow these issues to be addressed or to occlude/elide such a discussion. Lanham's writing course parody provides a good example of how an individual or a department (through its curricular structure) can occlude a serious discussion of one or more of these questions. For the purposes of brief illustration, I will focus on the questions in the production column, which focus on the value of writing, the value of digital media composing, and their relationship to each other. By setting up a binary opposition between traditional and digital forms of writing and assuming that only traditional forms of writing are worthy, Lanham's parody course elides a consideration not only of what is valuable about assigning digital media projects but also of the potential for digital media composing to be seen as a method of inquiry. Of course, this class is not real and it doesn't represent a unified departmental stance, just one course. However, it should not be difficult to imagine a departmental culture that shares many of these assumptions and thus structures itself in such a way as to make discussions of these issues difficult and, as a consequence, to make it difficult for individual instructors to consider these questions for themselves. So, understanding how a department structures the conversation about digital media is an important precursor to examining how individual instructors grapple with these questions in their own pedagogical practice.

Table 2.2. Questions to create an open discussion of digital media and teaching

Organizing questions	How do we define what counts as a text?	How do we approach reading texts?	How do we approach the production of texts?
Reframed questions	What kinds of texts do we assign as primary "readings"?	What methods of reading/research do we teach students?	What types of texts/genres do we teach/expect students to produce?
Questions for departments	What types of texts and genres should undergraduates be exposed to in their studies? When should undergraduates be exposed to new media texts? What can the department do to increase exposure to alternative texts/genres?	What lenses should undergraduates learn to bring to alternative texts/genres? When and how should undergraduates learn to read alternative texts? What are the best practices in teaching in your field?	What is valuable about assigning writing? What is valuable about assigning digital media projects? What skills should undergraduate students be able to demonstrate in writing? What would those skills look like demonstrated in another medium? How is writing a means of inquiry? How can digital media be used as a means of inquiry? Should undergraduates learn to produce alternative texts? When/where should they learn this (at what point in the curriculum)?

Print-centric Department

The print-centric department is a traditional English department consisting primarily of faculty in literary fields, with three in rhetoric and composition. According to Toby, an assistant professor in rhetoric and composition, digital media play an "ancillary role to pedagogy" in the department. Benjamin, one of Toby's advisees and a PhD student in rhetoric and composition, uses technology in this fashion, mostly as a supplement to his traditional pedagogy. He uses course websites to manage his classes, posting "[the] syllabus, handouts, assignment sheets, links to potential research, [and] links to all kinds of useful sites" and maintaining that "quite religiously." In addition, he says, "I always encourage, indeed require, my students to use that website because I'm not photocopying things for them. They're fully capable of going to a website, downloading, printing, reading." He notes the benefits of this approach: "Saves them money. Saves me money. Saves both of us time. . . . They're not losing their assignment sheets. It takes care of a lot of potential miscommunication and protest: 'You said that was due on such and such.' 'No I didn't, here it is clearly.' And so I rely on the website wholly to keep them up to date." The use of the technology doesn't change his pedagogy or cause him to rethink his teaching methods. His web syllabus space, for instance, is essentially unchanging, like a printed syllabus. The changes that are made are of a specific sort, additions: updates to due dates, the addition of links, the addition of texts to read or links to visit. Students can refer to the web syllabus as they would to a printed syllabus with unchanging information about the class. Web updates replace printed handouts; e-reserves replace a course pack (although he requires students to print out readings to bring to class, using the website almost like a photocopier for printed materials).

The facilities that are available contribute to these managerial uses of digital media. The department chair describes some "extraordinary wired classrooms" that the university has, which have "overhead projectors and computers so that we can immediately go into all kinds of applications, even beyond PowerPoint." He describes the configuration:

> It's really kind of interesting architecturally—if you can imagine an old dumbwaiter in the wall, which isn't a dumbwaiter, but it has a lock-down screen and you press it open and it pops up. And there's a password. And in that dumbwaiter is a DVD player; all the lighting and everything is from the computer. The overhead projector is from the computer. There's VHS in there. And then

there's interface with the computer in the podium, and therefore
you can give the discussion or the lecture and have access from the
podium to the DVD player, to the VHS player, to the lights and to
the sound, to the screens, to everything. And to the Internet, too.

This configuration sets up a particular relationship among students,
teacher, and technology and favors a particular pedagogy. There are
no computers for students; instead, everything is filtered through the
teacher. It does not allow for a particularly decentered teaching experience nor for student production of digital media texts. It does allow for
teachers to use the media in a presentational way, to show PowerPoint
presentations or provide visual aids with their lectures. It also permits
teachers to use digital or multimedia texts as objects of analysis in writing
or literature classes. For instance, a teacher could lead students through
a discussion of the rhetorical aspects of a photograph published in the
New York Times Online or have students analyze the reliability of various
websites, such as Wikipedia. Students might also discuss and analyze
film clips or entire films, as Toby has them do in some of his classes.

Although some in the department are using multimedia texts as
objects of analysis, the department chair says that this use "begs the
question, are web representations of reality objects of study appropriate
to English departments? To what extent is visual culture embraceable
under the broadest definition of the discipline of English?" He gives an
example of a professor in the department creating a "web representation
of reality" for an Asian American literature course: the professor worked
with a web designer to create a web tour of Chinatown and then had
students compare the web landscape to the descriptions of Chinatown
in novels. Although there are examples of individuals in the department who incorporate alternative texts and genres into their teaching,
the chair constructs such choices as controversial, in the sense that he
discusses such practices within the context of what "counts" as a text in
an English department and frames his comments not as statements of
what should count but rather as questions. He does not declare which
"side" he is on, so to speak, but rather points out that this is a question
facing the field, indicating either that a good number of individuals in
the department might still be wondering whether multimedia "representations" or "presentations" can even be considered "texts" or that this
is a conversation the department is having. His comments also, however, indicate the importance of his leadership in defining a disciplinary
identity for the department. He is a powerful local agent steering the
department in a particular direction; in this case, he constructs himself

not as a leader in integrating digital media but as more of a facilitator of the questions, which has the effect of maintaining a status quo or wait-and-see position on the issue of digital media texts as appropriate objects of analysis for English studies.

Benjamin directly addresses the issues of textuality, the appropriateness of different objects of analysis, and the appropriateness of different methods of composing, saying, "While I see multimedia presentations as texts, certainly, I'm not interested in my students producing them for a course; instead, I like to use them as texts for analysis." Although he does consider multimedia texts as suitable for students to read, there is still some question for him as to whether they are appropriate texts for students to compose:

> At the Computers & Writing conference in Indianapolis, there was much debate about "giving up" the traditional essay in favor of multimedia presentations. Great—but I don't think the place for that is necessarily in the composition (that is, writing) classroom (perhaps as a side project, perhaps as a project for which students then write an analysis, but not as a class focus). . . . Many students are already quite savvy with multimedia invention (Web, Power-Point, etc.) whether we have them produce such projects for classes or not. Analytical writing is where they need the education.

For Benjamin, the core skill he is to teach is analytical writing, and a particular form of analytical writing—the printed essay—which aligns with the discipline's valuing of essayistic literacy. It is the replacement of analytical writing with digital media production that worries Benjamin. He says, "If we (and I mean Compositionists, teachers of writing) start doing too much multimedia production in our praxis, then who is going to teach writing? Writing, I'd argue vehemently, is still a useful skill to have and process to explore. Unless, of course, the technology gets to the point that we must redefine (as opposed to complicate or extend) what a writing project is." He adds, "I am a strong believer in the analytical essay—a printed text composed of words. If a student wants to put images/figures into a paper, so be it, but I still teach writing." For him, placing images or figures into a paper might accomplish that complicating or extending move: to include other means of expression in a paper complicates what a paper is, thereby complicating what writing is. However, elevating those other means of expression above words (creating a Flash movie, for instance, that uses words marginally—printed words not at all—and makes its main argument through audio and video) redefines writing and goes too far.

Scholars in the field, though, argue that different forms of writing need not be mutually exclusive. In fact, some maintain that digital media production (or multimodal composition) teaches the same underlying skills as essayistic analytical writing: critical thinking, analysis, organization, focus, claim versus evidence, development, and so on. This philosophy has its roots in arguments about broadening the definition of literacy. Scholars, most notably Gunther Kress; Cynthia L. Selfe and Gail E. Hawisher; and Kress and Theo Van Leeuwen, have asserted that the new multimediated landscape of communication necessitates a redefinition of literacy to include communication in multiple media and modes, beyond the printed word. They further argue for the importance of teaching multimodal composing and, particularly, for writing teachers to teach it (Wysocki, Johnson-Eilola, Selfe, and Sirc).

Although Benjamin is interested in studying technology from a scholarly standpoint, he remains skeptical of pedagogical applications of technology and argues that there is still a lot of work to be done in studying the effects of technology before he feels comfortable integrating it into his pedagogy. Coming from this cautious standpoint, he sees the usefulness of digital media primarily as an add-on to traditional pedagogy: "And so if we're using these technologies in addition to what a lot of us are already doing, then they certainly have their advantages, and I think we need to maintain a large degree of skepticism. And I think we need to be very critical about our use of technology and continue to study it." This cautious and skeptical attitude is representative of the stance of the department toward digital media pedagogy, which contributes in large part to the supplemental role of digital media to pedagogy in this department.

There is nothing wrong with being cautious and critical about how to integrate digital media into pedagogy. But thinking about the implications of digital media pedagogy shouldn't prevent us from experimenting with digital media in order to figure out what works and what doesn't. Andrew Feenberg, for instance, argues that in addition to a critical interrogation of technology, we also need to have critical engagement, in which individuals are able to intervene in the design of technologies and shape them for their own purposes. In this department, such intervention happens rarely, and the department seems almost singularly focused on critical interrogation of technology. The central questions it is focused on are those pertaining to texts—which texts and genres are appropriate to teach and in which classes—and these questions are seen as primarily questions for individual instructors to answer for themselves; the question of how the department can increase exposure to alternative texts/genres is ignored. Additionally, the questions about reading/interpreting alternative texts and composing in digital media are beyond the pale of this department at the moment, although Toby and Benjamin engage somewhat with these questions because of their field identities. Partially, this lack of addressing questions in the second and third columns of table 2.2 (those dealing with reading/research methods and composing texts) is because there are few role models in the department for this type of engagement. Most individuals use technology in supplemental ways. But there is also an attitude that digital media need to be studied and figured out from a theoretical standpoint before being integrated into practice. Thus, the question of digital media as a means of inquiry—that experimental practice might lead to theoretical insight—is completely occluded.

Although digital media work is ancillary to pedagogy, Toby stresses that currently, it is "understood to be of importance" and that "instructors in areas *well beyond Rhetoric and Composition* are making use of, at the very least, DVD presentations and websites to some extent" (my emphasis). Although he is trying to argue that digital media are being used across the department, his statement has the effect of perpetuating the idea that it's normal or typical or simply assumed that scholars in rhetoric and composition would use digital media in their teaching and somehow notable or worthy of remark that those in literary fields would do so. The department chair reinforces this notion and specifically links digital media to rhetoric and composition. He says that his department is very different from English departments in other similar universities because "this department never really wanted to invest very much in professional and technical communication until very, very recently." He adds, "When I first arrived here twenty years ago, there were sixty-five faculty, only two or three of whom were actively involved in rhetoric and composition, let alone professional communication. It was not an investment this department, nor the college, wanted to make." He claims that this is changing because the department now has three specialists in rhetoric and composition and is hoping to hire a fourth, but in a large department such as this, three (possibly four) scholars in rhetoric and composition is not much of a change from the "two or three" that were there twenty years ago.

This department chair ties technology to a specific field within English studies (rhetoric and composition) as well as to a specific subfield within rhetoric and composition (professional communication), identifying a disciplinary home for technology that is extremely circumscribed. That technology should be linked with professional communication is not surprising, given that it is often seen as a "service" course to train students for professional and technical writing in business and industry. Neither is it surprising that technology should be linked so closely with rhetoric and composition as a field, given that the technologies of writing and conditions of access to those technologies have long been central to discussions in the field.

The print-centric department chair also ties technology to technical disciplines, however, indicating that the divorce of technology and English has a long history at his university. He explains that historically, other universities in the state system have developed technical programs like engineering and medical sciences, "so the onus on this department for generations was not to interface very well or very copiously with technology and with technical disciplines. . . . That was not our job." He adds that "it's a very slow process of trying to develop curricula, faculty, and classroom space and technologies for that kind of environment." Writing can't be taught in networked computer classrooms because the department doesn't have the facilities. Another university in the state, he says, has "several really beautiful wired classrooms on the same floor as the English department where writing is taught in that computerized environment. We have nothing that even vaguely resembles that right now," though he adds, "I think we will, but it really has been a very different kind of department in that regard." The print-centric department is facing an institutional constraint—the perceived mismatch of English and technology—that leads the department to uphold the stance that digital media are something for rhetoric and composition to contend with. At the same time, the chair is responding to historical and financial realities that maintain this separation, which also help to occlude the question of the potential for digital media as a means of inquiry. When technology and "English" are set in opposition in this way, it can be difficult to see the ways in which they might work together toward common goals. It can also be difficult, as the chair notes, to build a technological ecology in the English department at large because of the perception that it is "not their job" to deal with technology or provide the support that individual faculty need, which has serious repercussions.

In maintaining the status quo in his defining of English studies and keeping technology and English separate, the chair perpetuates the attitude that digital media are only part of the mission of rhetoric and composition, rather than of English as a whole, which contributes greatly to a departmental culture that posits digital media's usefulness as primarily for digital management in teaching, and sometimes perhaps analysis of digital texts. In this department, teaching is discussion-based but teacher-driven and analytical in nature and leads to analytical, essayistic academic prose. Digital media provide an interface to be used, maybe critically questioned and analyzed, but not created or designed. There is very little spirit of pedagogical experimentation and little acknowledgment that such experimentation or pedagogical scholarship about digital media could or should change our ideas about what constitutes good teaching. The department chair is almost completely focused on questions about digital media texts, at the expense of questions about methods of reading and genres/media of production (see table 2.3). It isn't fair to say he is ignoring these questions on purpose or that he wouldn't ask the questions if he knew which questions to ask. He is entrenched in the hierarchy of signs that Cushman argues is indicative of English studies and thus largely unaware of the issues involved in multimodal sign systems and digital media teaching. Toby and Benjamin as individuals are thinking about questions relating to reading and production, but the department chair is not equipped to articulate those questions in a way that those in the department can address them as a community. Consequently, individuals like Toby and Benjamin who might be interested in transformative digital pedagogies face an uphill battle and a lack of community as well as technical support; they are lone rangers in digital media pedagogy, and the departmental culture is slow to change to adequately accommodate them.

Parallel Cultures Department

The parallel cultures department is a large English department with a sizable rhetoric and composition program (approximately one-fourth of the department's faculty); in addition, a number of faculty members specialize in areas beyond literature, such as film, cultural studies, and folklore. This department is not as invested in the hierarchy of signs as the print-centric department is, valuing both printed and multimedia texts as important to English as a whole, rather than of importance to only one field of study. According to the department chair, "People think of the department of English as a center for the study of printed texts, and of course we will *always* have printed texts, but we're living in an age where we need to also be proficient with other kinds of texts, texts that involve imaging, video, sound and animation." In her reference to proficiency, there is a recognition not only of the importance of different media to the enterprise of English but also of a balance between critique and production, which Cushman argues tends to be lacking in constructions of the discipline.

Table 2.3. Print-centric department's framing of digital media and/in teaching

Organizing questions	How do we define what counts as a text?	How do we approach reading texts?	How do we approach the production of texts?
Reframed questions	What kinds of texts do we assign as primary "readings"?	What methods of reading/ research do we teach students?	What types of texts/genres do we teach/expect students to produce?
Print-centric department	*The department is focused on these two questions:* What types of texts and genres should undergraduates be exposed to in their studies? When should undergraduates be exposed to new media texts? *There is a sidestepping of this question:* What can the department do to increase exposure to alternative texts/genres?	*The department is less focused on these questions, assuming essayistic critical analysis is the appropriate method:* What lenses should undergraduates learn to bring to alternative texts/genres? When and how should undergraduates learn to read alternative texts? What are the best practices in teaching in your field?	*The department is well-versed in responding to these two questions, valuing the development of essayistic, analytical skill foremost:* What is valuable about assigning writing? What skills should under-graduate students be able to demonstrate in writing? *The department as a community is not equipped to address these questions, although individuals within the department are thinking in these terms:* What is valuable about assigning digital media projects? What would those skills look like demonstrated in another medium? How is writing a means of inquiry? How can digital media be used as a means of inquiry? Should undergraduates learn to produce alternative texts? When/where should they learn this (at what point in the curriculum)?

In fact, quite a few individuals in this department integrate digital media—from both critical and production standpoints—into their teaching. The director of the Center for Digital Media Studies (CDMS) —a departmental entity that maintains and supports five instructional labs, employs graduate students to provide pedagogical support for those teaching in the labs, provides professional development opportunities for faculty and graduate students, and maintains a centralized computer lab where faculty and graduate students have access to high-end equipment—says that in the department's computer classrooms, "there's huge diversity in what we teach. We have somebody who teaches I believe eighteenth century, or Renaissance would be a better description of his field. We have two of us in composition; we have somebody in business writing." However, even though the department maintains five networked classrooms, offering forty sections of computer-enhanced classes per term, there is still only a small niche of individuals who regularly teach in the labs and consistently integrate digital media into their classes.

Many are incorporating digital media in "critical mode," as in the print-centric department, using digital media mainly to deliver texts or as an object of analysis. According to the CDMS director, they use "digital media for demonstration purposes in teaching, and so we have a lot of people who are talking about historical artifacts, they're talking about theoretical concepts, and they're using technology as a way of demonstrating those ideas to their students. It's very much used in that presentational mode" and "just as a supplement to what they already do." Some examples include using a multimedia database tool to show students images of texts not physically available to them (such as pages from an original manuscript or a collection of papers housed at another institution's library), putting lecture notes and illustrations into PowerPoint, and demonstrating how to use the library's databases to search for information and articles. Emily, an assistant professor in nineteenth-century American literature, uses discussion boards in her classes in this supplemental way. She has used the discussion board feature of the university's course management tool for an undergraduate course in American realism. She says, "It was really bare bones what I set up. I like students to participate, so I basically say, 'If you contribute to the discussion board that counts as participation.'" In addition, for her graduate seminars, she uses the course management tool "as a place where the graduate students can get access to secondary essays as PDF files." Although the media is supplemental in this example, the CDMS director argues that the simple fact of incorporating some new media into their teaching shows that the instructors are "very interested in bringing what they know about class discussion to the technology and trying to figure out how it can be used in those ways."

A smaller segment of the department incorporate digital media production into their teaching and use it as a means of inquiry, according to the CDMS director. He says these individuals use it "as a way to teach, to improve the learning of students," and that in those classes, "digital media is used in both the idea of presenting information to students but also as a way of having students involved in production of digital media. Production of digital media is also a way of getting students to learn in deeper ways about the subject matter of the class." For instance, Chester, a PhD student in nineteenth-century British literature, has students in his introductory literature class create collaborative websites. As a "mini-step" toward creating the websites, he has the groups do PowerPoint presentations about their topics first, so they have the chance to draft their ideas and get feedback as well as "think about how color and text and [arrangement of elements] on the page influence how your readers respond." Two of the topics students focused on were "Representing the City: From Dickens to Doyle to Stevenson" and "Themes and Motifs in *Sister Carrie*." Chester says, "I want my students to get involved in what they are doing." The model for teachers of literature, he argues, has been "stand up in front of the room and talk; be the font of knowledge." He likes to break down this paradigm in his classes and have students create knowledge that will be available not only to the teacher but also to other students in the class and, potentially, to an even broader audience on the web. Other advantages to this, he says, are that students can offer new ways of looking at a text and can find that collaborating helps them learn how to negotiate different views and meanings of one text.

Another example of digital media production occurred in a graduate seminar that Cosmo, a PhD student in rhetoric and composition, took on composition pedagogy. Students explored theories about digital media production in first-year writing classes by creating digital "instructional assets" (including syllabi, assignments, and activities) for a first-year writing class, attempting their own drafts of the assignments they produced, and composing a final reflection about their work in the seminar. Cosmo created a digital campaign assignment that would require students to use Flash (an animation/movie tool) to design a public service announcement that would "persuade a target audience to take a particular action (ex: stop smoking or support a particular public policy)" or to produce a "parodic or satirical marketing campaign, which uses humor to critique the limitations of an already-existing corporate practice or product." He then made a sample PSA that "was designed to convince my students that it was un-American for CBS to refuse to run an anti-Bush ad during the Super Bowl."

Unlike graduate students in the other departments in this study, Cosmo had the opportunity to take a pedagogy class that specifically focused on digital media, modeling a studio workshop atmosphere in the classroom and providing him with the opportunity to study deeply the theoretical underpinnings of such a pedagogy and develop innovative assignments. It gave him the time to respond to his own assignment, helping him understand (by experiencing them) some of the problems that students might face when confronted with the assignment and, by extension, some of the issues he might have to deal with as a teacher assigning the project. Furthermore, the course allowed the students to address as a community questions similar to the ones in table 2.2, giving them time to think through questions about textuality, reading, and production as they pertain to integrating digital media into teaching writing. All graduate students in this department have unstructured opportunities to think about bringing digital media into their pedagogies, but because of the makeup of the faculty, rhetoric and composition students (and literature students who are interested in rhetoric and composition as a secondary specialty) have more structured opportunities for this kind of pedagogical work.

In this department, the focus is on creating a place for the digital alongside the traditional, or on peaceful coexistence, and the CDMS provides a space for experimentation with digital media pedagogy. The parallel cultures department does not force anybody to use digital media, however. Those who choose to integrate such work into teaching are supported, and that support is centralized in the CDMS. According to the center's director, "The current administration is funneling a great deal of funding to this program, as a way of making sure that there's a resource center with high-end equipment for everybody involved." The CDMS receives this funding because "currently our administration has a philosophy that they would like to centrally locate higher-end technology rather than spread mediocre-level technology widely." So for example, rather than giving inexpensive scanners to ten professors who request a scanner, the department prefers to spend that money on one or two high-end scanning stations and place them in the CDMS, where everyone has access.

This philosophy supports everybody. It allows for faculty who have requested high-end equipment to have access to that equipment, and it also allows graduate students and auxiliary faculty access to that equipment; the department does not have to duplicate equipment, in other words. It supports individuals who need access to basic technology infrequently, and it also supports those who value digital media production and experimental pedagogies and need access to higher-end equipment more often. Faculty and graduate students are able to experiment with digital media production in their classes because of the CDMS: it supports the labs in which they teach, offers professional development workshops on digital media and pedagogy, provides access to other material resources like video cameras and audio equipment, and fosters informal conversations among graduate students and faculty about their teaching strategies. For example, Chester uses the CDMS to "make connections and network" with others informally. He finds that talking about what he's doing with others helps him integrate the technology into his pedagogy and make it meaningful to students. Similarly, Cosmo says the CDMS "is a space where I feel a lot of support for what I do" because he has "seen a community of teachers develop here" and gotten a lot of help from people who were, like him, using the computers there or "just hanging out" before and after their classes. In other words, the CDMS provides a space in which individuals can discuss questions about textuality, reading/critical methods, and production as a community. The CDMS is the locus—the nucleus, if you will—of the technological ecology in the department; it is the place that organizes the people, resources, and spaces that support digital pedagogy in the department.

Besides the benefits for graduate students and faculty who are interested in incorporating advanced multimedia projects into their classes, the director of the CDMS notes some of the benefits of his center for the department as a whole:

> There are lots of things that digital media is doing in this department right now. One is that it's catching people's attention who would normally think of English studies in very traditional terms. . . . Digital media obviously has buzzword status right now, and it also has become one of the key initiatives at the university, to improve education through technology and through technological literacy. And so the fact that it's happening in the English department is a way of keeping us competitive.

He specifically ties digital media to literacy, which brings together university initiatives and one of the implicit roles of the English department. But he also argues that the "buzzword" status of digital media keeps the English department visible and thus competitive in terms of funding and attention within the university. Additionally, for graduate students, the ability to work with faculty on digital media pedagogy and to experiment with multimodal assignments in media-saturated classrooms keeps PhD students competitive on the job market and the program competitive within the field of rhetoric and composition.

The chair's attitude that the digital is equally important to the printed, coupled with the department's investment in the CDMS, makes a statement about the importance of digital media to the department and, consequently, about digital media's relationship to the discipline at large: this department sees digital media as an important part of its future and an important part of the discipline. Unlike the chair of the print-centric department, the chair of this department does not construct a disconnect between older-mediated and newer-mediated texts. Digital texts are just as appropriate an object of study for "English studies" as books or illuminated manuscripts or any other kind of text; furthermore, her statement that we need to achieve proficiency with digital texts implies that teaching digital media production is also an important part of the new definition of "English studies."

In this department, teaching consists of many methods—from lecture-based to discussion-based to multimedia studio format; it incorporates process pedagogy, especially in composition classes, but also in other classes like Chester's; it incorporates all kinds of texts in all kinds of media; and for some, it incorporates student production of multimedia texts. This department cultivates a community of individuals with technical and pedagogical expertise and employs faculty who are leading the department and the field of composition to a new, expanded definition of writing and what it means to teach writing. They see the value of having students engage in multimodal composing and are redefining composition pedagogy because of what they are learning about multimedia. Because so many of the CDMS classrooms are scheduled for first-year writing, graduate students in many fields are learning about multimodal pedagogy and using that knowledge to rethink teaching in their own fields. Because of the community in the CDMS and the chair's leadership, the department is thinking not only about questions of digital media textuality but also about questions of production (see table 2.4). While there is an extent to which this department, like the print-centric department, assumes essayistic critical analysis is the preferred method of inquiry, the CDMS community is exploring alternatives.

Table 2.4. Parallel cultures department's framing of digital media and/in teaching

Organizing questions	How do we define what counts as a text?	How do we approach reading texts?	How do we approach the production of texts?
Reframed questions	What kinds of texts do we assign as primary "readings"?	What methods of reading/research do we teach students?	What types of texts/genres do we teach/expect students to produce?
Parallel cultures department	*The department focuses on all of these questions:* What types of texts and genres should undergraduates be exposed to in their studies? When should undergraduates be exposed to new media texts? What can the department do to increase exposure to alternative texts/genres?	*The department as a whole is less focused on this question, assuming essayistic, critical analysis is the appropriate method:* What lenses should undergraduates learn to bring to alternative texts/genres? *The department, particularly the community in the CDMS, is addressing these questions, particularly the one about best teaching practices with digital media:* When and how should undergraduates learn to read alternative texts? What are the best practices in teaching in your field?	*The department is well-versed in responding to these two questions, valuing the development of essayistic, analytical skill foremost:* What is valuable about assigning writing? What skills should undergraduate students be able to demonstrate in writing? *The department is moving in the direction of addressing these questions, with the CDMS community at the forefront of these discussions:* What is valuable about assigning digital media projects? What would those skills look like demonstrated in another medium? How is writing a means of inquiry? How can digital media be used as a means of inquiry? Should undergraduates learn to produce alternative texts? When/where should they learn this (at what point in the curriculum)?

Integrated Literacies Department

The integrated literacies department is not an English department, like the other two departments discussed above, but a department combining rhetoric and composition with cultural studies, two areas of scholarship included in the larger print-centric and parallel cultures departments. Because of its focus on writing (in fact, the word "writing" is in the department's official name), it already balances producing texts with critiquing, theorizing, and historicizing them in a more systematic way than the other departments. It is also somewhat more balanced in terms of the hierarchy of signs, though there are particular material constraints to achieving that balance—namely, a lack of computer classrooms, spaces such as the CDMS, and forums for discussion and development of digital pedagogy outside of formal curricular structures— which will be explored more fully in a later chapter. The department maintains one computer classroom and has a research center focused on digital scholarship but no center comparable to the parallel cultures department's CDMS. A crucial part of the department's philosophy is that digital media are seen as part and parcel of the academic enterprise of the department rather than as an add-on or something outside the purview of most members of the department or as something only a few instructors really need to think about. According to the graduate director, "You just have to do it. It may not be your research focus, and it may not be your principal identity, but there's sort of a certain level of competency and skill and ability that you have to have. And that includes teaching in computer-based environments." So though digital media work may not be specifically tied up in the individual professional identities of each of the members of the department, it is part of the professional identity of the department as a whole. The graduate director is a tenured faculty member whose research is in digital rhetoric, so he is a powerful local agent working toward redefining his field not only at the disciplinary level but also at the department and curricular levels.

Because of the graduate director's advocacy, the department chair is on board with this agenda. He echoes the graduate director's comments and sees the department as very focused on technology and encourages faculty to use "writing technologies and involve students in digital media projects" at all levels and in all types of writing classes. He also describes recently developed "vision documents" that emphasize the importance of digital media use in first-year writing. He stresses that, although functional computer literacy and digital management are important, analysis of digital texts and digital media production are far more important. For instance, he connects the analysis of digital texts to a course that represents the overall stance of the department toward digital media as well as the cultural studies foundation of the department:

> In no way is it a skills course. Technology is not skills. It involves skill, and it's used by skillful people and by skilled people, but our emphasis is always on studying it as part of culture and its impact on culture and in fact the way the technology itself is determined by the culture and mediated by the culture and maybe even in some cases trying to be controlled by the culture or directed in some way.

It is this department's stance that faculty and graduate students should encourage the students in their classes to think about technology as a cultural artifact, about the ways it designs their communication/reading/writing experiences, and about how different tools/audiences/media design those experiences differently. So, not only is the department at large entertaining questions about textuality, reading, and writing in regard to digital media, but those questions are also incorporated, when appropriate, into undergraduate courses.

The chair's comments echo recent scholarly conversations that point out that formal and technical considerations have a rhetorical dimension. For instance, in her article analyzing/reflecting on an extended multimedia project in which she was involved, Jennifer Sheppard maintains that "careful attention to practices of production can demonstrate the critical negotiations writers/designers must undertake as they compose multimedia texts" (122). She argues that many colleagues and administrators in fields other than digital media often don't understand the intellectual work of digital media composing, seeing courses that focus on production "as simply a matter of passing on computer skills rather than doing the more valued work of theory, analysis, and argumentation" (123), and she demonstrates through her case study the rhetorical and intellectual work that is accomplished in multimedia production projects.

The chair of the integrated literacies department clearly understands multimedia production as intellectual and rhetorical work and, as a result, values the incorporation of technology into writing courses. He points to the department's 200- and 400-level courses in web authoring as a place where digital media production is valued, saying that "all of the necessary skills and techniques that are involved" in web authoring are taught in the course, but he also highlights that creative dimension, that innovative dimension. You know, what can you do that's really different here? What can you do that's exciting? What can you do that actually contributes something that other people can learn from, that other people can use, that will advance knowledge, that will advance cultural understanding, that will advance a perspective on the role of technology and the media in our society? And also, how is what you're doing part of the larger culture? So that's the one thing that I think we decided very early that was an absolute connection.

He adds that even in technical writing classes, "There's always that consciousness, that understanding, so you're constantly reflecting on the work that you're doing. You're not just learning it for the sake of saying, 'I'm becoming a very skillful technical writer.'" The chair and the graduate director are pushing a philosophy that digital media should be integrated into the curriculum, rather than simply be an add-on, and that new ways of thinking about and using digital media should push their respective fields to new understandings of those fields.

The way that Ava, an assistant professor in digital rhetoric, teaches document design is an example of this philosophy in practice. One of her course modules focuses on Photoshop and design strategy. The students read about postmodern identity and design, including cheapskate design and clutter as a design strategy, and for one of the assignments, she says, "they had to start with a headshot of themselves and work with it to create either a sense of their unified or fragmented sense of identity." Additionally, each module in the class requires students to also reflect upon their work. So through the module's activities, the students learn how to use Photoshop, but they also learn about the rhetoric of design and how design choices relate to culture. In these examples, the analysis of technological artifacts and multimedia texts goes hand in hand with the production of texts using all kinds of media.

In addition, the department chair constructs digital media work as a means of inquiry and encourages its use for knowledge production and teaching. He says, for instance, he admires the creativity and imagination of faculty who use digital media "for [their] own purposes, for [their] own needs, to [their] own vision" and who "experiment with them and do creative, exciting things with them" and "incorporate them into [their] own system of instruction." An example of this creativity is the way Ava uses PowerPoint. When she was in graduate school, she worked with a group of middle school teachers who produced a *Jeopardy*-style game with PowerPoint that was hyperlinked and interactive. She says, "They ruptured that linear, default template design of PowerPoint [and] did some really cool stuff with it" that influenced her thinking about how to use PowerPoint as an instructional tool. She also uses the program in nonlinear ways that avoid the use of templates: "I couldn't imagine another tool to get information conveyed in a way that lets you pull in video clips, audio clips. I don't use [the built-in] transitions or sounds because I think they're cheesy. But I'll embed my own sounds or create my own transitions. And because I know how, I can do all my own designs. So I create all my own PowerPoint templates." She is not only able to assess the limitations of a particular technology and understand how it is culturally constructed, but she is also able, as Feenberg puts it, to critically engage with the technology and redesign it for her own purposes.

Feenberg argues that we need to move beyond critical assessment of technology toward critical engagement, teaching students how to analytically and creatively engage with technological systems in order to change them for the better. Richard Selfe calls this process technological activism, and Ava is a technological activist, intervening (in this case) in the technology of PowerPoint, which is often used in repetitive and unimaginative ways, by designing her own way of using it in her teaching. This redesigning involves both a rethinking of her teaching methods and *how* she teaches as well as modeling for students ways that they can intervene in the technology and redesign it for their own purposes. She is able to engage in this type of digital production and incorporate it easily into her teaching because of the leadership of the graduate director and chair in pushing a technological agenda, but also because the department chair views the process of integrating digital media into teaching as generative and requiring academic labor, not just technical expertise. He therefore values that productive labor as part of the pedagogical enterprise of the department.

The graduate director, Ava, and others in the department participate in scholarly communities that focus their teaching agendas on technology and could (and, indeed, should) therefore be seen as (functional) specialists in digital media. But they define their work in ways that resist traditionally functional or technical emphases, stressing instead the ways in which digital media force us to rethink traditional categories: rhetoric, literacy, pedagogy, various theoretical approaches to texts, and the nature of text itself. Indeed, the graduate director stresses that he sees rhetoric as becoming *digital* rhetoric in the graduate curriculum— as he puts it, it is "just the way the field operates":

Eventually the new curriculum will simply come into the old. So, when we do our methodology course, it will just be methodology of computer-based writing; that's what writing is. Or, if we do a composition pedagogy course, it will be just teaching in computer classrooms because of course you teach writing in computer classrooms. So I see that merger as sort of happening, as being where the field has to go, not as sort of an add-on or a special topic or a specialization in the field.

The department chair reinforces the graduate director's comments when he explains that digital media are becoming an integral part of the curriculum: "Almost all of the courses are built around various aspects of that. . . . Also, part of our new thrust for undergraduate writing is to move to a much greater degree in terms of making writing technology or writing with technologies as part of the undergraduate instruction." The integrated literacies department's official position on technology use in writing classes is that it is more than merely teaching skills in a decontextualized manner, that is, how to use a particular software program. Instead, it is a method of critical inquiry, allowing students to explore the relationships between texts of all kinds, the cultures that produce them, the technologies used to create them, and the technologies that mediate them. Because it is a means of inquiry, as well a cultural artifact, it is easily diffused, or integrated, into a department that defines its mission as that of teaching critical inquiry, writing, and cultural studies. The department chair plays an important role in defining the disciplinary sea in which the faculty and graduate students must swim. He defines digital media as part of the environment in such a way that digital management, analysis of digital texts, and digital media production are integrated. His approach stresses digital management in that technology "involves skill, and it's used by skillful people," but he also emphasizes analysis of digital media (technology is "determined by the culture and mediated by the culture") and digital media production (faculty and students as designers, creating multimodal texts and reshaping the tools made available to them). Moreover, there is not a separation between digital media activities and other activities. In other words, digital media work is integrated; it is like salt in the sea rather than a ship on the sea.

Of all three departments, this one is the most active in addressing questions about production and methodology, and faculty seem to have come to a consensus on questions about digital media textuality, encouraging integration of digital media texts into courses at all levels (see table 2.5). Although this department is philosophically integrated and most faculty have the support they need to develop digital pedagogies, graduate students have a more difficult time with this endeavor because of a lack of physical resources and spaces (this will be explored in more detail in chapter 4). Thus, the seeds of a robust, sustainable technological ecology for digital pedagogy are just being planted in the soil fertilized by the department's philosophical stance.

Table 2.5. Integrated literacies department's framing of digital media and/in teaching

Organizing questions	How do we define what counts as a text?	How do we approach reading texts?	How do we approach the production of texts?
Reframed questions	What kinds of texts do we assign as primary "readings"?	What methods of reading/research do we teach students?	What types of texts/genres do we teach/expect students to produce?
Integrated literacies department	*The department has seemingly already reached a consensus on these questions, integrating digital media vertically in the curriculum:* What types of texts and genres should undergraduates be exposed to in their studies? When should undergraduates be exposed to new media texts? What can the department do to increase exposure to alternative texts/genres?	*The department is well-versed in exploring questions about reading/ methodology and teaching:* What lenses should undergraduates learn to bring to alternative texts/genres? When and how should undergraduates learn to read alternative texts? What are the best practices in teaching in your field?	*These are the questions this department seems most focused on:* What is valuable about assigning writing? What skills should undergraduate students be able to demonstrate in writing? What would those skills look like demonstrated in another medium? What is valuable about assigning digital media projects? How is writing a means of inquiry? How can digital media be used as a means of inquiry? Should undergraduates learn to produce alternative texts? When/where should they learn this (at what point in the curriculum)?

Negotiating Technological Ecologies:
Building Digital Pedagogies in Local Contexts

Departments, consciously or not, maintain stances on the role of digital media in teaching, which emphasize some aspects of digital work over others. As a result, individuals must negotiate these stances and situate their digital media teaching in particular ways in order to "fit" with the department's culture. The department chair plays a crucial role in framing the conversation about digital media, greatly influencing the departmental culture of support for digital media teaching. Some chairs, like the one in the parallel cultures department, set a tone of acceptance and support (both philosophical and financial) that helps to carve out a space in which digital media work can occur. Some chairs, like the one in the integrated literacies department, take a proactive role in not only creating a space for digital media work to occur but also providing leadership in integrating digital media throughout the curriculum and providing language with which to view digital media as already integrated into the disciplinary identity of the department. Other chairs, like the one in the print-centric department, construct a more limited space for digital media in the curriculum and, by eliding questions about reading methods and textual production, uphold the hierarchy of signs Cushman describes, which have the effect of creating a culture that makes digital media work more difficult or less desirable to do.

Cushman argues that this hierarchy of signs could be leveled by teachers incorporating multimodal assignments into their teaching because multimodal compositions value other sign technologies as equal to the letter for knowledge and meaning making. She explains:

> As with the production of new media scholarship, the teaching of new media maps onto the activities already undertaken as routine practices of textuality: when producing multimedia products, students can engage in historicizing the signs they are using in order to draw upon the historically rooted meanings and values attached to those signs; they could theorize the works they are interpreting and produce multiple ways of representing this interpretation. Taken together, then, producing meaning through composing and teaching with new media might help level the hierarchy of signs through both recognition of the problem and a concomitant change in intellectual activities that have sustained it. (77)

The next three sections examine how individuals are using digital media in their teaching, how their uses intervene in this hierarchy of signs, and how such intervening raises tensions. Specifically, I consider the ways that instructors negotiate different constructions of digital media teaching and the disciplinary and departmental forces that are at work in those negotiations. Although all of the instructors in this study use multimedia in the ways that Cushman suggests, not all of them are comfortable with the notion of leveling the hierarchy of signs. I trace their relative (dis)comfort to the extent to which their engagement with the disciplinary and pedagogical questions outlined in table 2.6 mirrors or is in tension with their department's engagement with similar questions. Whereas table 2.2 introduced questions I argue are important for departments to address as a community regarding digital media pedagogy, table 2.6 introduces questions I contend are important for individuals to reflect on as they incorporate digital media into their teaching. These questions will help to frame my discussions of the ways in which individual instructors situate their digital media teaching within the contexts of their departmental cultures and disciplinary value systems.

Reading Critically and Writing Analytically about Digital Media: The Print-centric Department

Toby, a second-year assistant professor in the print-centric department, reflects on all of the questions in table 2.6. His teaching and research is "heavily invested in bringing the rhetorical tradition(s) to bear on contemporary issues of selfhood, identity, and agency." In addition, he coordinates the professional writing program, which focuses on visual literacy and document design. Although he says his "primary pedagogical responsibility is to share with them stuff about writing," he also is interested in exploring the rhetoric of new media with students.

He uses the Internet in his classes in ways that are consistent with this pedagogical philosophy. For instance, in his professional writing classes, he uses the Internet to point students to interesting resources and sample documents. Toby says, "When I teach them reports and proposals, I tell them to go to the Internet and type 'proposal,' Google it, search for a report on a topic that interests you. Get a bunch and look them and ask, 'Why are they reports? What sorts of commonalities are there across the genre?' Stuff like that." In his rhetoric and democracy class, he has students "listen to Lee Greenwood lyrics and look at old *Schoolhouse Rock* episodes about the American melting pot. I do a lot of that just 'cause I like the plurality of media representation to see what that does to both the rhetorical intent of a text and the way it's assembled, the design of it." His choices are motivated by his disciplinary training in rhetoric and composition; no matter what texts he

Table 2.6. Questions for individuals to reflect on regarding digital media and/in teaching

Organizing questions	What counts as a text?	How do we approach reading texts?	How do we approach the production of texts?
Reframed questions	What kinds of texts do we assign as primary "readings"?	What methods of reading/research do we teach students?	What types of texts/ genres do we teach/ expect students to produce?
Questions for individuals	What kinds of texts do you typically assign/ make available as primary readings? As secondary readings? As supplemental/ optional texts? Do you have students look at or analyze cultural artifacts as texts? Technology as a text? What teaching methods or philosophies of teaching guide you in your choices of texts to teach?	What methods of textual analysis/ interpretation do you teach undergraduates? Do you teach other approaches to texts? How do you define critical analysis? What research methods do you teach? Critical analysis? Bibliographic? Ethnographic? Statistical? Other? What teaching methods or philosophies of teaching guide you when you teach students to approach texts in particular ways?	What types of texts do you ask students to produce? For formal assignments? For informal assignments? For in-class activities? Do you use writing as a means of inquiry in your classes? Do you use digital media as a means of inquiry in your classes (like writing)? If so, how? What teaching methods or philosophies of teaching guide you in your teaching of digital media production?

has students analyze, he focuses on rhetorical concerns such as form, genre, message, audience, and the design of discourse.

Toby says that the Internet has changed some of his expectations when he teaches, particularly about what he can assume students will know and how they go about research. For instance, he spends more time talking about research skills because of the influence of technology and "the ease of access to certain kinds of information that may not be the best information." He says he feels a pedagogical responsibility, especially in an expository writing class, to incorporate "the kinds of technology that they live with and function with and turn to to get the work of their daily life done." He also addresses "nuts-and-bolts questions" such as "How do you do something in Word—how do I get a horizontal line on the page in this report?" But he tries to blend the technical instruction with a rhetorical stance toward technology. Again, his choices are largely motivated by disciplinary rather than departmental concerns. His focus on blending the practical with the rhetorical and incorporating texts and technologies that are "of the moment" mirrors the way his field approaches the teaching of writing—starting where the students are; valuing a variety of texts, particularly popular or non-canonical texts; focusing on rhetorical concerns and addressing "nuts-and-bolts" concerns through a rhetorical lens (for instance, focusing not just on how to get a horizontal line in a report in Word but also on why and when it might be beneficial to do so from a rhetorical standpoint).

One way Toby achieves this blend is by using technologically focused and multimedia texts as texts for students to analyze in his courses. In Rhetorics of Technology, a course about new forms of communication, for instance, students read "You and the Atomic Bomb" by George Orwell, *Brave New World* by Aldous Huxley, and "Can Technology Replace Social Engineering?" by Alvin M. Weinberg. The students are then asked to write analytically and rhetorically about technology. For instance, the first paper requires students to analyze the 2001 movie *A.I. Artificial Intelligence* "in order to articulate its representation of technology." Furthermore, as the assignment sheet explains, students must "use [their] analysis as the basis for some rhetorical speculation about this representation—that is, some speculation as to what the filmmaker (Steven Spielberg) might be trying to accomplish in representing technology in this way." The second paper requires students to compare and contrast the representations of technology in *Brave New World* and a written or filmic text they choose. The final paper assignment involves developing a rhetorical analysis of a text's representation of technology, using outside sources to help students support their arguments about the rhetorical intent of the text. These assignments ask students to consider the ways in which technology is represented, culturally and rhetorically, in a variety of texts. They also ask students to consider the ways in which media affect the rhetoric of texts by having them read, view, and listen to texts and, in one of their papers, to compare texts composed in different media.

In this class, taught in a non-networked classroom without computers, Toby uses online discussion boards as an out-of-class supplement. He says he does this because "it seems really appropriate that a class on technology would have some sort of technologically mediated form of communication. That process itself is of interest to me, and we talk about that." In addition, he notes it is "more opportunity to pursue more questions" and "another opportunity to get people talking." He requires that students post a 500-word analytical response to a course reading twice during the semester and a 250-word analytical response "to any kind of post that's up there" twice during the semester. This use of the discussion board is heavily influenced by a model of print literacy— namely, asking students to produce essayistic analytical responses to articles they have read. But Toby also uses the postings to spark face-to-face discussion in class. He says, "When we start to have a discussion about a text, we usually use the responses of people who had to offer their commentaries for that day as the jumping-off point." Even though Toby uses this online form of communication, it is still a supplement to traditional face-to-face pedagogy. In fact, it enables traditional face-to-face pedagogy by preparing students for class time and attempting to ensure that they actually talk during class discussions. Most of the real communication and discussion happens in class, face-to-face, not on the discussion board. The discussion board is more like a container that holds their essayistic, analytical responses to readings, which everybody, not just Toby, can access, read, and respond to.

Toby uses online discussions as a bridge between reading and writing and to teach the students about composing. In these discussions, he says he tries "to ask questions about what we're reading as a way of getting them . . . to read the thing a little more closely, question their own readings of it, [and] just to find ways to get them interested in any kind of question that can feed a writing project that they'll participate in." This sort of questioning and encouraging students to read texts is consistent with the model of traditional academic literacy that the print-centric department heavily values. But it also allows Toby to connect the texts students are reading to the texts they are writing for the class. This approach to the discussion board thus allows Toby to concentrate on teaching academic writing. Although Toby uses digital discussion boards to spark discussion and as a container for students' analytical writing, ultimately the digital form has little effect or input on the form/media in which he asks his students to write. They write as if writing for print, even when posting the writing online, and he says his role in the discussion forum, "first and foremost, is to be a writing teacher."

His reflection that he is to be a writing teacher, above all, in these online discussions seems to be more motivated by departmental rather than by disciplinary forces. This class is not a "writing class." It is an upper-level class called Rhetorics of Technology. How many English faculty would say that in discussions (online or not) in upper-level courses, their primary role is to be a "writing teacher"? I suspect very few, even if they assign a lot of writing or set up discussion forums in the same way Toby does. While it certainly could be an issue of field identity—it is the nature, I think, of rhetoric and composition specialists to see most assignments as occasions for learning something about composing—I think he is also responding to the culture of the department, which values essayistic, analytical writing and hired him as a writing specialist. The kind of writing he teaches is the analytical, academic essay. This definition of writing and his assignments (formal, analytical writing, even when posted on the discussion board) are consistent with the department's stance toward digital media as a supplement to support traditional writing and analytical activities. This definition of writing is also consistent with his primary professional identity as a rhetoric and composition specialist. Traditionally, the field of rhetoric and composition has valued academic writing, but more recently, visual rhetoric (the analysis of visual texts) has become central to composition curricula in many universities. Although Toby has his students analyze films and other nonprint media, the writing that is encouraged is traditional academic prose with visual texts as the object of analysis. There is a subfield within rhetoric and composition arguing for the valuation of alternative types of writing, particularly digital media productions (also known as multimodal texts). This subfield follows in a tradition of scholars who have endorsed valuing other nonacademic forms of writing and other literacies in composition classes. In Toby's department, however, the standard is the academic, analytical essay.

Toby pushes against this departmental stance by reflecting on questions about production and the potential future of academic composing. Walking a middle-ground position on writing and multimedia production, Toby envisions "a program with word-processing abilities but with an explicit design component [becoming] the gold standard for what the students write their papers in" because he sees writing pedagogies trying to respond to the visual and digital culture in which students now grow up. This type of writing technology could support multimodal composing and different kinds of writing tasks. So while it still assumes a printed product—Toby says it will be the "gold standard for what the students *write* their *papers* in" (my emphasis)—it does complicate what a writing project is by allowing for multiple means of expression, not just words. Thus, it doesn't completely redefine writing to allow for multiple means of expression *and* multiple means of delivery, though it does incorporate a design element. Again, as an untenured member of the department only in his second year, Toby is responding to the culture of his department.

In addition to the department's definition of "writing" being traditional, there are also material constraints preventing him from teaching different forms of composing. He doesn't have a computer classroom available to him, for instance. So even the class Rhetorics of Technology can't lend itself to digital media production activities, although it might in another department. He's constrained, trying to see beyond the traditional essay, but enmeshed in the department culture. He's trying to respond to forces in his field to transform notions of writing and rhetoric to incorporate the digital, but he can't fully "go there" in this department.

Toby has clearly articulated reasons for doing what he does, indicating he has thought through questions of textuality, reading, and production in order to determine how to best incorporate digital media into his teaching (see table 2.7). There is little tension between his responses to questions about textuality and his department's because the department relegates digital media work to the field of rhetoric and composition, which is Toby's field. Therefore, his use of digital media in classes at any level is, in a sense, sanctioned by the department because that is where it "belongs." His responses to questions about reading mirror the department's stance that critical/rhetorical analysis is the preferred lens for reading any kind of text; Toby has not made a move to complicate the questions of reading or introduce other lenses or methods of reading new media texts (and neither has anybody else from his department involved in this study). There is, however, a tension in responding to questions about production; while the department either is not equipped or has decided not to address these questions as a community, Toby does reflect on these questions as they relate to his teaching and constructs a future in which digital media composing is central to, at the very least, rhetoric and composition classes, if not any class in which students must write a paper.

The Internet and Canonicity: The Parallel Cultures Department

Two individuals in the parallel cultures department are struggling with tensions raised by the question of which texts should be assigned as readings in English classes. Roxie is a first-year PhD student focusing on nineteenth-century American literature and works as a consultant in the Center for Digital Media Studies. She understands her field as valuing the study of printed, alphabetic texts. She positions herself squarely in her field but says she sees her research and teaching interests as

Table 2.7. Toby's reflections on digital media and/in teaching within the framework of his department's culture

Organizing questions	What counts as a text?	How do we approach reading texts?	How do we approach the production of texts?
Reframed questions	What kinds of texts do we assign as primary "readings"?	What methods of reading/research do we teach students?	What types of texts/genres do we teach/expect students to produce?
Toby	*There is little to no tension over these questions because of Toby's field:* What kinds of texts do you typically assign/make available as primary readings? As secondary readings? As supplemental/optional texts? Do you have students look at or analyze cultural artifacts as texts? Technology as a text? What teaching methods or philosophies of teaching guide you in your choices of texts to teach?	*Toby's responses to these questions mirror the department's, focusing on critical/rhetorical analysis in the form of an essay:* What methods of textual analysis/interpretation do you teach undergraduates? Do you teach other approaches to texts? How do you define critical analysis? What research methods do you teach? Critical analysis? Bibliographic? Ethnographic? Statistical? Other? What teaching methods or philosophies of teaching guide you when you teach students to approach texts in particular ways?	*There is tension because Toby sees these questions as central to his field, but the department is not equipped or ready to address them:* What types of texts do you ask students to produce? For formal assignments? For informal assignments? For in-class activities? Do you use writing as a means of inquiry in your classes? Do you use digital media as a means of inquiry in your classes (like writing)? If so, how? What teaching methods or philosophies of teaching guide you in your teaching of digital media production?

cutting-edge within that field. Yet, she admits that technology makes her "feel very traditional and very old-fogey" because "it reveals to me how old-fashioned some of my beliefs really are, and that makes me uncomfortable. I'm not accustomed to thinking of myself as an old-fashioned person. I always think I'm sort of radical and on the cutting edge, but technology makes it very clear to me, 'no, you're not that radical.'" Because she works in the CDMS, Roxie's experience exemplifies the clashing of the two communities in the parallel cultures department—the traditional majority that values primarily print literacy and the experimental minority that also values digital media production. She says the reason she decided to teach in a CDMS classroom was because she had to in order to land the administrative assistantship there, so she is new to digital media pedagogy. She is trying to come to terms with occupying that space as she confronts her own disciplinary identity in the face of digital media.

In her class, she asks students to analyze digitally mediated visual texts, such as websites, and says they seem to be more comfortable analyzing these visual texts than traditional alphabetic texts. Roxie suggests a benefit of this comfort is a certain kind of empowerment:

> It gives them a sense of authority, especially because of my area. I'm asking them always to look at texts that they feel very alienated from. Nineteenth-century language can be very off-putting, and the themes are often very sentimental. It's unclear to students what kind of a relationship they can forge with these texts. Whereas with the websites I think they feel much more in a position of mastery.

Having students analyze visual texts, however, makes her "itchy," she says, and has negatively affected her teaching:

> It makes me really sad! It does, it makes me very sad. Has it changed the way I approach teaching? Yeah, it has, and begrudgingly, honestly, because I do a little bit with visual culture. I don't do a whole lot with it. It's a secondary interest of mine. My primary interests are textual. So, I find it frustrating that in order to produce what I would consider even passable analyses, I have to turn to visual texts that I'm not necessarily as interested in.

She worries about whether digital texts are appropriate to study in an English department. Why should they make her "itchy" unless there is something inappropriate about analyzing them in an English class?

Her discomfort stems, possibly, from the feeling that asking her students to analyze nonliterary or nonalphabetic texts goes against a core aspect of her discipline. Roxie does not professionally identify with alternative or nonliterary objects of study as Toby does or some of her rhetoric and composition colleagues would. As a literary scholar, she values traditional literary objects of study, but as a composition teacher, she incorporates these alternative objects of study to keep her students interested and to help them learn analytical essay writing. On a certain level, however, she views the analysis of digitally mediated visual texts as a cop-out. Her scholarly field identity and teaching identity are clearly in conflict. Additionally, she is responding to an attitude that exists in the discipline but also in research universities that instructors should teach their scholarly interests, even in lower-level classes. Veering from her own interests to what interests the students thus causes her inner conflict over her pedagogy. Additionally, she is a graduate student and has very little agency in determining what courses she will teach, which likely adds to her frustration.

Not only are tensions raised for Roxie by questions about texts, but tensions are also raised for her by questions about reading methods. Her reflection that analysis of visual texts in English is somehow inappropriate is partly motivated by what she perceives as a "dismissive attitude from older professors, like, 'Oh, that's neat that you can do that, but there's no place in *my* class for that kind of activity.'" But she also senses that the methods of reading/interpreting those texts might also be an issue. In her reflection about why "older professors" might be so dismissive, she constructs a tension between two different philosophies of teaching, one she attributes to her literary colleagues, who value talk as inquiry, and one she attributes to her digital media colleagues, who also value writing and digital media composing as inquiry:

> I think in some ways, particularly among more traditional professors, there's really a sense that using technology is a kind of way to avoid the real work of teaching. So that, you know, instead of having a class discussion where you ask the hard questions and really try to pull answers out of your students, you just have them post to a discussion board. And I think that there's a sense that that's less valuable than what's perceived as the nitty-gritty of teaching.

Roxie senses that the kind of teaching she is doing in her computer classroom is not seen as valuable by senior colleagues in her field in the department. The inner conflict over her pedagogy in the computer classroom is intensified because she thinks her field will view some of her activities as not real teaching or as not the appropriate reading methods to teach students.

At the same time, while she has internalized the view of older professors in her field, she has been introduced to different constructions of digital media pedagogy through her work in the CDMS, particularly for composition classes. And so rather than characterize the traditional professors as "correct" in their view about digital pedagogy, she labels them "dismissive," indicating that she's questioning their view and trying to reconcile her field's more traditional ideas about pedagogy with the CDMS's ideas about pedagogy. In particular, she finds a tension in the last question in table 2.8 in the methods of reading column, "What teaching methods or philosophies of teaching guide you when you teach students to approach texts in particular ways?" While the CDMS community is exploring different methods of approaching texts and teaching students to interpret texts, the discipline at large remains tethered to one method instead of providing students with a canon of methods, which is what Scholes endorses.

Emily (an assistant professor in Roxie's field) is somewhat more accepting than the "traditional professors" Roxie alludes to. Though Emily says she began using technology in her teaching because of "the proliferation of wonderful materials that are out there" and because she wanted "to make them available to the students," she also notes that this is an idealized situation because "there's tons of amazing stuff out there, and then of course there's lots of dross. Right? That's always the problem." She adds, "Ideally, I'm showing [undergraduates] what are acceptable and interesting sites and places so that they don't go to the dross. Although, I'm not sure that that in fact works." As a literature teacher, she draws the line between acceptable and unacceptable materials, which is reminiscent of canonicity: some texts are worthy of study; some are not. And although she blurs traditional canonical lines by making alternative texts available via the course management system—including photographs and magazine articles—these are not the core texts of the course, and those core literary texts are *not* natively digital or made available digitally. This example illustrates the department chair's statement that though digital texts are important, the study of English will always involve printed texts. *Which* printed texts, though, continues to be a central debate in the discipline and influences how both Emily and Roxie frame the discussion of their feelings about using digital media for teaching. *Which* digital texts are worthy of inclusion in class (either as supplemental materials or as objects of analysis) is foremost in their minds when they think about digital media and teaching. Thus, Roxie and Emily are almost singularly focused on questions about the appropriateness of different kinds of texts, at the expense of questions about reading methods and production (see table 2.8).

Table 2.8. Roxie and Emily's reflections on digital media and/in teaching within the framework of their department's culture

Organizing questions	What counts as a text?	How do we approach reading texts?	How do we approach the production of texts?
Reframed questions	What kinds of texts do we assign as primary "readings"?	What methods of reading/ research do we teach students?	What types of texts/ genres do we teach/ expect students to produce?
Roxie and Emily	*Roxie and Emily are most focused on these questions:* What kinds of texts do you typically assign/ make available as primary readings? As secondary readings? As supplemental/ optional texts? Do you have students look at or analyze cultural artifacts as texts? Technology as a text? What teaching methods or philosophies of teaching guide you in your choices of texts to teach?	*Roxie and Emily's responses to these questions tend to mirror the department's, and so there is little tension:* What methods of textual analysis/interpretation do you teach undergraduates? Do you teach other approaches to texts? How do you define critical analysis? What research methods do you teach? Critical analysis? Bibliographic? Ethnographic? Statistical? Other? *This question causes tension for Roxie because her field tends to value one method while the CDMS encourages a variety of methods:* What teaching methods or philosophies of teaching guide you when you teach students to approach texts in particular ways?	*Roxie and Emily's focus on questions about texts occludes these questions:* What types of texts do you ask students to produce? For formal assignments? For informal assignments? For in-class activities? Do you use writing as a means of inquiry in your classes? Do you use digital media as a means of inquiry in your classes (like writing)? If so, how? What teaching methods or philosophies of teaching guide you in your teaching of digital media production?

*Digital Media Production as Means to a Rhetorical
End: The Parallel Cultures Department*

Others in the parallel cultures department, like Cosmo, are more focused on questions of reading methods and production, as they experiment with incorporating digital media as a means of inquiry into their
teaching. A second year PhD student in the parallel cultures department, Cosmo is studying rhetoric and composition and is also a staff
member in the CDMS. He recently taught a second-year writing class[1]
on the role of marketing in American life, in which students read texts
by marketers as well as texts critical of marketing. The class focused on
"marketing in the broader sense as it affects all aspects of our culture"
and asked students to think about "how we understand our subjec-
tivities, looking at the broader material conditions underneath that."
He began the class with critical academic analysis, looking at digital
texts, such as websites and Flash movies like *The Meatrix*, an animated
activist Flash movie available online that exposes factory beef- and
pork-farming techniques. In class, he and his students "talked about
[the texts'] persuasive effects and how they were connected to broader
marketing campaigns." Students then wrote about new media texts in
traditional academic prose.

Cosmo notes that there is a strong component of visual rhetoric but
not digital media production built into the writing curriculum in the
parallel cultures department. He says the curriculum involves "teaching
students to critically analyze and read visual texts and other kinds of
digital multimodal texts" yet still asks them "to write about them in
very traditional, academic print ways" rather than to author digital or
multimodal texts. His class follows this pattern at first, responding to
the official curriculum in the department, but then his class departs
from the pattern by incorporating digital media production. Cosmo
says that he sees a disconnect for students when they are asked to write
academic prose about visual texts because "even though the texts we're
studying may be close to their lives, a lot of the academic print discourse
conventions may not be." But he claims that digital media production
helps students, for instance, "to understand the rhetoric of how digital
texts are manipulated." He adds, "You don't tend to believe in the reality of the image after you've selected a bunch of images, manipulated
them, put them together, and combined them with music and text in
other ways to make a persuasive point." Consequently, he says, "I found
once my students had engaged in that kind of production work, they
were much more able to be critical of the rhetorical work of design."

He argues, however, that while students have a great deal of experience *reading* new media texts, "often they don't have experience with digital production in any great way."

Because of this reflection, he decided to give his students some experience in digital production. For their final projects, students created "digital marketing campaigns." Cosmo required, however, that "it couldn't be for a product. It had to be an idea, a concept, some kind of social change; the *kind* was up to them. And so they really got to put into place this notion of making change through persuasive multimodal texts." For instance, one group of students made a movie "trying to advocate that people use alternative forms of energy or use energy-saving models." The goal for the campaign assignment was twofold: to persuade an audience and to "consider the material effects of what it is they were attempting to do." The alternative energy movie attempted to persuade the audience using classical rhetorical appeals to logos (including statistics about "electricity, how it may not be so good for you"), pathos ("with continued voice-over about the problems of it . . . a very haunting classical music soundtrack and . . . images of pollution and destruction"), and an enthymeme: "And then they turned to some happy family image in front of the wind-powered home, and then some information on more ways that people could be involved with alternative energy. And then they ended on an American flag and a patriotic appeal."

Cosmo says that the students employed these rhetorical appeals deliberately because of their focus on trying to persuade a particular audience, their class members:

> The students were very conscious of the rhetorical manipulation of this. They ended on the American flag, but they were ending on it partially because they really saw the rest of the class as their audience, people who probably didn't really care much about this. We talked a lot about enthymemes, and they were looking around for enthymemes to associate this with. And so when they ended with a normative vision of the family and a normative vision of the flag, they were conscious of this as a kind of rhetorical manipulation, which I thought was very powerful.

Additionally, the students' movie showed an understanding of marketing as tied to broader material conditions. Cosmo says, "There are some ways in which [appealing to traditional family values and patriotism] might be reinforcing certain norms I wouldn't necessarily want to reinforce, but [in this case], they really understood that as a core manipulation and used it in a pretty savvy way."

Cosmo is clearly experimenting with teaching students to use digital media as a means of inquiry and as a rhetorical tool. Students are not only learning to produce digital media texts but also learning underlying rhetorical skills. In fact, he says this type of production project gives him "a great way to teach rhetorical analysis." He has assigned production projects—from collaborative websites to Flash movies—in both a required composition class and a business communication class. He always includes reflective writing as part of production assignments: "Whenever I've done a production project, I've always had a strong reflective component, where students actually had to write about all their rhetorical choices, analyze their rhetorical situation." This reflective component allows Cosmo to teach rhetorical analysis by bringing a critical component to the production projects. Students do not just learn how to make Flash movies; they also learn how to craft a persuasive message that displays their understanding of rhetorical concepts. The reflective essay also provides an opportunity for them to think about how the medium of composition influences and constrains their creativity, how a different medium might influence them in different ways, and who might be the "ideal user" of the medium. The written component of the project gives them a chance to reflect on their rhetorical choices, both those that are dependent upon the medium and those that are not.

His choices are clearly influenced by rhetorical pedagogy. Cosmo, a rhetorician/compositionist, defines two of the central concerns of his field as rhetorical theory and civic participation, which are traditional concerns in rhetoric and composition pedagogy; these are the skills and values he tries to teach his students with the digital marketing campaign assignment. He is also heavily influenced by his subfield of digital media studies or "computers and composition." For Cosmo, the core skill he is supposed to teach is critical/rhetorical thinking; the products by which students express their critical/rhetorical analyses are less of a concern to him. He combines analysis and design, teaching critical thinking through design and making rhetoric the centerpiece. In other words, he uses rhetoric as the bridge between multimodal composing and traditional writing, suggesting that he would have students transfer their thinking about digital media to more traditional forms of writing to help them write better.

As a scholar in the "computers and composition" community, Cosmo is familiar with much of the most recent scholarship on digital media production and composition. The way he incorporates digital media production and discussions of the materiality of texts is influenced by Anne Frances Wysocki's argument that "new media needs to be informed by what writing teachers know, precisely because writing teachers focus specifically on texts and how situated people (learn how to) use them to make things happen" ("Opening New Media" 5). Cosmo focuses specifically on the materiality of texts—the fact that they can persuade people to change their behavior—as well as on the particular material effects that the particular production students were planning would have on a particular audience, their classmates, who were situated in a particular context and a particular time. This materiality was a constant theme throughout Cosmo's class, not only with this assignment but also with the more traditional writing assignments in which students analyzed multimedia texts, like *The Meatrix*, for their persuasive effects and their connections to broader marketing campaigns.

The departmental culture is also an important component facilitating Cosmo's pedagogy. For instance, his department values print literacy but creates a space for digital media production and experimental pedagogy, allowing him to try out different ways of using digital media in his pedagogy. Both of these decisions require reimagining what it means to teach writing and answering the question "What business are we in?" differently than it might have been answered in the past. Furthermore, the department paid for the space in which he taught his recent second-year writing class, the CDMS's newest and most powerful lab. This space enabled a student-centered, studio pedagogy that allowed him to incorporate digital media production into his class in the way he did. The classroom has sixteen student stations with G5 Macintosh computers and four iBooks available for use. The sixteen workstations are set up in pairs, with five empty desks strategically placed around the perimeter and two circular tables near the center of the room. This setup worked especially well for group projects, according to Cosmo, because students had the option to work individually on machines, together on one machine, or individually or together without a machine. The class took two days learning Photoshop and Flash and then spent five days of studio time working on projects. Most people chose to work in groups, Cosmo says, although a couple of people worked alone. During studio time, students were free to do what they felt was most pressing. He says, "One group would be writing the script, another group would be working with images, another group would be thinking about sound. . . . I spent a lot of time running from group to group asking a lot of questions about their rhetorical intent, solving the technology crises as they happened."

Besides reflecting on the processes of teaching and learning in the class, Cosmo also reflects on the students' engagement with each other's work. He says, "What I noticed was very different in this course is that the students all really wanted to see each other's work." Because of this engagement and their willingness to talk about each other's texts and give constructive feedback, he says that in the future he wants to start with the digital media project rather than end with it: "I think the students were so engaged in thinking about the rhetorical consequences of this digital work because they really saw it as a kind of text audiences they know really would read. I'd rather have them start with that. If it were a course where I had to teach print, I would actually want them to transfer their thinking from the digital text to print." Cosmo is taking on the role of a pedagogical scholar, as his graduate program has trained him. He is rethinking and redefining rhetorical pedagogy, transforming it into digital rhetorical pedagogy.

For Cosmo, it is important to allow digital media to help us rethink or redefine what we do:

> I would like to see us move beyond what I would call the additive model of technology, where technology is valued and considered a good thing, but the notion is, take what we already do and put technology in it. I think that that puts a great burden on people who do technology because they end up having to do everything else everyone already does in a class, "Oh, and now I have to learn all this tech stuff." . . . I think if we're really going to develop as a field, we have to let digital composition change what we think teaching looks like, and not see it as additive but as transformative.

A singular focus on questions about which texts are appropriate elides this issue of transforming pedagogical methods and transforming English by focusing on an additive model—which texts to add to a canon. While Roxie and Emily are focused on questions about the appropriateness of new media texts as primary course readings, Cosmo is focused on methods of reading and textual production (see table 2.9), which is not surprising given that his field is rhetoric and composition and theirs is literature. Because of this focus on production, particularly the question about using digital media as inquiry, and because of the experimentation that the CDMS encourages, Cosmo is helping facilitate a rethinking of what teaching looks like and helping the field and the department see composition pedagogy and English studies in new ways.

Table 2.9. Cosmo's reflections on digital media and/in teaching within the framework of his department's culture

Organizing questions	What counts as a text?	How do we approach reading texts?	How do we approach the production of texts?
Reframed questions	What kinds of texts do we assign as primary "readings"?	What methods of reading/research do we teach students?	What types of texts/ genres do we teach/ expect students to produce?
Cosmo	*There is little to no tension over these questions:* What kinds of texts do you typically assign/make available as primary readings? As secondary readings? As supplemental/ optional texts? Do you have students look at or analyze cultural artifacts as texts? Technology as a text? What teaching methods or philosophies of teaching guide you in your choices of texts to teach?	*While the department as a whole is not focused on these questions, Cosmo and the CDMS are:* What methods of textual analysis/ interpretation do you teach undergraduates? Do you teach other approaches to texts? How do you define critical analysis? What research methods do you teach? Critical analysis? Bibliographic? Ethnographic? Statistical? Other? What teaching methods or philosophies of teaching guide you when you teach students to approach texts in particular ways?	*Cosmo is primarily focused on these questions:* What types of texts do you ask students to produce? For formal assignments? For informal assignments? For in-class activities? Do you use writing as a means of inquiry in your classes? Do you use digital media as a means of inquiry in your classes (like writing)? If so, how? What teaching methods or philosophies of teaching guide you in your teaching of digital media production?

Critical Framing of Creative Tools: The
Integrated Literacies Department

In the integrated literacies department, production and consumption are more balanced, and the discussion of questions surrounding digital media use are more visible. Ava, whose teaching focuses on the impact of the Internet and the web on North American culture, is an assistant professor in the integrated literacies department. When I interviewed her, she was completing her third year at the university and was going through early tenure review. She had passed the department- and college-level reviews and was waiting to hear the final word from the university committee. She was teaching a class called Visual Rhetoric for Professional Writers, one of four core courses for the undergraduate professional writing program. Ava organized the course around modules that help the students learn software applications and put into practice design theories. For instance, one module has students read and discuss articles on document design and typography and analyze documents' designs. The module also asks them to experiment with design principles they have read about and discussed by using Microsoft Word to design song lyrics or a poem and to reflect on their work by writing a brief statement explaining their interpretation of a song or poem and how their design complements that meaning rhetorically—why they chose certain features and fonts, what effects they think it will have on an audience, and so on.

Like Cosmo's, the pedagogy of Ava's class is heavily influenced by her field identity in computers and composition, incorporating reflective writing alongside nontraditional composing in order to focus students' attention on the rhetorical features of composing in different media and forms. "The focus of the class is a twofold focus," Ava explains. "The . . . most important purpose is developing a vocabulary, an ability to speak in rich ways about writing and design and the intersections of form and content. So we do a lot of analysis." An activity that helps students develop a critical vocabulary through analysis is something Ava calls the Visual Example Presentation. She asks each student to bring in an object and deliver a brief analysis of it; the class then responds with questions and discussion of the object. In the class I observed, one student brought a perfume bottle. The student gave an analysis of the bottle that focused on its color scheme and packaging, and the class, led by Ava's questions, discussed the significance of those choices—why color matters, how packaging is related to the economics of shelf space, and how design decisions are related to society's constructions of gender.

Ava balances critical and productive uses of digital media in this class. She explains, for instance, that she wants students to understand not only the mechanics of design but also the cultures of production that influence design choices, so the students work with software programs (which she calls "tools"). However, she stresses, "The critical and analytical *always* frames the use of the tools. It is like my nightmare to be stuck teaching Dreamweaver MX for fifteen weeks or a class *on* Adobe Photoshop, because that is just meaningless and uninteresting to me. Because the tools, I mean, they're *nothing* unless they're framed." Critical and cultural theory and discussions of cultures and histories frame the tools in Ava's visual rhetoric class. The module exercise that asks students to design a poem or song lyrics in Word is an example of this critical framing. This assignment is coupled with a reading about the font Hitler decided would be the defining marker of the Nazi party.[2] According to Ava, "He's talking about how we can design hate, that designs come to us, in some sense, as a blank slate and we embed them with this cultural and historical and social meaning. . . . I hope that they never look at font faces the same again, that they have to kind of push and wonder why that was the way it is." Again, Ava's reflection about her pedagogy is motivated by her field identity; she focuses on the development of a vocabulary for *writing* and on how design concerns reflect rhetorical choices. At the same time, she focuses on analysis of cultural artifacts, which is consistent with her department's mission of cultural studies and analyzing digital media in relation to cultural context. So her pedagogy is highly influenced by both her disciplinary identity and her department's culture.

In order to explore the critical and analytical frameworks, Ava says, "We use some pretty conventional tools, but I try to push at the margins of them." Ava's pushing at the margins of software programs represents her resistance to the programs' conventional uses, which are steeped in particular cultural frameworks. In her feminist analysis of technology, Billie J. Wahlstrom argues that multimedia technologies have implicit frames built into them by their manufacturers/designers that we can choose to simply accept or teach our students to recognize and reflect upon. Others have argued that technological applications have implicit, often uncritically accepted political perspectives built into them that encourage us to work in particular ways rather than others or, in other words, that frame our work in particular ways and not others (see, for example, Howard; Selber; C. Selfe; and Selfe and Selfe). The framework that is typically associated with software packages in classrooms, and which Ava is resisting, is a particular functional approach to computer literacy—simply teaching students how to use the tools in conventional and uncritical ways—which Stuart Selber critiques in *Multiliteracies for a Digital Age*, redefining a functional approach to computer literacy that understands technology as embedded in social and rhetorical contexts.

Selber's tripartite digital literacy framework can aid in interpreting the pedagogical value of Ava's assignments. She employs an approach to digital media "tools" that suggests the type of functional approach Selber advocates: she frames the tools as a method of inquiry and argumentation rather than as an end in and of themselves as she teaches the students how to learn to use the tools to complete the assignments. Her analytical framework requires students to adopt a critical stance toward designs and the contexts in which they are created and consumed, which fulfills the requirements of the critical literacy component of Selber's computer multiliteracies curriculum. In addition, she promotes rhetorical literacy by using critical and rhetorical concepts to frame not only the learning of functional skills but also critical thinking about the ways in which design and persuasion (and, by extension, writing in/for various media) work in real contexts. Furthermore, she has students produce assignments with digital media, creating their own designs rather than just writing about digital media texts. She does not ask students to create new interfaces, as Selber does with hypertext assignments in which students become redesigners of media/reading/writing interfaces; however, the reflective writing that she assigns prompts students to think about how the application and the medium influence their design choices, thereby encouraging them to understand the applications themselves as designed. This rhetorical, rather than functional, approach to teaching in digitally mediated environments—production of digital media texts, reflection, critical/analytical framing of technological tools, and pushing the boundaries of traditional/mainstream software packages—echoes the way the chair of the integrated literacies department describes the department as focused on technology and encouraging of faculty to use "writing technologies and involve students in digital media projects" at all levels and in all types of writing classes. In stressing the creative aspect of digital media production, both the chair and Ava emphasize Selber's rhetorical literacy—reshaping the tools/interfaces to better meet individual needs, as in her creation of her own PowerPoint templates. In addition, if a tool in the university's course management program doesn't work for her, she can use something else: "[Our course management tool's] chat interface sucks so bad. But, again, I have access to a couple of different MOOs [multi-user virtual spaces], and I just create accounts and we go dork around in the MOO. So, I don't have to use that interface." Or she can change it: "I know enough about [our course management system]; I can go in and tweak and revise areas so that it fits my needs. Obviously, not that many people can do that." That she has the functional skill to do this only partially explains why she does it. It is also important that her department values this kind of work with technology, and the chair asserts that the department does. Her professional identity as a technology specialist also influences her reshaping of writing technologies to fit her needs; her field values this kind of technical expertise.

As a result, digital media saturate Ava's work. It is impossible to really separate "digital media" from her work. It is not even accurate to say that what she does integrates digital media. Digital media is central to her work; her work wouldn't exist without it. The way she teaches and what she teaches wouldn't exist without it. And yet, her teaching is nonetheless heavily invested in and informed by traditional rhetorical concerns such as context, purpose, audience, and critical-analytical frameworks. Unlike Toby, she is not alone in her explorations of questions about digital media use (seen in table 2.10); unlike Roxie and Emily, whose field is not having an open discussion about the questions raised by digital media, Ava is involved in an open discussion about these issues both in her field and in her department. The fact that the department has actively pursued conversations about digital media teaching as a community creates a culture that allows Ava's teaching to flourish.

Conclusion: Negotiating a Place for Digital Media Teaching in the Discipline

In "Made Not Only in Words: Composition in a New Key," Kathleen Blake Yancey argues that we are facing a moment of change in the writing public that is similar to the change in the reading public in the nineteenth century. Writing outside of the academy has gone digital, people are writing more and more, and the writing they do outside of school bears less and less resemblance to the writing they do inside of school. Because of this situation, she wonders if we are becoming anachronistic and reports "disturbing data [that] suggest that traditional English departments already are" (302), including a decrease in the number of departments called English and a rise in departments called something else, like communication or humanities or rhetoric. She likens these shifts in departmental definition and writing practices outside the academy to tremors but asks, "Are they minor tremors signifying routine academic seismic activity that makes the world more stable? Alternatively, are they tremors occurring along the fault lines of

Table 2.10. Ava's reflections on digital media and/in teaching within the framework of her department's culture

Organizing questions	What counts as a text?	How do we approach reading texts?	How do we approach the production of texts?
Reframed questions	What kinds of texts do we assign as primary "readings"?	What methods of reading/research do we teach students?	What types of texts/ genres do we teach/expect students to produce?
Ava	*There is little to no tension over these questions:* What kinds of texts do you typically assign/ make available as primary readings? As secondary readings? As supplemental/ optional texts? Do you have students look at or analyze cultural artifacts as texts? Technology as a text? What teaching methods or philosophies of teaching guide you in your choices of texts to teach?	*Ava actively complicates traditional notions about reading methods, incorporating traditional rhetorical lenses as well as lenses from other fields such as art and design:* What methods of textual analysis/ interpretation do you teach undergraduates? Do you teach other approaches to texts? How do you define critical analysis? What research methods do you teach? Critical analysis? Bibliographic? Ethnographic? Statistical? Other? What teaching methods or philosophies of teaching guide you when you teach students to approach texts in particular ways?	*Ava actively reflects on these questions, which the departmental community has also engaged:* What types of texts do you ask students to produce? For formal assignments? For informal assignments? For in-class activities? Do you use writing as a means of inquiry in your classes? Do you use digital media as a means of inquiry in your classes (like writing)? If so, how? What teaching methods or philosophies of teaching guide you in your teaching of digital media production?

tectonic plates that will in the not-too-distant future change the very topography of higher education?" (303).

She is speaking specifically to compositionists, but what she says is relevant to everybody under the umbrella of "English studies." As discussed in chapter 1, "English studies" is a deliberately imprecise term, and not all of the departments in this study are "English" departments. Scholes describes a historical split in the culture of "English" between literature and composition, which—along with Yancey's analysis—can help to explain the existence of departments like the integrated literacies department, which came about because of a literal institutional split between literature and composition. However, Scholes calls for a reconstruction of "English" around the notion of textuality.[3] According to Scholes,

> under this sign, there is no difference between the theory of composition and the theory of literature—and there is precious little difference between theory and teaching at all, since the practice of teaching is based upon the teaching of theory, and this theory itself rests upon the shared stance of students and teachers as practitioners of reading and writing—textuality. (36)

He further argues that "the one thing a curriculum in English *must* do, whatever else it accomplishes on the way, is to lead students to a position of justified confidence in their own competence as textual consumers and their own eloquence as producers of texts" (66). The instructors in this study are all practitioners of this kind of textuality; furthermore, they all seem to have this goal of helping students become "competent textual consumers" and "eloquent producers of texts" at the heart of their teaching. What their experience helps us better understand are the ways that digital media forms of reading and composing can be an integral part of a study of textuality.

Accomplishing such integration, as these cases have demonstrated, is not without tension, however. Within the contexts of their departments' cultures of support for digital media, individuals must contend with questions about texts, reading/teaching methods, and composing in order to situate digital media within their teaching in ways consistent with their field identities and values. Likewise, departments as a whole must also contend with these questions in order to figure out how to situate digital media within their curricula in ways that reflect their understanding of curricula and pedagogy in their disciplines. While digital media teaching can help to level the hierarchy of signs and help the discipline engage in a complete study of textuality, it is not enough for individual teachers to do this in their classes. There needs to be a departmental commitment to discussing issues of textuality, reading and teaching methods, and composing practices—specifically the questions I have identified throughout this chapter, assembled in table 2.11—in order for change to occur at the departmental and curricular levels and in order for multimedia teaching to be appropriately supported and evaluated.

Table 2.11. Compiled matrix of questions to facilitate departmental discussions about digital media and/in teaching

Organizing questions	What counts as a text?	How do we approach reading texts?	How do we approach the production of texts?
Reframed questions	What kinds of texts do we assign as primary "readings"?	What methods of reading/research do we teach students?	What types of texts/ genres do we teach/ expect students to produce?
Questions for individuals	What kinds of texts do you typically assign/ make available as primary readings? As secondary readings? As supplemental/ optional texts? Do you have students look at or analyze cultural artifacts as texts? Technology as a text? What teaching methods or philosophies of teaching guide you in your choices of texts to teach?	What methods of textual analysis/ interpretation do you teach undergraduates? Do you teach other approaches to texts? How do you define critical analysis? What research methods do you teach? Critical analysis? Bibliographic? Ethnographic? Statistical? Other? What teaching methods or philosophies of teaching guide you when you teach students to approach texts in particular ways?	What types of texts do you ask students to produce? For formal assignments? For informal assignments? For in-class activities? Do you use writing as a means of inquiry in your classes? Do you use digital media as a means of inquiry in your classes (like writing)? If so, how? What teaching methods or philosophies of teaching guide you in your teaching of digital media production?

A discussion of these issues should not focus only on teaching, however. As Cushman argues, the hierarchy of signs might be leveled "if professors in English studies could produce multimodal scholarship *and* create more assignments that ask for multimodal products" (65–66, my emphasis). Additionally, as Sheppard argues, misconceptions about the rhetorical and intellectual aspects of engaging in and teaching digital media composing "have repercussions for how faculty are evaluated, for

Table 2.11. (*continued*)

Organizing questions	What counts as a text?	How do we approach reading texts?	How do we approach the production of texts?
Reframed questions	What kinds of texts do we assign as primary "readings"?	What methods of reading/ research do we teach students?	What types of texts/ genres do we teach/ expect students to produce?
Questions for departments	What types of texts and genres should undergraduates be exposed to in their studies? When should undergraduates be exposed to new media texts? What can the department do to increase exposure to alternative texts/genres?	What lenses should undergraduates learn to bring to alternative texts/genres? When and how should undergraduates learn to read alternative texts? What are the best practices in teaching in your field?	What is valuable about assigning writing? What is valuable about assigning digital media projects? What skills should undergraduate students be able to demonstrate in writing? What would those skills look like demonstrated in another medium? How is writing a means of inquiry? How can digital media be used as a means of inquiry? Should undergraduates learn to produce alternative texts? When/where should they learn this (at what point in the curriculum)?

how resources are allocated, and most importantly, for what learning experiences are available to students" (123). Departmental/community attention to the questions I have identified in table 2.11 can help to reveal the rhetorical connections between "traditional" and digital work, help departments to better understand their role in supporting such work through the allocation of resources and sustaining a robust and supportive technological ecology, and help departments come to terms with how to evaluate digital work, particularly digital scholarship. The next chapter will explore how these departments position themselves toward questions of textuality, reading, and composing when it comes to scholarship; how those questions are inflected differently in the realm of scholarship; and the tensions that arise for individuals and departments over the question of how to evaluate new forms of scholarship for promotion and tenure.

3

Scholarship through a New Lens:
Digital Production and New Models of Evaluation

> I'm not sure if I published a piece in *Kairos* versus in *Computers and Composition*,[1] . . . [it] would necessarily be considered better. *I* think it would be because I would think you'd want your technology specialist to be publishing innovative digital work. But there are times when I'm not sure that it would be.
> —Cosmo, PhD student, parallel cultures department

> The department and the college are so much more traditional than the university. But the college is the gatekeeper. It doesn't matter how progressive the university is if it doesn't trickle down.
> —Ava, assistant professor, integrated literacies department

Chester, a PhD candidate in Victorian literature in the parallel cultures department, was preparing for the job market when I interviewed him. He noted that although people had told him he was positioning himself well for the job market by learning about digital media, he did not see much disciplinary reward for producing new forms of scholarship in multimedia or developing a multimedia pedagogy for literature classes. He attended a department-sponsored lecture by a "big name" from another university who "talked about how he and a few other people had to fight to get tenure for somebody who had primarily digital and electronic type of publications and editorial work" that the university was not recognizing. Chester said, "And my response is, 'I don't want to be a guinea pig.' The job market's really bad. I don't want to have to trust that my senior colleagues at some future point in time are going to fight for me because they believe [in my work]—It's just too risky."

Rebecca Rickly discusses this issue in her 2000 article in *Computers and Composition*, "The Tenure of the Oppressed: Ambivalent Reflections from a Critical Optimist," noting a discrepancy between what graduate students are told about technology and what is expected once they land tenure-track positions:

> Most of us, as graduate students, were encouraged to learn about, experiment with, and use technology as long as it didn't inhibit our progress towards a degree. In fact, I'll wager that many of us got interviews and, subsequently, positions based on our work with technology. But once we've been hired, then what? Do we continue to spend as much time with technology? Should we continue to include it in our teaching, our scholarship, and our service? (21)

Like Chester, Rickly frames the issue in terms of evaluation, questioning whether work with digital media will be valued at the department level and, consequently, whether it is "worth" doing, whether it is worth being a "guinea pig."

Rickly's article came out the same year as the MLA's "Guidelines for Evaluating Work with Digital Media in the Modern Languages," which laid out responsibilities of departments and candidates in dealing with digital media work. However, by the middle of the decade—when my data was collected—faculty engaging in digital scholarship were still venturing into uncharted territory. The "Report of the MLA Task Force on Evaluating Scholarship for Tenure and Promotion" (first published online by the MLA in December 2006, later published in print by *Profession*) indicated an overwhelming lack of experience and confidence in evaluating digital scholarship for tenure and promotion, and the key administrators of the departments in this study showed a lack of consistency across programs regarding the question of new forms of publication. The chair of the print-centric department, for instance, said that the profession "is not ready to change." He argued that "somebody else will lead the change sometime in the future, but far in the future, not now." The chair of the integrated literacies department, on the other hand, said, "We're changing. We're leading the change. We have to change. Change is now." Somewhere in the middle of this spectrum is the parallel cultures department, whose chair recognized that evaluation criteria were not clearly delineated and that discussions were needed: "This is a question that we're trying to figure out, we need to figure out, but we're not really leading the fore on figuring it out." She and the chair of the department's promotion and tenure committee both expressed optimism that new forms of digital scholarship have a place in the department and would be accepted in tenure cases but that specific policies would likely need to be adapted as cases arose.

Although the MLA has suggested guidelines for evaluating digital scholarship since 2000, departments have been slow to officially adopt those guidelines and codify them in written promotion and tenure policies. Even in 2011, humanities scholars were still arguing for the recognition of basic aspects of digital scholarship that the MLA had been advocating for years, such as recognizing/valuing collaborative work (Nowviskie) and reviewing work in the medium for which it was produced (Rockwell; Anderson and McPherson). The conversation has, however, changed in tone, moving from arguments that tried to help scholars understand how new forms of scholarship fit into the print-centric structures of the humanities to arguments that recognize the centrality of digital structures to scholarly communication in the discipline. Steve Anderson and Tara McPherson, for instance, write:

> Whether we are willing to admit it or not, all humanities scholarship is now digital. From our electronic resources at the library to the software systems that produce our paychecks to our course management software, networked information flows are the terrain of the twenty-first-century university. If we choose not to engage in a deep and sustained manner with the digital infrastructures that shape our universities, our presses, the media, the health care system, and the very engines of late capitalism, if we persist with the business of the humanities in the old and familiar forms, we also cede the opportunity to work as agents of change in those networks. (150)

This and many other current arguments stress the importance of re-imagining the methods and products of scholarly inquiry in order to keep the field vital.

The intent of such arguments is to create a much-needed dialogue around digital scholarship in the discipline, a dialogue that should also take into account local contexts and ways departments can create technological ecologies for digital scholarship. In thinking about the approaches the departments in this study take toward such scholarship and the technological ecologies they create, it is necessary to return to the three big questions that digital media have forced the discipline to reconsider and ask how these questions manifest themselves in relationship to scholarship. The question of what counts as a text, while certainly an item of theoretical interest in scholarship, also has a practical side to it. Which texts departments see as scholarly and count as scholarship is a question that directly relates to the kinds of work that departments encourage and value (and expect to see in tenure dossiers). So, the question of what counts as a text needs to be rephrased as "What counts as a *scholarly* text?" The question of how scholars should read texts takes on a slightly different significance in the realm of scholarship, focusing more on how to approach the processes of research and scholarship. That question can be rephrased as "Which methods of scholarly inquiry are appropriate?" Last, the question of how to approach textual production becomes incredibly complex because the variables of publication and peer review are so important. This question needs to be broken down into two: "What counts as being published?" and "How do we engage in peer review?" (See table 3.1).

This chapter explores the stances on these questions of the three departments in this study and also their technological ecologies for digital scholarship by examining the tenure/promotion policies of the departments and analyzing interviews with the chairs of tenure and promotion committees, department chairs, and individual faculty and graduate students within these departments. I am not examining these questions merely for the purpose of advocating changes to promotion and tenure policies (although my analysis will point out issues for departments to consider in that regard) but also to discuss what these policies reveal about what departments value most about scholarship and how individuals position their work within such value frameworks. The first section, "The Textuality of Scholarship," considers the ways these departments define scholarship and the extent to which departmental policies and practices make space for seeing nontraditional forms and genres of scholarship as scholarly texts. The second section, "Methods of Scholarship," looks at how the departments either embrace or limit various scholarly methods and in what senses the departments

Table 3.1. Organizing questions reframed in the context of digital scholarship

Organizing questions	Questions reframed for scholarship
What counts as a text?	What counts as a scholarly text?
How do we approach reading texts?	What methods of scholarly inquiry are appropriate?
How do we approach the production of texts?	What counts as being published?
	How do we engage in peer review?

are poised to value a "more capacious" definition of scholarship, as advocated by the MLA. "Production, Publication, and Peer Review" examines how these departments define what counts for publication and peer response and in what ways they make room for alternative visions of these concepts. Finally, in the chapter's conclusion, I extend the matrix with sets of questions for two different groups: individuals creating digital scholarship and departments seeking to update their policies toward digital scholarship. The questions for individuals encourage deep thinking about the scholarly value of specific projects and ways to describe those projects to colleagues, while the questions for departments are prompts for localized discussions about what is valuable about different types and forms of scholarship.

Ellen Cushman's arguments about the hierarchy of signs are especially relevant to a discussion of digital media scholarship in English. Cushman and others, most notably Cheryl E. Ball, have noted that much scholarship that digital media specialists produce is published in printed rather than digital or multimodal formats. Ball distinguishes this printed *scholarship about new media* from *new media scholarship*, which makes meaning through multiple media or modes, including words, images, sounds, and so on. However, many promotion and tenure committees have little experience evaluating new media scholarship, falling back on print standards of evaluation, which often are not appropriate and fail to recognize the intellectual work encoded in different ways in digital scholarship. Cushman recognizes that "knowledge production in print alone reinforces the supremacy of letters, the habits of mind cultivated with this tool (textuality), and the artifacts of knowledge produced and delivered with this tool (print)" (68). She further argues, following Ball, that in order to level the hierarchy of signs for scholarly production, more scholars must produce new media scholarship. She states that, because tenure committees often do not value alternative forms of scholarship, "tenured professors are better situated to produce new media scholarship" (70).

But there is a lot at stake even for tenured faculty producing digital media scholarship. It's true, their jobs are not at stake in the way that the jobs of untenured faculty are. However, the same scholarly evaluation standards that fail to account for or value digital forms of scholarship for tenure also tend to hold for promotion. So, tenured associate professors might be leery of producing digital media scholarship that won't count in their bids for promotion to full professor. However, tenured faculty are in a better position than untenured faculty to push for their departments to have discussions about new or alternative forms of scholarship, and throughout this chapter, I will further build the matrix with questions to help departments in this endeavor. Similar to the questions in the previous chapter, which encourage departments to look at teaching through a new lens, the questions revealed in this chapter will help individuals and departments look at scholarship through a new lens and create sustainable technological ecologies for new media scholarship.

The Textuality of Scholarship

What counts as a text, in a general sense, is a question that most of these departments answer broadly. When it comes to thinking of texts as objects of scholarly analysis, most would include visual and audio works, as well as many cultural artifacts. The integrated literacies department even considers culture itself, not to mention technology, as a text to be read. However, when it comes to scholarly production, particularly the production of digital media scholarship, the definition of text narrows.

According to the chair of the print-centric department, the question of digital media publication "is moot as long as the monograph is king." He said that articles of all kinds, digital or otherwise, are just icing on the cake. However, he was very clear that the type of digital scholarly production that "counted" for tenure and promotion was the peer-reviewed article in an electronic journal. In fact, throughout the interview, while I used the more general term "digital scholarship," the chair repeatedly reframed it more narrowly as "peer-reviewed electronic articles," indicating that in order for a text to count as scholarship in this department, it must have a recognizable print analog (in this case, the article). Further cementing his point, the chair noted that the department had recently had a tenure case in which a faculty member had two electronic peer-reviewed articles, but because he also had a book published by a university press plus other "regular articles," the digital media work ended up being, in the chair's words, "unimportant to the tenure case." Toby, an assistant professor whose research is in the field of rhetoric and composition in the same department, saw the department's stance in similar terms and said that it "is grasping for a standard to put [digital scholarship] up against," noting that faculty are "still having a discussion on how to evaluate multimedia, still figuring out the questions to ask." But he added that although "communal standards are needed, . . . the department won't create policy criteria; they will come from the outside."

This example illustrates a central problem that scholars doing work in digital media face and that several of the participants in this study mentioned as a difficulty: that digital media scholars must often do their digital work *on top of* more traditional work. This has the effect of shutting down or postponing a lot of potentially innovative or important work while individuals create the scholarship that their departments will value (in this case, a scholarly monograph) and relegating their digital work to a place of "unimportance" in terms of tenure and promotion. Furthermore, because of their untenured status, many scholars doing digital media work are not really in a position to help their colleagues develop the "communal standards" that Toby says are necessary. They have to walk a fine line between teaching their senior scholars how to read and evaluate their digital work (or, in Toby's terms, what questions to ask) and meeting the long-held standards for tenure and promotion in the department. The fact that there are only a handful of faculty, all untenured, doing digital media work in the department is likely one reason Toby imagines policy criteria will have to come from the outside, from a more authoritative source such as the MLA or perhaps from the college or university level.

Although Toby, as an untenured professor, might not be well situated to advocate strongly for the department to come up with communal standards for evaluating digital media scholarship, he is well situated to frame a discussion of his own work for his colleagues. Table 3.2 suggests two questions that might point to ways for Toby (and scholars in his situation) to explain his work and encourage his colleagues to read his work in ways that focus on the scholarly activity he has engaged in as opposed to the form his scholarship takes. Jennifer Sheppard's observations about the misperceptions of the work involved in digital media production are relevant to this discussion. Although her arguments were made in the context of teaching digital media production, they easily extend to producing digital media scholarship. The rhetorical nature of technical production and the intellectual work involved are just as true for scholars creating new media scholarship as they are for students crafting new media compositions and for faculty teaching production. Considering the questions can help the discipline refocus its lens on the theoretical and analytical aspects of digital scholarship and on the particular ways that such intellectual work is encoded in digital scholarly texts. Attending to these questions can also aid in better understanding the contribution a particular text makes to scholarship in the author's field.

The parallel cultures department has begun to examine these issues and sees the importance of creating new criteria internally and broadening the scope of the kinds of texts that are considered scholarly. The chair, for instance, said that "greater types of texts should count" for tenure and that "the debate over how to assess new products" was currently going on, not just in the profession but also in the department. At the same time, the department was in a moment of tension trying to

Table 3.2. Questions for individuals to consider to help explain the scholarly activities that are enacted in individual scholarly texts/projects

Organizing questions	What counts as a text?	How do we approach reading texts?	How do we approach the production of texts?	
Reframed questions	What counts as a scholarly text?	What methods of scholarly inquiry are appropriate?	What counts as being published?	How do we engage in peer review?
Questions for individuals	In what ways does your text/project exhibit scholarly activity? How does the text/project contribute to scholarship/scholarly conversations in your field?			

figure things out. While the chair of the department was looking toward the future and at what has to change, the chair of the promotion and tenure committee explained that while members of the department appreciate the article "as a substantial publication," the department "does have a fetish for the old-fashioned, single-authored book." Much like the print-centric department, this one defines scholarly text in a way that privileges printed alphabetic-text-based analysis, though its promotion and tenure policy document allows for other types of texts in certain cases: "Where appropriate, evidence of scholarship may also include textbooks and journal articles on pedagogy, recordings, videotapes, films, and works in electronic or other media, singly or collaboratively produced." The promotion and tenure committee chair stressed, though, that this criterion is field-dependent (hence the "where appropriate" specification). Though this policy is certainly more accepting of digital scholarship and broader in its definition of scholarship in general than the print-centric department's, it still reflects the construction of digital media scholarship as not centrally a part of the discipline and only sometimes appropriate and makes it clear that digital scholarship alone will probably not earn a faculty member tenure.

Being part of a major research institution, like the print-centric and parallel cultures departments, the integrated literacies department also requires a "major body of substantial published scholarship," which the department chair noted is "ordinarily a book" but added that "that's not a specific requirement," as it seems to be in the other two departments. A body of articles also would count. As for texts beyond print, the chair said that the department was "moving toward establishing some clearer guidelines," but "the basic thrust of it is that work in digital media is evaluated as a major contribution to the field." He also noted that work in digital media can take many forms, including "publications in refereed electronic journals, digital media projects that are exhibited in a lot of different kinds of venues—at conferences, technical shows; certainly there are many more venues in which one's work can be demonstrated—and it can be creative or scholarly, as well." Additionally, in a section that includes "examples of materials or activities by which research and creative activity may be evaluated," the department's revised policy includes "multi-media production, computer software, websites, or other technological contributions" as well as "reviews, abstracts, and public and community documents, including teaching materials meant for internal circulation," expanding considerably the notion of scholarly text.

The chair indicated that the department was interested in more than just broadening the idea of what kinds of texts can be considered scholarly:

> Basically, we're looking at a different model and a different kind of paradigm for thinking about scholarship, thinking about contributions to a field, thinking about innovation, thinking about creativity, thinking about how one takes a set of tools and works with them toward a product or a performance or whatever it might be, or incorporates it into something, some format, markets it in some format other than a published book.

This department really sees itself as a leader in the field on this issue of new forms of scholarship. This view came about, however, because of a tenure case in which the candidate had a great deal of scholarship that the old policy could not handle. According to the chair, because there were several individuals in the candidate's field of digital media on the committee, they were able to "mediate and negotiate away from the bylaws and articulated the kind of criteria that were appropriate and necessary in terms of the evaluation" while maintaining the spirit of the policy. Through that process, they were able to create new criteria and benchmarks, which then were approved by the department at large.

While the committee members did take the MLA's "Guidelines for Evaluating Work with Digital Media in the Modern Languages" to heart, including, for instance, the guideline that work should be reviewed in the medium for which it was composed, the department went beyond that, as well, foreshadowing some of the issues that are now being brought up in the MLA's "Evaluation Wiki." Currently, the MLA committee working on this issue has gone beyond general guidelines and is providing a list of questions to be asked about digital work and a list of best practices for digital work (both of which are, because of the wiki format, still under creation and open to revision and discussion).

At the time that I was writing this chapter, the MLA wiki included several sections, the following of which are relevant to the issue of the textuality of scholarship:

- "Types of Digital Work—A list of types of academic digital work with thoughts as to how they might be presented for evaluation and how they might then be evaluated."
- "Short Guide to Evaluation of Digital Work—A list of questions evaluators can ask about digital work being assessed for tenure and promotion" (n. pag.)

Within "Types of Digital Work," editors have added online, peer-reviewed publications; scholarly electronic editions; specifications; research tools; hypermedia and hyperfiction; instructional technology, computer-assisted instruction, and computer-assisted language learning; and research blogs. In the discussion page for this section, someone has also added social networks. The text at the top of the page promises that "this section is a list of types of digital work with brief discussion of how it can be evaluated." However, the section actually focuses on describing the different types of texts—in particular, describing what it is about these kinds of texts that makes them important work—and on reflecting on the difficulties associated with evaluating the texts.

The task of laying out standards for evaluating digital texts is taken up in the "Short Guide to Evaluation of Digital Work," which provides two lists of questions to ask about a digital work. The first set of "questions to ask about a digital work that is being evaluated" reads as follows[2]:

- Is it accessible to the community of study?
- Did the creator get competitive funding? Have they [sic] tried to apply?
- Have there been any expert consultations? Has this been shown to others for expert opinion?
- Has the work been reviewed? Can it be submitted for peer review?
- Has the work been presented at conferences?

- Have papers or reports about the project been published?
- Do others link to it? Does it link out well?
- If it is an instructional project, has it been assessed appropriately?
- Is there a deposit plan? Will it be accessible over the longer term? Will the library take it? (n. pag.)

What is striking about these questions designed to evaluate digital texts is that they are primarily focused on issues outside of the text itself—such as whether or not it has been reviewed, presented at conferences, or competitively funded and whether or not the library will take it—rather than on the scholarly work that the text accomplishes in and of itself. Questions like those above are certainly asked about traditional printed scholarship and are likely important in determining quality; however, ultimately it is the scholarly work that a book or article does that is (or should be) the most important factor in its evaluation. This is the question that needs to be addressed about digital scholarship, as well: how do different types of digital texts accomplish scholarly work? If digital scholarship is to be seen as *scholarship*, the question of how digital texts make scholarly moves must be explicitly addressed.

James P. Purdy and Joyce R. Walker address this issue in their recent article in *Profession*, "Valuing Digital Scholarship: Exploring the Changing Realities of Intellectual Work." They acknowledge that, while the discipline has begun "to recognize the importance of digital work, discussions have tended to focus primarily on establishing digital work as equivalent to print publications to make it count instead of considering how digital scholarship might transform knowledge-making practices" (178). Rather than pitting print and digital publications against each other or creating a hierarchy of publication media, they argue that both print and digital publications must be considered "in relation to larger, more systemic issues regarding the nature and value of various kinds of scholarly work: design and delivery, recentness and relevance, and authorship and accessibility" (179). They explain in detail these three categories, demonstrating how to read the contribution and intellectual activity of digital scholarship through this framework. Their framework opens up a space for defining the scholarly activities the discipline values and for making these activities visible regardless of the form the final product takes. They maintain that such a focus on scholarly activities not only avoids a simple print-digital binary but also allows for evaluation to focus on what a text "produces, participates in, or does" (191). They then suggest several questions to help develop a robust assessment model that would focus on scholarly activities—such as knowledge production, genre, expertise, audience factors, and whether the text has been vetted—a model that they recognize would look very different from the current promotion and tenure evaluation models in place at most institutions. This model would, as Purdy and Walker argue, allow for consideration of more than just the "textual artifact," giving us access "to an exploration of the activity systems in which people interact (with various tools, institutions, and individuals) to create texts that disseminate information, make arguments, explore ideas, and even contribute to the ways the discipline sees itself," ultimately rewarding faculty for "a more comprehensive range of scholarly contributions to our institutions and discipline" (192). In their digital text "Scholarship on the Move: A Rhetorical Analysis of Scholarly Activity in Digital Spaces," Purdy and Walker demonstrate how such an assessment model might work. They analyze the ways in which scholarly rhetorical moves are made in specific webtexts, blogs, discussion boards, and Twitter, and conclude that it is important to recognize the different ways that scholarly moves are made in digital texts and to create evaluation frameworks that resist print-based models.

Unfortunately, the MLA wiki does not break out of this print-based framework to recognize the scholarly work and contribution of ideas that can happen in other ways through scholarly digital texts. The print-centric and parallel cultures departments are still both focused on form rather than on scholarly activity and, like the MLA wiki, focused on questions somewhat external to the scholarship demonstrated by the texts—such as venue reputation. They know that digital texts should count, but they don't know how to read the scholarliness of such texts in order to evaluate them. Purdy and Walker's analysis in "Scholarship on the Move" provides a good foundation to build on in terms of figuring out what questions digital media scholars and departments can ask to discover if a digital text is doing the work it needs to do to be considered scholarship. The integrated literacies department, having gone through the process of holding digital texts up to a set of evaluation criteria based on printed scholarship, has been able to rearticulate its definition of what constitutes scholarship in broad enough terms that the scholarly work accomplished in all kinds of texts can be made visible and thus evaluated.

In addition to Purdy and Walker's questions, which are useful for evaluating individual pieces of scholarship, table 3.3 suggests questions for departments to consider to help them (re)develop community standards for scholarly production and evaluation. These questions can help departments articulate what it is about scholarship that they value, how the scholarly activities or moves that they value are encoded in different kinds of texts in different fields, and how those scholarly moves might be encoded differently in different media.

Methods of Scholarship

The question of textuality is intimately related to the questions of which scholarly methods are appropriate and, indeed, what counts as a scholarly process. Textuality and scholarship methods are so intertwined it was sometimes difficult for me to decide whether a particular example belongs in this section or the previous one because if one has a method that leads to particular types of texts but those texts are not considered scholarly, then that method will likely not be valued either or, if it is, will be less valued than other methodologies that lead to the types of texts that are considered most scholarly. Teasing out the differences between how the discipline defines scholarly texts and scholarly methods requires an exploration of what we mean by the terms we use to describe our methods, such as "critical analysis." It also requires an exploration of a range of methods whose scholarliness is under discussion, such as

Table 3.3 Questions to help departments define the scholarly activities they value and to help imagine those activities enacted in different media

Organizing questions	What counts as a text?	How do we approach reading texts?	How do we approach the production of texts?		
Reframed questions	What counts as a scholarly text?	What methods of scholarly inquiry are appropriate?	What counts as being published?	How do we engage in peer review?
Questions for departments	What scholarly activities do you value? What do those activities typically "look like" in published scholarship (in your field)? What might those activities look like if enacted in another medium?				

bibliographic inquiry, and a consideration of the scholarly processes involved in certain teaching and service activities. These scholarly methods are not new, and discussions of their scholarly worth have been ongoing in English studies; however, digital media scholarship has renewed interest in and raised new questions about these methods.

The print-centric and parallel cultures departments are quite similar in the scholarly methods they privilege, both placing critical analysis—defined as the interpretation of some kind of text or set of texts through a theoretical lens (typically critical or rhetorical theory)—that leads to a peer-reviewed publication at the top of their list. Other kinds of scholarship are considered in both departments but lead to gray areas that each department negotiates slightly differently. The scholarship of teaching is a prime example. In both departments, the scholarship of teaching counts when it results in a peer-reviewed publication, such as a journal article or textbook. However, there is a difference in these two departments on whether a textbook can count as equivalent to a scholarly monograph in tenure deliberations or not. According to the chair of the print-centric department, some of the deans in the college "contend that the scholarship of teaching and learning isn't a viable research category," but the department "resists that view." When I asked Toby about this issue, he said the department "wants to value it but doesn't know how," particularly when it comes to digital work in the scholarship of teaching and learning, such as an online textbook.

This question about the scholarship of teaching was especially salient for Toby, an assistant professor in the print-centric department, because he was working on a project that challenges the definition of scholarship as theoretical work. His project involved building a website for the training of first-time professional writing instructors, and Toby wanted this to count, not as service or teaching, but as a kind of research: "It is departmental service because it grows out of my responsibility to train these instructors, but it's a certain kind of research and creative work that requires a kind of expertise that I don't think a whole bunch of other colleagues in the department would be able to put forward." He said that working on the project has given him a better perspective on how technology inflects his pedagogical aims, but he was concerned about the reception of such a project and whether others would accept his argument that it should count as research/scholarship.

In addition to explaining the ways in which the project crosses the traditional categories of teaching, research, and service, Toby offered his reasons for creating the training website himself and noted the time and effort involved in the endeavor:

I'm doing it [instead of having the Teaching with Technologies Lab do it] because I have greater control over it. I have a vision about it I don't want to have to translate to somebody else. And I want to be the person who maintains the site and has that kind of access to it. But to pay for that I have to invest all this time. . . . I've gotta go to three workshops on more advanced features of Dreamweaver and Image Ready so my files aren't too large. I think that ought to be valued. There ought to be some sort of currency that that's given as an effort to be up to speed pedagogically with the options that the university gives us and as a kind of research because now I have a much better perspective on how technology inflects certain pedagogical aims of mine. I think it's valuable [and] should be valued; I just don't know how.

Toby recognizes that how the discipline values creative applications of technology depends on how the discipline defines them. Is his project service? Is it teaching? Is it research on teaching? Realistically, it is all three of these. And it is valuable *because* it is all three—teaching, research, *and* service. However, although the chair said that the scholarship of teaching and learning counts as scholarship, the way the department evaluates such work is by looking at the products that result. Because the department and—even more so—the college privilege a certain kind of published and peer-reviewed product, Toby was convinced that this particular project would count only as service to the department or perhaps as further evidence of teaching because of the lack of traditional peer review and dissemination.

Toby's experience is a good example of Sheppard's arguments about the rhetorical work of digital media production not being recognized. The technical issues Toby references—having authorial and design control of his text, creating files that are quick to load for the accessibility of his audience—are rhetorical concerns that he is learning to enact through a new technology. Furthermore, creating the site has helped him better understand his pedagogical goals, revise his pedagogy to better reflect those goals, keep up with the pedagogical advancements in his field, and train future teachers to do the same—in other words, to engage in scholarly teaching and perhaps, if we are willing to see his website as akin to a textbook, the scholarship of teaching.

A similar kind of hesitancy or uncertainty about the scholarship of teaching exists in the parallel cultures department, particularly if the teaching under study has a digital media component. The chair of the promotion and tenure committee said that the scholarship of teaching is scholarship and is "given full credit." At the same time, the department's policy document marks the production of pedagogy-centered publications and textbooks with the limiting words "where appropriate." The case of the scholarship of digital media teaching muddies the waters even more. When I interviewed the chair of the promotion and tenure committee, I showed him some examples of nontraditional publications, including Anthony Ellertson's "Some Notes on Simulacra Machines, Flash in FYC & Tactics in Spaces of Interruption," published online in *Kairos: A Journal of Rhetoric, Technology, and Pedagogy*. It was created using Macromedia Flash to organize its elements and consists primarily of text but also utilizes several images, moving text, side-by-side text blocks, pop-out windows, a video of the author speaking part of his analysis, and a graphical, interactive interface that allows the user to navigate multiple paths through the text. Even though the piece is composed primarily of words, because of its multimedia elements, it seemed quite foreign to the chair of the promotion and tenure committee. When asked how something like that would be evaluated, he responded:

> I'm gathering that there's a professional protocol for this kind of thing. I'm gathering that there's now a group of scholars who are in a position to tell us what's a good presentation and what isn't a good presentation, one that's taking full advantage of the resources peculiar to the technology. I've never seen anything like that before, at fourth- or sixth-year review. But that's not to say that it wouldn't be welcome as yet more evidence of either teaching or research, and I think that this is an area, sometimes like the border between service and teaching, that is a little more difficult to define as one or the other.

In addition to placing the burden of proof on the candidate to explain how the nontraditional project fits the traditional value system, this chairperson of the promotion and tenure committee also places some burden on scholars in the field. He assumes that there is a group of scholars that can educate those outside of their field about digital research, and that recognition indicates an openness to learn about digital media research and the potential to accept it on its own terms.

This comment, though, also points to the ways in which both digital media scholarship and the scholarship of teaching are undervalued by traditional evaluation criteria, particularly at research-oriented universities. This particular multimedia publication utilizes traditional composition methodology and represents as much work as an ethnography presented in print and published in a journal; in fact, *Kairos*, the online journal in which the piece appears, has a reputation for publishing quality scholarship—it has a rigorous peer-review process and a 10 percent acceptance rate, for instance. The difference is that the piece uses multimedia to present the research findings; it is not in print, and it is not linear. Thus, the chair of the promotion and tenure committee, though he claims it would be accepted as evidence of work, says it would be evidence of *either* teaching *or* research, suggesting that this project is not clearly "scholarship." If it were printed, even with its focus on the classroom and ethnographic methodology, there would be no question; it would count as published scholarship. This example demonstrates how the old question of the scholarship of teaching is renewed but inflected differently because of the digital media element. This department has composition and folklore programs, and several faculty in those areas do ethnographic research. So there is a history of faculty educating their peers about ethnography; the use of the methodology is established in the department. But because of the "article's" multimedia elements, suddenly the focus on the classroom and the medium of presentation become an issue, and it might not classify as scholarship.

Another example of a scholarly gray area in these two departments is collaborative work. Toby said that in the print-centric department, this is the "hardest to get to count," particularly collaborative digital work because "it's just one more layer of difficulty to assess." Likewise, in the parallel cultures department, the chair of the promotion and tenure committee said that "collaborative work counts but not as much as single-authored work," although the policy document seems much more open to collaborative work: "Evidence of scholarship should consist of published writing, singly or collaboratively authored, or, where appropriate, recordings, videotapes, films, and works in electronic or other media, singly or collaboratively produced." Although the language of the official policy suggests that collaboratively authored works have parity with single-authored works, the chair of the promotion and tenure committee's comment suggests that this is still a point of negotiation within the department and that in practice, the department values single-authored works more highly.

Digital media makes this old question about collaborative authorship more salient if only because so much digital scholarship is necessarily collaborative, and not just because so much of it is produced by composition scholars, who tend to collaborate more on scholarship anyway. But collaboration is an issue not only in terms of authorship but also because of the technical complexity of much digital scholarship. It is likely that a scholar producing a digital text will collaborate with a technical expert on issues of production, display, and design, which, as Sheppard argues, have a rhetorical component to them. An example of this type of collaboration is "This Is Scholarship," a multimedia text created by me and Kenneth L. Gilbert, whose major argument is accomplished in a short movie. I created the original visual track of the movie and the website that houses it, wrote the introductory framework, and compiled the list of suggested readings and selected works referenced. Gilbert, an audio technician by profession, created the audio track for the movie and handled the technical aspects of compressing the movie for web delivery. He composed the music to fit with the visual track and to be an aural interpretation of the visual arguments. The movie, in part, argues that the form of a text is often what makes it appear scholarly (for example, in a particular journal, edited for the page, looking the way we "expect" a piece of scholarship to look), and I see the (co)authorship of the piece as a part of its argument. We do not often think of editorial technicians as coauthors of our work. However, because they are in charge of the ultimate form of our scholarly publications (for example, the way an article looks in print), they are in a sense our coauthors, as the form of a work helps to define, from a promotion and tenure evaluation standpoint, whether it is "scholarly." Digital media production reveals that the form a text takes influences whether it is seen as scholarly, and I wanted the authorship of this text to expose rather than perpetuate this content/form (composing/editing) division.

A third gray area in these two departments is bibliographic/editorial scholarship, which has seen a resurgence in recent years because of digital media and the ability to create online collections that are easily accessible to scholars around the world. Toby indicated that his print-centric department would "love" this kind of work and give it full credit, whereas in the parallel cultures department, the chair of the promotion and tenure committee said that this kind of work would count "not as scholarship but as editorial service." Only published critical analysis of the works contained in the collections would count as scholarship, not the compiling and editing of the collection itself.

All of these examples point to a larger issue that English as a discipline (or set of interrelated disciplines) needs to consider: the privileging of one method, namely critical/theoretical analysis, over other methods of inquiry and the print-culture bias that goes along with it. Among fields (like composition) that value the scholarship of teaching, for instance, such work is indeed seen as a kind of scholarly inquiry, in addition to "yet more evidence of effective teaching." In the other fields of English studies, there is very little pedagogical scholarship produced, likely in part because there are few venues for such work, but also because teaching is not typically seen as a site of inquiry (or as a place where critical analysis is applied) in the same way that critical analysis of texts is valued as a site of inquiry.

Entangled with this narrow view of critical analysis is the similarly narrow model of the solitary scholar, who writes alone. In their historical account of how the concept of authorship has been constructed in the Western world, Andrea Lunsford and Lisa Ede show convincingly "just how deeply entrenched in our culture"—and, I would add, in English studies—"is the assumption that authorship is inherently an individual enterprise" (73). They demonstrate that the concept of individual authorship is a relatively new cultural construct, one that was able to arise, in part, because of the development of printing and one that has been *theoretically* "problematized, deconstructed, and challenged to such an extent that discussions of the problem of the author are decidedly old hat in literary circles" (87). And yet, while these discussions have destabilized the definition of text (literary texts and criticism share the same status, for instance, as text), such discussions have not, as Lunsford and Ede recognized in 1990, destabilized the idea of the solitary author in writing classrooms.

Nor have such discussions destabilized the notion of the solitary scholar. Despite decades of social-constructivist thought, English departments still exalt the solitary scholar interpreting texts and then writing up and publishing those interpretations. The scholarly "conversation" that is typically referenced in such interpretations is constructed as a conversation between published words, not as a part of the process of *composing*. While constructing that conversation might be a part of the interpretive process, it occurs at the stage of analysis and is best thought of as "influential" rather than "cooperative" in the composing process. The implications of this failure to consider the construction of the singular scholarly author are great and have a disproportionate effect on scholars creating digital media works because so much digital scholarship is by its very nature collaborative.

Furthermore, scholarly methods that don't emphasize writing/interpretation as a solitary act have been consequently devalued. Bibliographic and editorial scholarship, for instance, are often seen not as scholarship but as service to the profession. This situation is addressed in the "MLA Evaluation Wiki," and the contributor makes a case for, specifically, scholarly electronic editions:

> Scholarly electronic editions represent significant careful and informed work that can be accessed widely. The work of the electronic editor is not trivial—he or she has to make a series of decisions informed by knowledge of the context and original about what to show and hide, how to enrich the material, and how to represent it online. The opportunities and fluidity of the electronic form mean the editor must master two fields, the intellectual context of the work and current practices in digital representation. Ironically, if the editor gets the form right so that the electric version can be searched and easily read, no one will notice, and their delicate work will be unappreciated in evaluation, but this is true of translation and editorial work whatever the medium. The real issue here is that editorial work is viewed as of less value than theoretical work. (n. pag.)

This argument for scholarly electronic editions focuses both on the medium and on the scholarly moves such projects make. It necessarily imagines a definition of scholarship that is not method- or medium-specific, highlighting the intellectual work the editor engages in and the contribution to scholarship such texts make, as well as the creative digital work the editor engages in.

Purdy and Walker explore this notion of scholarly moves in much greater detail, providing numerous examples of the ways that digital texts make these moves in ways that are different from printed texts. The five rhetorical moves that Purdy and Walker propose as basic characteristics of scholarly texts—explicit argumentation, speculation, implicit association, dialogic exchange, and formal enactment—complement the seven "scholarly primitives" John Unsworth identifies as the basic functions (or methods) of scholarship across disciplines as well as across media: discovering, annotating, comparing, referring, sampling, illustrating, and representing. While Purdy and Walker's focus is on the ways that different scholarly moves happen in digital texts themselves, Unsworth focuses on the activities a scholar engages in to create a piece of scholarship (the scholarly composing processes, if you will). In the example of scholarly electronic editions, the editor's work would necessitate several (if not all) of the scholarly primitives:

- discovering information about the context of different versions of a text
- annotating each version in particular ways so that it can be searched by others

- creating a means of representing the texts (and portions of the texts) in a way that others can compare different versions (formal enactment, in Purdy and Walker's scheme)

These scholars concentrate on characterizing scholarly *activity*, which should be the focus of any assessment of scholarship. Such a focus allows departments to value multiple methods and multiple forms without sacrificing scholarly excellence or any quality indicators that departments set up. Standards of quality should be medium- and method-independent in order to value a range of methods.

The integrated literacies department provides a model of a policy that enacts a broader notion of not only scholarly products but also scholarly methods and frees the definition of "scholarship" from both method and medium while still considering method and medium as part of the context of (but not the conditions for) scholarship. The textbook question is not even an issue in this department, for instance. Its revised policy[3] lists all of the types of texts and processes by which scholarship is to be evaluated. Though the list does create a hierarchy and states that the list "should be viewed as most valued in descending order of importance," the very first line reads, "A scholarly, belletristic, or textbook of substantial quality." A textbook is clearly equivalent to a monograph in this department. Likewise, the question of collaboration is not an issue. The document states, "In all cases, collaborative work is to be valued as a legitimate form of inquiry and production and as co-equal with single authorship." The department chair reinforced this position, describing the recent tenure case that occasioned the department's revision of its policy. The candidate had a great deal of collaborative work, and the case hinged on the department's coming to an understanding of the importance of collaborative work to the candidate's field and on the nature of collaborative work. Finally, editorial scholarship is also rewarded as a legitimate form of inquiry in and of itself: the third line of the list of what counts as scholarship includes "other scholarly contributions such as editing a scholarly book, an edition of letters, or editing an anthology or reader."

Even beyond these more common yet debated forms of scholarship, the integrated literacies department policy lists items that are not routinely thought of as scholarship in the other two departments, such as "consulting with government, non-profit, or private organizations," "creative activities such as public readings, performances, or showings" (the university's creative writing program is not housed in this department, so the department is actively recognizing a creative component to scholarship in certain fields as well as alternative types of venues), and "editing journals, magazines, and newsletters." The policy also states that "research which is not published or incorporated in a delivered paper, yet has a demonstrable effect upon the classroom, and projects of particular significance to the teaching mission of the Department may be eligible to be considered." Many of these items, which might be considered service in other departments, have a scholarly element to them, which this department recognizes.

This is especially true for digital media work that is often considered as service, such as pedagogical workshops focused on digital media. In the integrated literacies department, such workshops can count as research and scholarship. The chair explained that the recent tenure candidate conducted a lot of these workshops, which require not only a lot of preparation but also a lot of work in managing "the dynamics of the workshop itself and doing some kind of evaluation of the effect, [measuring] the impact of those workshops at a high level." He continued:

> In the past we would have said, that was a lot of good service, in the same way you might give service by sharing your expertise in some way. But this is different in the sense that it actually requires research in order to produce a workshop that's going to move people significantly ahead in terms of their skills, their facility for using it in their classroom and their instruction, their ability to use it in research, their ability to actually try out some new formats themselves, in creative ventures.

This department takes seriously Ernest L. Boyer's category of the scholarship of teaching. In his book *Scholarship Reconsidered*, Boyer reconceptualizes scholarship as consisting of four separate yet overlapping functions—discovery, integration, application, and teaching—and argues that this broader definition of scholarship "brings legitimacy to the full scope of academic work" (16). Though Boyer doesn't specifically integrate multiple media into his redefinition of scholarship, his argument for recognizing a diversity of scholarly functions can be easily extended to include a diversity of forms, genres, and media, as well. Certainly, digital media work brings this issue to the forefront, as in the case with the digital media workshops that the chair of the integrated literacies department described.

This department chair also recognizes the transformative potential of digital media and realizes the need for a transformation of tenure policy based upon a new model of scholarship. The department's policy lists four criteria for judging the quality of work:

Scholarship: to what extent is the effort consistent with the methods and goals of the field and shaped by knowledge, understanding, and insight that is current or appropriate to the topic? To what extent does the effort generate, apply, and utilize knowledge?

Significance: to what extent does the effort address issues that are important to the scholarly community, specific constituents, or the public?

Impact: to what extent does the effort benefit or affect fields of scholarly inquiry, external issues, communities, or individuals? To what extent does the effort inform and foster further activity in instruction, research and creative activities, or service?

Attention to context: to what extent is the effort consistent with the university mission statement, issues within the scholarly community, the constituents' needs, and available resources?

These criteria present a vision of scholarship that is medium- and field-independent and that values the particular methods and conversations in an individual's field yet can be applied to a range of different kinds of work in a range of different media and for multiple areas of study.

It is no surprise, then, that the integrated literacies department is the only department in my study in which individuals are actively developing technologies to enact new research methodologies. Alan, for instance, a PhD student in the department, was "doing a lot of work with online citations and how they're being used in print publications." His project was developing "methodologies for seeing where these things were when they were originally cited," which involves the development of database technologies. This project provides an example of a different kind of analysis of digital texts that upsets traditional methods of scholarship because it requires the creation of digital media tools. It is a collaborative project exploring citation practices of both print and online publications to understand whether, where, and how much online sources are cited.

In addition to using the Wayback Machine,[4] an Internet archive enabling users to see old versions of websites that might no longer exist "live" on the Web, he and his colleagues also "developed a database to put the data into and then get information out of it based on the queries we give it." He had "been working a lot on developing the web interface of the database, structuring the database and getting that to work, which is kind of new stuff for me but interesting," and said it "could be really functional in a lot of different ways for research." This project pushes at disciplinary boundaries. In addition to analyzing digital texts, Alan also created a new methodology that does not resemble traditional methods in his field of rhetoric and composition. Furthermore, this new methodology required the creation of digital tools to perform the analysis. Whereas many individuals interviewed certainly use digital tools to acquire the texts they will analyze, few actually use digital tools to *perform* part of that analysis. Moreover, nobody else in this study has *created* their own digital applications. Alan's project is thus unique in this study for its production of digital media for research purposes, and it represents an example of the kinds of computer applications that this department would value as a major scholarly contribution, in part because it is a tool that has the potential to be used by other scholars for other projects.

Certainly, in all three departments, almost anything is a text that can be interpreted for scholarship, but there is still an expectation in the print-centric and parallel cultures departments that the interpretation will be "written up" and published in a peer-reviewed venue. Such a definition excludes a great deal of work that could be considered scholarly, and it forces a strict relationship between scholarly methods and scholarly product; understanding scholarly texts as marked by a fixed medium, typically print, limits the scholarly process to those methods that produce such texts. However, the integrated literacies department provides a model for valuing other types of scholarship that result in different products, as well as examples of these other types of scholarship.

Some of these different types of products have pages devoted to them on the "MLA Evaluation Wiki," including scholarly electronic editions, research tools (like Alan's project), and "specifications" (guidelines or standards, the development of which is often seen as service work). The guidelines for them are emergent; their entries right now consist mostly of arguments for why they should be considered scholarly. And although the MLA wiki claims that it "does not represent the official positions of the Modern Language Association," it does represent where the conversation is headed: toward a rethinking of what constitutes scholarship from the standpoint of method.

Table 3.4 suggests questions to help departments create assessment criteria that represent not only disciplinary but also local values about scholarly activity or scholarly methods. The questions for individuals focus on process and can help to illuminate the intellectual and rhetorical work put into any piece of scholarship. The questions for departments can help frame a community discussion of what is valuable about various methods of scholarship, pointing to how evaluation criteria can be developed that, while not ignoring the textual artifact, allow for a consideration of a range of scholarly activities that might be enacted in a variety of forms and media.

Table 3.4. Questions about methods of scholarly inquiry

Organizing questions	What counts as a text?	How do we approach reading texts?	How do we approach the production of texts?	
Reframed questions	What counts as a scholarly text?	What methods of scholarly inquiry are appropriate?	What counts as being published?	How do we engage in peer review?
Questions for individuals	In what ways does your text/project exhibit scholarly activity? How does the text/project contribute to scholarship/ scholarly conversations in your field?	Describe the scholarly methods you employed in this text/project. Why did you choose these particular methods? How are these methods appropriate for your field and for this text/ project in particular? How much time did you spend on various aspects of your text/project, including research, data analysis, encoding/writing, interface design, etc.?		
Questions for departments	What scholarly activities do you value? What do those activities typically "look like" in published scholarship (in your field)? What might those activities look like if enacted in another medium?	What activities or methods of inquiry can be considered scholarly? What is valuable about each? What sorts of products or outcomes can be expected to result from such activities or inquiry? What constitutes the scholarship of teaching? What is valuable about the scholarship of teaching? What kinds of products can be expected to result from the scholarship of teaching? What constitutes editorial scholarship? What is valuable about editorial scholarship? What kinds of products can be expected to result from editorial scholarship? What is valuable about scholarly collaboration? Under what circumstances should digital media "service" work be considered a contribution to scholarship? What kinds of products or outcomes can be expected to result from such scholarship? Under what circumstances should it be considered service and not scholarship?		

Production, Publication, and Peer Review

Just as the question of textuality is intimately related to the question of which scholarly methods are appropriate, so is the question of method intimately related to the question of production, as Roxie's case exemplifies. Roxie, a PhD student in the parallel cultures department, was also working on a project that disrupts the traditional methods and format of scholarship. Her field is nineteenth-century American literature, and she explained the benefits of hypertext for rethinking her approach to literary analysis:

> I've been working on one story for probably four years now and have a really hard time trying to analyze and interpret this story in a scholarly essay because there's so much going on in it. So for me to scan that text [and] do hypertext and link is a much easier way and in some ways I think does more justice to the ambiguities and complexities of that story, rather than writing a traditional essay about it. So, yeah, [digital media work has] made me rethink the way I approach literature in some cases.

Roxie envisions a basic "remediation" of scholarly literary analysis. In their book *Remediation: Understanding New Media*, Jay David Bolter and Richard Grusin argue that new media present themselves as "refashioned and improved versions of other media" (15). "Remediation" is thus defined as this act of refashioning, which depends, they argue, on the twin concepts of immediacy and hypermediacy. Media seek "to achieve immediacy by ignoring or denying the presence of the medium and the act of mediation" (11); at the same time, hypermedia call attention to the process of mediation and ask the audience "to take pleasure in the act of mediation" (14). This "double logic of remediation" means that "our culture wants both to multiply its media and to erase all traces of mediation: ideally, it wants to erase its media in the very act of multiplying them" (5). All media, they argue, remediate older media in an attempt to get the audience closer to the actual thing represented, which is the very reason Roxie imagines hypertext would work so well for her analysis. On the one hand, the immediacy of hypertext would allow Roxie to do the sorts of literary analysis she thinks is appropriate, bringing the audience closer to the ambiguities and complexities of the story and thus erasing the fact of mediation (whereas print is inadequate to the story's complexity and thus calls attention to itself). On the other hand, hypertext, as an unconventional scholarly medium (in Roxie's field, at least), would call attention to itself too much for faculty in her field, who struggle to see past the medium and recognize the scholarly work that is encoded there in ways different from the linear (printed) textual analyses they are more familiar with.

Roxie must negotiate, then, a position in between her department's stance on digital media and her own experience. For instance, she indicated that while there could be opportunities for reward for this kind of work "out there," she said she didn't think they existed very much in her department because it was "very divided." She continued: "I think that there is a small group of professors who would go, 'Oh wow, that's great!' But the majority would be a little uninterested, like, 'That's great, maybe you should submit an article about it to this journal and be published,' [implying] that the online work isn't enough; it has to be authenticated by appearing in a print journal." Though in many ways, Roxie's potential project maintains many of the traditional hallmarks of literary analysis, particularly close reading of a text, the very fact that it is hypermediated raises red flags. Furthermore, Roxie indicated that many professors in her department have set up a binary opposition between printed scholarship and hypertextual or digitally mediated scholarship, considering only the former truly "published."

Though Roxie's project is one that could potentially diversify the methods and media of literary analysis, she has in fact imagined it not as a research project that she would publish and share with other scholars but rather as primarily a teaching strategy: "This is actually not a project that I myself have been working on, but I have been thinking about requiring it at some point from my students. Which means, in effect, that I would do the project first so that I could better guide them. But no, I haven't done it yet." Though she was teaching in the parallel cultures department's networked classrooms, had worked in the department's Center for Digital Media Studies, and had role models for teaching first-year writing with digital media, she didn't have role models for digital research. So she was clearly walking a middle ground between her perception of the usefulness of the medium and her perception of her faculty mentors' (and, by extension, her field's) response to such work.

In making their argument that the discipline should attend more to scholarly activity as opposed to scholarly forms, Purdy and Walker specifically address this print culture bias that Roxie must negotiate. Like the authors of the MLA wiki, faculty in Roxie's field have a hard time imagining alternatives to the print-based processes of scholarship that Purdy and Walker observe: coming up with ideas and developing research agendas, moving through conference presentations of preliminary findings, and ultimately arriving at a print-based product. For these colleagues, the digital production takes the place of the "middle" stage, presentation of preliminary findings, and so is devalued. Roxie clearly both recognizes and disagrees with this viewpoint, but there is very little she can do about it. Roxie's experience also underscores the interconnections between scholarly processes/methods and the resulting products. Not only are textuality and scholarly methods bound up together, but publication is also an incredibly important aspect in understanding what ultimately can be considered a scholarly text, and the entire enterprise of scholarly publishing, not to mention tenure and promotion, hinges on the twin concepts of the medium of dissemination and the perceived rigor of the peer review process.

According to the chair of the print literacies department, the medium of publication is already a central concern in tenure decisions:

> If scholar X publishes his or her articles at well-known presses or in well-known journals, at least those of us who know the discipline reasonably well ask no questions; we know what those are. Whereas, if that same person's publishing in electronic journals, unless they're extremely well known, nobody knows what they are. Now, let's hope that the next generation of scholars will know. But I think for right now, it prompts questions that are not raised if scholarship is published in traditional venues. I assume that's gonna change in the next ten years.

But how will the next generation know about online venues? If those venues are not valued now, rising scholars are not likely to publish in them. If rising scholars don't publish in them, they will never gain a reputation and nobody will ever know about them. Toby echoed his chair's sentiment about online publishing, saying that the press or venue is incredibly important and that he believed that something published in conference proceedings would actually fare better in tenure deliberations than something published in an online journal, even if it were refereed.

If the medium of publication matters so much, then defining the media of scholarship is crucial. In other words, the discipline needs to rethink the concept of publication and recognize how biases toward particular media are written into tenure policies and thus influence the kind of work that does and does not get done, not to mention where it does and does not appear. Previous research has found that the aforementioned print/digital binary structures many promotion and tenure policies. In a discourse analysis of promotion and tenure policies, for instance, I found that the MLA guideline to make explicit reference to medium in tenure and promotion policies led to departmental policies that specifically tied the definition of scholarship to the medium of production, privileging production in print and taking the scholarliness of printed production for granted, while stipulating the conditions under which digital productions could be considered a valuable contribution ("Guidelines for Evaluating Work"). Furthermore, the policies conflated medium with genre, suggesting, for instance, that an e-book would be considered to fall under the genre of "digital publication" rather than the genre of "book" (although no specific examples were spelled out, the policies left a great deal of gray area open to interpretation). I concluded that while the spirit of addressing digital media publication in the guidelines is to be inclusive of digital media scholarship, the way the guidelines are worded actually reinforces "the binary between print scholarship and scholarship not in print, where only the former is considered 'published'" (Braun 197). Likewise, Valerie Lee and Cynthia L. Selfe tell the story of how their department revised the wording of its promotion and tenure policy to remove print-culture biases. They provide specific examples of the passages that were laden with print biases and the reworded passages that provided "parity for digital media works" (56).

Departments often struggle to think of publication in nonprint or medium-independent terms, but the language that scholars like Purdy and Walker, Lee and Selfe, and Unsworth use gives individuals creating digital media scholarship a way of framing their work to colleagues who aren't sure how to interpret and evaluate such work. It also provides departments with a way of connecting traditional and new forms of scholarship and making visible the common rhetorical moves that scholarship makes across a range of forms/genres/media. In table 3.5, I suggest specific questions that individuals can reflect on to help articulate the rhetorical elements underlying their publication decisions (for example, why a particular medium or venue was chosen) that focus on the scholarly aspects of publication rather than on merely the form or venue of publication. Likewise, I suggest specific questions for departments to consider as a community to help them recognize the media biases in their promotion and tenure policies and discuss how their shared values about publication can be applied to scholarship in a variety of forms.

At the time of my interviews, faculty in the parallel cultures department were beginning to think about some of these questions, particularly the ways that their policies were biased toward print. The department chair, for instance, said that she and her colleagues were in the process of thinking about how to change the language of assessment, noting that they "can't have the university press requirement anymore" because it creates bias against digital publication. The chair of the promotion and tenure committee also said that the venue is important but "not the decisive factor." However, when asked whether it would matter if a person

Table 3.5. Questions about scholarly publication

Organizing questions	What counts as a text?	How do we approach reading texts?	How do we approach the production of texts?	
Reframed questions	What counts as a scholarly text?	What methods of scholarly inquiry are appropriate?	What counts as being published?	How do we engage in peer review?
Questions for individuals			Why did you choose this particular venue? Why did you choose this particular medium? What other texts/projects in your field are similar to this text/ project?	
Questions for departments			What elements go into determining a venue's reputation? How can we determine the reputation of a new or unfamiliar venue? Which online or nonprint venues are reputable in your field?	

had only online publications and no print publications, he said, "I can't tell you that it wouldn't matter. What's most important is the book. And by that I mean a thing like this"—he held up a bound book—"not in cyberspace." He later added, "Now, we've had debates about what a book is. I think we're very broad-minded about what constitutes a book. As long as it's doing the sorts of work that important scholarship does, then I think it satisfies the senior members of the department." But what work does important scholarship do? A book in cyberspace, or an e-book, arguably does (or has the potential to do) much the same scholarly work as a printed book. A collection of photographs making a visual argument or a documentary film chronicling an ethnographic research project or a software program that allows classes to write poetry collaboratively or even a teaching module for new professional writing TAs also has the potential to do much the same intellectual work as a book full of words. Yet he specifically pointed to a bound, printed book and specifically said "not in cyberspace." This indicates that the conversation in the department about what constitutes a book has been focused on other issues, not the medium of dissemination. The chair's comments indicate that the department was moving toward having some of those discussions, but the promotion and tenure committee chair's comments point to the history of tenure decisions in the department and the expectations that many in the department might still hold.

One thing is clear, and that is that in order for something to be considered published, it would have to be "fixed" in some medium and refereed. I asked, for instance, how a digital film documenting an ethnographic study would fare if it were not published in an online venue but were displayed or exhibited, and the promotion and tenure committee chair said it would most likely count similar to a conference presentation. This is problematic and shows a limited understanding of the work that is involved in digital media production and of the types of venues that are appropriate for exhibiting/distributing it. In "Are you ready to assign multimedia projects? A pedagogical question/naire," a handout for teachers to use to decide if they are ready to assign multimedia projects, Cheryl E. Ball writes:

> A *proficient* producer of digital video has a typical editing-to-finished product ratio of *200:1* minutes. That's 200 minutes of editing for every 1 minute of finished video. And that's JUST the editing part. Add in all the research, story-boarding, scripting, filming, and capturing parts involved in the "writing" process, and you're looking at more like *2000:1. Consider a 2–3 minute video as equivalent in scope and purpose to a 10-page, double-spaced paper.* (1, all emphases original)

Although meant to give teachers a rule of thumb for understanding how much work students (novice producers) put into multimedia assignments, this statement also provides a guide for understanding the amount of work that goes into scholarly multimedia projects, such as an ethnographic film. If a scholar created a feature-length film, the amount of work would be at least as much as that required for a book, and it would be unrealistic to expect that a scholarly journal's web server would be equipped to handle a file that large. The film would have to be exhibited in another type of venue, and given the amount of work that went into it, it doesn't seem right for it to have parity with a conference presentation. It should have parity with a book. But in order for that to happen, a different model of peer review would have to be in place to prove that the film was of the appropriate scholarly quality and scope of a book.

The bigger issue here, though, is not counting how many hours an individual puts into a particular piece of work but being able to talk about the scope of effort required for different genres in a variety of media and the wider scholarly impact of that work in the scholar's field. I think we generally understand, for example, that the effort to create a book is usually larger in scope than the effort to create a journal article. Because books are typically longer than journal articles and separated into chapters, the differences in scope are visible in a manner particular to the medium of print. But this method of judging the scope of a publication breaks down when we try to compare across media (as in the above example of scholarly video). Consequently, this concept of scope needs to be teased out in order to create policies that are appropriate for evaluating the scholarly quality of different genres of texts produced in media other than print and how scope of effort is related to venue and peer response. The notion of scope is tied to Purdy and Walker's notion of scholarly activity. Scholarly activities can find expression in many different media and in many different venues and can address scholarly questions of many different reaches (that is, the equivalent in scope of a book, an article, a review, and the like). While we shouldn't ignore issues of venue (such as durability, reputation, peer review procedures, and so on), we should not put them above the scholarly activity expressed in the text itself, and scope is yet another way to describe a text's reach and impact.

In its effort to evaluate digital media scholarship as a major contribution on par with printed scholarship, the integrated literacies department broadened its conception of both venue and peer review. Besides understanding that digital media projects can be "exhibited in a lot of different kinds of venues" and that some scholars may want or need to market their work "in some format other than a published book," the chair also said that he has had to rethink the way he and his colleagues go about finding external reviewers for tenure candidates who present digital work in alternative formats:

> We may need different people to evaluate that [digital work] other than internally within the department. That is, we may need to vet some of that out, in the same way that we would vet out scholarship for tenure review, to people to provide commentary and analysis on the significance of it as some kind of contribution to the development of a particular media or media style or generally to electronic formats.

Here he recognizes that in addition to getting experts in the field to review the work for its scholarly contribution, the department might need to get media specialists (who might work in a different profession) to provide context about the media aspects of the work separate from the scholarly aspects (such as the editing-to-finished product ratio or similar issues of production and distribution).

In addition to this type of peer review, the chair said that as he and the faculty were revising their policy, it was imperative for them to come to understand "more about the history of [particular] electronic journals and their review process and their peer evaluation process." It is this prepublication peer review that the chair of the promotion and tenure committee in the parallel cultures department said is "the paramount issue in evaluating online work," and the chair of the print-centric department said that for an online publication (or any publication) to be taken seriously, "colleagues would have to be convinced of the rigor of the peer review process."

A problem arises in that many online venues use peer review processes that are necessarily different from traditional peer review processes for printed venues. Ava, assistant professor in the integrated literacies department, addressed this issue:

> I would imagine electronic publication is only going to continue to grow, but I think the journals and the sites that anchor their identity and stay alive and afloat are going to be those that have peer review processes that pull the *good* things from print publications and apply those in new realms. Maybe in new ways, like *Kairos* has a really open, interesting review process. But it's a fascinating process; it's a process that wouldn't be possible were it not an online journal. And I think that's why it's prestigious.

The review process of *Kairos: A Journal of Rhetoric, Technology, and Pedagogy* happens in three stages or "tiers." First, the coeditors decide if a submission is appropriate for the journal and of high enough quality to go through their editorial review process. If so, they send it to the next stage, where over the course of two weeks, the entire editorial board—approximately forty members at various institutions—discuss (presumably in an online forum of some kind) the submission and three members write formal review letters based on the discussion. If the submission is accepted, then it moves on to tier 3, where "the editors work with authors, as needed, to guide/facilitate revisions based on the editorial board's comments and evaluation" ("Kairos Editorial Review Process" n. pag.). The journal has reshaped peer review to fit its needs and to take advantage of digital media while clearly explaining its process in terms that make clear how rigorous it is.

Still, though not double-blind, *Kairos* works on a model of prepublication peer review that is "closed," that is, only the authors and a few editorial board members are involved. Kathleen Fitzpatrick argues that we should open up the process even more and do peer-to-peer review instead, publishing work online in draft form and engaging in a conversation that ultimately shapes the final version. She has engaged in an experiment in this kind of peer review. A draft of her book *Planned Obsolescence*—which argues for reforming peer review to better reflect the publishing realities of the digital age—was hosted online by MediaCommons, and members were asked to comment and help shape her revisions. The book in draft form—which also received blind reviews and in its final form was published in print by New York University Press in 2011—still exists online, and the community conversation is visible. Fitzpatrick participated in the conversation as well, responding to her responders and blogging about the benefits and limitations of the particular technical tools and the general experience of the open review process. Figure 3.1 shows the format of *Planned Obsolescence*. On the left is Fitzpatrick's text, and on the right is a threaded discussion organized by paragraph. The highlighted paragraph on the left is the one to which the comments on the right directly respond, and one of Fitzpatrick's responses to a commenter can be seen in the screenshot. Though often written in a more casual tone than might be seen in a traditional review, the comments are substantive and constructive, and it is easy to see how the conversation helped Fitzpatrick to further shape the text.

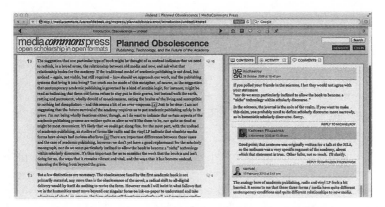

Figure 3.1. Screen capture of *Planned Obsolescence*, Kathleen Fitzpatrick and MediaCommons' foray into peer-to-peer review

Shakespeare Quarterly also engaged in a successful partially open peer review experiment for four articles being considered for an issue on Shakespeare and new media. From 10 March to 5 May 2010, editors "invited thoughtful feedback from Shakespeare scholars and other readers on any essay that fell within their areas of expertise—in terms of its originality, accuracy, and stylistic and rhetorical merits" ("*Shakespeare Quarterly* Open Review" n. pag.). The editors also asked readers to register using their own names, so that the scholars whose work was reviewed could "show that experts in the field participated in this process" (n. pag.). Additionally, this requirement demonstrates that *Shakespeare Quarterly* was sensitive to the fact that scholars needed to represent the rigor of the process to their colleagues and institutions. The comments on the papers are archived on the MediaCommons site, and while commenting is closed on the essays, it is still possible to comment on the experiment itself. That a flagship journal in the field would recognize that a shift in models of publication and review is necessary and would put its reputation behind an experimental form of review demonstrates the flexibility of the discipline to respond to the rhetorical exigencies of new media while maintaining scholarly values.

Such an open approach to peer review has the benefit of allowing work to get out faster, which is especially important with work that focuses on digital media topics or pedagogies because the technologies change so quickly. It also allows for the work to be reviewed in different contexts for different purposes. Many have argued that institutions need to stop outsourcing peer review to publishers. For instance, in "On the Future of Academic Publishing, Peer Review, and Tenure Requirements," Fitzpatrick writes:

The granting of tenure should not be reliant on whether the vagaries of any publishing system did or did not allow a text to come into circulation, but rather on the value of that text, and on the importance it bears for its field. Peer-review thus demands to be transformed from a system of gatekeeping to a mode of manifesting the responses to and discussion of a multiplicity of ideas in circulation. (n. pag.)

In addition to placing more emphasis on the scholarship enacted by texts, such a model of peer review would allow for a consideration of some types of scholarship whose impact is often thought to be felt only locally, such as the scholarship of teaching and administration, and it might make visible the ways in which these types of scholarship can have an impact beyond the local institution.

Of all the issues raised in this chapter, rethinking peer review practices is likely to be the most difficult for the discipline because of how longstanding and entrenched the traditional model is. As many of the preceding examples have shown, it is the peer-reviewed status of digital texts that often gives them respect and helps them to "count" for promotion and tenure. However, the traditional model of peer review is not appropriate for some types of digital scholarship, such as some editorial/bibliographic or database projects. To remedy this situation, we can look to other disciplines for ideas about how to understand peer review. As Mills Kelly notes:

Already other disciplines that are not as resistant to change have embraced the digital world to a much greater extent. For example, work posted on the *Social Science Research Network* "counts" in many academic departments around the country despite the fact that peer review takes place *after* the fact, not before. And in other disciplines—computer science, biology, physics, etc.—peer review increasingly takes other forms entirely. (n. pag.)

Kelly calls for a "serious discussion in our profession about what peer review means, what its value is to the process of advancing knowledge, and how it can change to take into account the new realities of the digital world" (n. pag.). In table 3.6, I suggest questions to help frame this kind of discussion, questions that can help individuals and departments understand what is valuable about different forms of peer review and how different methods might be appropriate for different kinds of scholarship.

Table 3.6. Questions about peer review

Organizing questions	What counts as a text?	How do we approach reading texts?	How do we approach the production of texts?	
Reframed questions	What counts as a scholarly text?	What methods of scholarly inquiry are appropriate?	What counts as being published?	How do we engage in peer review?
Questions for individuals				What is the venue's peer review process? Why is that process appropriate for this venue?
Questions for departments				What is it about prepublication peer review that you value? What values do you see embedded in other forms of review (e.g., peer-to-peer or postpublication reviews)? Under what conditions might other forms of review prove to be valuable (e.g., peer-to-peer or postpublication reviews)?

Conclusion: Digital Media and Discourses
of Professional Evaluation

In her *PMLA* article "Obsolescence," Fitzpatrick argues that the system of academic publishing as we know it no longer serves our purposes. She provocatively calls the first academic book (that is, the first book a scholar writes, typically in order to gain tenure) "undead" because, while it is no longer viable/sustainable, it is still required. Promotion and tenure policy might be said to be similarly undead, at least at research-intensive institutions, because in its current form, it requires a sustainable model of academic publishing in order to evaluate scholars fairly. But as Fitzpatrick and many others argue, the current model is not sustainable. It is not the physical object, the materiality of the first academic book, that she argues is obsolete, however. She recognizes that

> a radical shift to all-digital delivery would by itself do nothing to revive the form. However much I might insist that we in the humanities must expand our focus beyond ink on paper to understand and take advantage of pixels on screens, the print form still functions well, and numerous studies have indicated that a simple move to electronic distribution in the current system of academic publishing will not be enough to bail the system out, since printing, storing, and distributing the material form of the book represent only a fraction of its production costs. (720)

Instead, what is obsolete is "the system, the process, through which the book comes into being" (720). By the system, she means the current system of peer review and evaluation standards that place more emphasis on the physical form of the text than on its scholarly merit or, in Purdy and Walker's terms, on the scholarly activities it evidences. Fitzpatrick argues that the gatekeeping function of prepublication peer review is obsolete because "scarcity is over." What we need, she contends, is a means of "coping with abundance, of working in a living system of scholarly communication." She envisions a peer-to-peer system to facilitate this process of scholarly communication, arguing that "peer review needs to be transformed from a gatekeeping system into a postpublication system that doesn't determine whether a text should be published but instead measures how it has been (and how it should be) received and what its place in the ecosystem of scholarly communication is." The biggest obstacle to such a revised system of scholarly communication, as Fitzpatrick recognizes, is "the academy's conservative governing structures, whose motto, like that attributed to defenders of tradition everywhere, could be 'we have never done it that way before'" (721).

In *Hacking the Academy*, Fitzpatrick and others argue that in order to save scholarly publishing in the humanities, we need to embrace not only new forms of peer response but also open-access publishing, which allows scholarship to be published and accessed outside of a market-driven system. She contends that this is the best way to ensure that our scholarship will continue to flourish:

> We are, after all, already doing the labor for free—the labor of research, the labor of writing, the labor of editing—as a means of contributing to the advancement of the collective knowledge in our fields. We should value our labor sufficiently to ensure that we, our institutions, our colleagues, and our students, have full and perpetual access to the results of our work—and promoting the development of open-access publishing venues, and contributing all of our work to them, are the best ways to meet that ethical imperative toward the widest possible distribution of the knowledge that we produce. ("Open Access Publishing" n. pag.)

Of course, open-access publishing raises concerns about peer review, but new forms of peer review processes can easily address these concerns and, in Fitzpatrick's words, break down "some of the roadblocks to a broader acceptance of open access publication" (Cohen, Ramsay, and Fitzpatrick n. pag.).

Purdy and Walker provide a way to rethink promotion and tenure criteria to focus more on a text's place in the ecosystem of scholarly communication Fitzpatrick discusses and on the scholarly activities of the text rather than on its form. Such a model of assessment, Dan Cohen suggests, might help us "reorient ourselves to our true core value—to honor creativity and quality—which will still guide us to many traditionally published works but will also allow us to consider works in some nontraditional venues such as new open access journals, blogs, articles written and posted on a personal website or institutional repository, or non-narrative digital projects" (Cohen, Ramsay, and Fitzpatrick n. pag.). In addition, the questions I have identified throughout this chapter (compiled in table 3.7) can help guide departments in discussing the issues raised in this chapter and to devise standards that are more sustainable, better serve our needs/purposes, and grow out of our shared values.

Table 3.7. Compiled matrix of questions to facilitate departmental discussions about evaluating digital media scholarship

Organizing questions	What counts as a text?	How do we approach reading texts?	How do we approach the production of texts?	
Reframed questions	What counts as a scholarly text?	What methods of scholarly inquiry are appropriate?	What counts as being published?	How do we engage in peer review?
Questions for individuals	In what ways does your text/project exhibit scholarly activity? How does the text/project contribute to scholarship/scholarly conversations in your field?	Describe the scholarly methods you employed in this text/project. Why did you choose these particular methods? How are these methods appropriate for your field and for this text/project in particular? How much time did you spend on various aspects of your text/project, including research, data analysis, encoding/writing, interface design, etc.?	Why did you choose this particular venue? Why did you choose this particular medium? What other texts/projects in your field are similar to this text/project?	What is the venue's peer review process? Why is that process appropriate for this venue?
Questions for departments	What scholarly activities do you value? What do those activities typically "look like" in published scholarship (in your field)? What might those activities look like if enacted in another medium?	What activities or methods of inquiry can be considered scholarly? What is valuable about each? What sorts of products or outcomes can be expected to result from such activities or inquiry? What constitutes the scholarship of teaching? What is valuable about the scholarship of teaching? What kinds of products can be expected to result from the scholarship of teaching? What constitutes editorial scholarship? What is valuable about editorial scholarship? What kinds of products can be expected to result from editorial scholarship? What is valuable about scholarly collaboration? Under what circumstances should digital media "service" work be considered a contribution to scholarship? What kinds of products or outcomes can be expected to result from such scholarship? Under what circumstances should it be considered service and not scholarship?	What elements go into determining a venue's reputation? How can we determine the reputation of a new or unfamiliar venue? Which online or nonprint venues are reputable in your field?	What is it about prepublication peer review that you value? What values do you see embedded in other forms of review (e.g., peer-to-peer or postpublication reviews)? Under what conditions might other forms of review prove to be valuable (e.g., peer-to-peer or postpublication reviews)?

I have sought in this chapter to foreground the values that the language of departmental and disciplinary policies (both explicit and implicit) emphasizes. Digital media scholarship is dynamic and varies depending on the field, but if departments adjust their lenses only slightly, they can recognize the ways that many different kinds of texts make scholarly moves and the ways that many different methods demonstrate scholarly inquiry, and as a result, they may recognize and seek to change print-culture bias in their own tenure and promotion policy documents.

At the same time, unless there are social spaces within departments for scholarly communities to discuss, debate, and share digital work, nothing is going to change. In other words, faculty aren't going to change what they do if they don't participate in these conversations and if they don't have the appropriate support for learning how to engage in digital media scholarship and teaching, both from philosophical and technical/material standpoints. Tenure and promotion policy is only a part of that support. Faculty and graduate students also need material resources, spaces, and low-stakes opportunities to learn (and the time to devote to learning). So, the next chapter examines different approaches to providing material support and professional development opportunities focused on digital media.

4

Professional Development in/with Digital Media:
Sustaining a Technological Ecology

Students at the University of Denver recently created a video parody of a technologically unfriendly classroom and a technologically inept teacher.[1] In the style of the television show *The Office*, the plot of *The Class* centers on "Michael," a teacher who knows very little about technology yet is teaching a class about technology in education. In a small classroom not well equipped with digital technology, Michael attempts to lead a discussion on new technologies. The students seem distant and uninterested; one student sleeps. After class, his student assistant tries to encourage Michael to make some changes. She approaches him tactfully but honestly: "Now, the class is about technology, and you're really not using any" (fig. 4.1). She explains further: "The board doesn't really count. Maybe you could add more technology to the classroom, like, show them actual uses of the technology. . . . You know what I'm saying?" (fig. 4.2). Although Michael responds "Yes," he clearly does not know how to "add more technology to the classroom" and appears rather at a loss for what to do (fig. 4.3). In the next scene, he explains to the students that in an effort to incorporate more technology into the class, he has decided that they will Skype, and we see his face on a screen at the front of the room (fig. 4.4). But when the camera pans across the room, we see that Michael and all of the students are together in the classroom; he didn't even move to a different room on campus (fig. 4.5). One student raises his hand (fig. 4.6) and asks, "Michael, if you are here, why are we Skyping?" Michael responds haltingly, "I'm not sure. I have a, I have a lesson plan, actually." As the camera zooms in on her, the student assistant shakes her head.

Ultimately, the explicit argument of *The Class* is that teachers need to collaborate with students in order to use technology in ways that meet the

Figures 4.1–4.6. Screen captures from *The Class*, a video parody of *The Office*, created by students at the University of Denver portraying a technologically unfriendly classroom and a technologically inept teacher

students' needs and expectations. However, the video also demonstrates the importance of professional development opportunities specifically focused on digital pedagogy as well as of investments in material technologies and spaces appropriate to those pedagogies. If Michael had been able to consult with mentors or support personnel in his discipline, he might have been more successful in incorporating technology into his class in ways that were not only pedagogically sound but also more interesting and satisfying for students. There is a wealth of resources online and in scholarly journals about integrating technology and teaching, and Michael could have begun there if only somebody knowledgeable had pointed him in that direction. Furthermore, he could engage in the scholarship of teaching to systematize such an investigation and discover not only what the students like but also which applications of technology help them learn and develop their skills; he could, in effect, turn his classroom into a research lab in which he and the students could explore together the potentials that different technologies might offer.

Related to the issue of how to support faculty in learning new forms of pedagogy that incorporate new technologies is how to support faculty in learning about new forms of scholarship. For obvious reasons, *The Class* doesn't address digital media scholarship, but imagine what an *Office*-style parody of current scholarly practice might look like. In *The Graduate Seminar*, Michael, this time teaching a graduate course on digital media scholarship, would likely end up in a traditional classroom with little or no technology. He would probably jump in without familiarizing himself with published digital scholarship or consulting colleagues who have created digital scholarship. In asking students to create digital scholarship for the course, he might include requirements that are based on print culture and either difficult or not workable in multimedia contexts, such as banning collaboration, expecting that the projects make linear arguments, or requiring students to produce the equivalent of a thirty-page research paper without defining specifically what that means or forcing them to print out segments of their projects to meet the arbitrary "page" length. After the by now exasperated graduate students turn in their multimedia compositions, Michael would most likely have no idea how to "read," respond to, or assess their work. And, having never created a multimedia text himself, he would probably have little to no conception of how much work the students put into their projects.

These three issues of difficulty that Michael would struggle with—understanding the nature of different kinds of multimedia texts, learning ways of reading different kinds of multimedia texts, and learning what goes into producing different kinds of multimedia texts—are the focus of this chapter. These three issues map onto the three organizing questions of the book but take on a slightly different character in the context of professional development (see table 4.1), focusing on how departments introduce their faculty and graduate students to new types of texts/genres and prepare them to apply this new knowledge to their pedagogical and scholarly practice. *The Class* and the imaginary *The Graduate Seminar* make it clear that in order to use digital media in ways consistent with disciplinary values, faculty and graduate students must engage in professional development opportunities focused on digital media. However, financial and other material constraints, including a department's investment in digital media (both as a field of study and as physical technologies), have a profound impact on a department's culture and its ability to provide these opportunities.

It is incredibly important that departments provide these opportunities. Many scholars have recognized that students today live in a highly digitally mediated literacy environment, and our classes must prepare

Table 4.1. Organizing questions reframed in the context of professional development

Organizing questions	Questions reframed for professional development
How do we define what counts as a text?	How do we introduce grad students and faculty to new types of texts/genres?
How do we approach reading texts?	How do we prepare grad students and faculty to read and teach students to read different types of texts/genres?
How do we approach the production of texts?	How do we prepare grad students and faculty to produce and teach students to produce different types of texts/genres?

them to live and work in that context. Consequently, in order to provide such an education, Meredith Graupner, Lee Nickoson-Massey, and Kristine Blair argue that faculty need preparation for working in a range of spaces, not only teaching spaces but also spaces within and outside of the academy. They assert that graduate students need professionalization in digital media to prepare them for the various "knowledge-making spaces" they will encounter after graduate school, which exist in a digitally mediated context. Specifically, they contend that doctoral programs need to "take a multimodal approach to teaching and research" (13). Although they recognize that "it is admittedly unrealistic to expect that all faculty will jump on the digital teaching and research bandwagon, we nevertheless explore the possibilities of graduate education in experiencing a paradigm shift from print to digital," which they maintain is vital to the continued relevance of the discipline (13–14).

Debra Journet also recognizes the changing student population and reflects on what it means to her pedagogy:

> I have begun to realize that what I and my students consider "writing" are very different phenomena. Young people today move more fluently among words, sound, and image; they report experiences with technologies I only dimly understand; and they write in genres I have never heard of. Confronting this sea change—trying to understand what might be called the new work of composing—I am striving to reconsider how I define my core responsibilities as a teacher. (107)

Later she asks how teachers can "find appropriate opportunities for professional development" to help them learn about and incorporate digital media into their teaching (108). Her answer is using her teaching as a means of educating herself, to learn by doing as well as by theorizing and reflecting. Michael in *The Class* could be said to be learning by doing; however, he's missing the theoretical structure that Journet recognizes is also important to successfully incorporating digital media into teaching in meaningful and pedagogically sound ways. Journet also understands that integrating digital media and teaching can be "messy" and is often experimental, no matter how much theoretical preparation goes into it, but that such messiness is often productive. She therefore introduces the concept of "rough edges," which indicates that such learning is happening, and encourages faculty to accept the "rough and messy places that characterize growth and learning," advocating for a "pedagogy of rough edges." However, she notes that there are material complications in digital media pedagogy that don't exist in traditional pedagogies. Furthermore, she says it is a challenge "to place their skills and experience within an academic context centering on rhetorical activities such as critique, analysis, argument, and research" (116). In keeping with Journet's stance about the importance of learning about digital media work, Graupner, Nickoson-Massey, and Blair argue that it is important not just for graduate students (that is, future faculty) to be professionalized in digital media but also for current faculty:

> For faculty to attend to students' needs and experiences as they assist students in developing their professional identities, both students and faculty must work in a variety of face-to-face and virtual spaces that promote a balance between student initiative and faculty support. Such spaces, which span the curriculum and professionalization activities beyond the curriculum, should demonstrate the value of developing and sustaining new skill sets, whether technological in nature or not, and the responsibility students have to the ongoing development of digital literacy skills throughout and beyond their programs. (15)

To respond to their call for thinking about how best to provide such professionalization, this chapter looks at some of the ways departments are responding to questions surrounding professional development in digital media. Because of their different stances toward providing technical/material and communal support for digital media work, the three departments in this study locate financial responsibility for digital media differently and place different levels of importance on different aspects of digital media work (functional literacy, scholarly integration, pedagogical experimentation). As a consequence, the departments also offer varying types of rough spaces for faculty and student experimentation with digital media pedagogy and research. These material and philosophical decisions determine the choices available to faculty and graduate students and, ultimately, have a significant influence on the work they are enabled to do.

Three Cultures of Support for Developing Digital Media Pedagogy and Scholarship

These material and philosophical decisions can be thought of, as Richard Selfe suggests in *Sustainable Computer Environments: Cultures of Support in English Studies and Language Arts,* as cultures of support for digital media. In defining the concept of a culture of support, Selfe stresses the importance of long-term sustainable practices that support integration of digital media. The cultures that create such sustainable practices might also be thought of as "technological ecologies," environments that grow and change with time but sustain themselves over the long term. Citing "the growing number of ads for composition specialists that stress computers and writing and new media specialty as a desirable credential," Graupner, Nickoson-Massey, and Blair argue for the importance of creating in graduate programs "sustainable technological ecologies not only to enhance graduate student professional development but also to make the current rhetoric of multimodal composition a reality in undergraduate writing programs across the country" (19). Each department in this study has a different historical relationship to digital media defined by faculty research and teaching interests, institutional missions, and departmental funding priorities, and the technological ecologies of each grow out of these histories, emphasize different methods of providing learning opportunities surrounding digital media, and offer different levels of integration of digital media with departmental curricula.

Table 4.2 lays out the questions that are important for a department to consider to create an intentional technological ecology or culture of support for professionalization in digital media. The reason for the questions' significance will become apparent as I analyze how each department sets the stage either to allow these issues to be addressed or to occlude/elide such a discussion. Understanding how a department structures the conversation about professionalization in digital media is an important precursor to examining how individual instructors learn to develop digital media pedagogies and scholarly agendas.

Table 4.2. Questions for departments to consider to create a robust and intentional technological ecology for professionalization in digital media

Organizing questions	How do we define what counts as a text?	How do we approach reading texts?	How do we approach the production of texts?
Reframed questions	How do we introduce grad students and faculty to new types of texts/genres?	How do we prepare grad students and faculty to read and teach students to read different types of texts/genres?	How do we prepare grad students and faculty to produce and teach students to produce different types of texts/genres?
Questions for departments	What types of texts and genres should grad students be exposed to in their studies?	What interpretive lenses should grad students learn to bring to alternative texts/genres?	Should grad students learn to produce alternative texts? When should they learn this and how (coursework, workshops, on their own, etc.)?
	When should grad students and faculty be exposed to new media texts in their field's scholarship? In other fields' scholarship? As texts with which to teach?	When and how should grad students learn to read alternative texts in their field's scholarship? In other fields' scholarship?	Should grad students and faculty be encouraged to have their students produce alternative texts? In which classes would this be most appropriate?
	What support structures exist in the department/university to help introduce grad students and faculty to new texts and genres? Are they/can they be made sustainable?	Should grad students learn to teach undergraduates to read alternative texts? When? How?	Should faculty be encouraged to produce alternative texts?
	What support structures exist to help grad students and faculty apply knowledge about new media to their scholarly and pedagogical practice? Are they/can they be made sustainable?	What support structures exist in the department/university to help grad students and faculty learn to read alternative texts and genres? To teach undergraduates to read alternative texts? Are they/can they be made sustainable?	What support structures are needed to encourage faculty and grad students to produce and teach their students to produce alternative texts? Do these support structures exist in the department or university already? Are they/can they be made sustainable?
	What can the department do to increase exposure to alternative texts/genres?	What can the department do to increase support for learning to read alternative texts/genres?	What can the department do to increase support for faculty and grad student production of alternative texts or the incorporation of alternative text production into teaching?

The Print-centric Department

As I argued in chapter 2, the chair of the print-centric department identifies a disciplinary home for technology that is extremely limited and
links technology to technical disciplines, indicating that the divorce of
technology and English has a long history at this university and in this
department. Consequently, new technologies and digital environments
for writing and learning are not integrated into the department, and
most people who use digital media use it for digital course management—such as distributing texts, collecting assignments, and posting
grades—or for analysis of digital texts. Few incorporate digital production into their teaching or scholarship, and few have digital media as a
primary scholarly interest. The department's stance toward supporting
digital media teaching and scholarship in the department runs parallel
to its stance toward the role of digital media in the discipline.

As a consequence of this definition of support, there is no sustainable
departmental mechanism for providing individuals opportunities to
learn about and explore pedagogical and research applications of digital media. Benjamin, a PhD student in rhetoric and composition, says,
"There is nothing that I know of that is English department–sponsored
that is specifically geared to teaching instructors to use technology in
the classroom." Although the university offers technical training and
twenty-four-hour technical support, there is no structured pedagogical
training to teach graduate students or faculty how to effectively integrate
technology into their courses or their research. The department thus
relies upon the university to provide interested individuals with learning
opportunities, and those learning opportunities are purely technical,
not pedagogically or methodologically oriented (that is, they offer "how
to make a website" rather than "how and why to integrate composing
for the web into your classes").

This dependence on the university makes sense given the department's stance toward digital media in the discipline: digital media studies is a small, nontraditional pocket within rhetoric and composition,
not a force affecting the texts and/or research methods of the discipline
at large. Furthermore, the acceptance of technical training instead of
pedagogically focused training reinforces the widespread use of digital
media as primarily tools for the management of professional activities,
tools that do not necessarily change, fundamentally, the tasks being
performed or the central questions or methods of the discipline.

"Support" in the department is defined mainly as functional technical
support and physical access to equipment. Toby (an assistant professor

in rhetoric and composition in this department), for instance, calls the university "tech-friendly" and notes, "There's as much support there as I could want, really. Certainly, the university makes it very easy. I feel like no matter what tech question I have, there's someplace on campus where there are people that are at the phone to answer that, or at email." He defines support as a help-desk, technical matter that is the university's job; he does not include opportunities for learning about integrating digital media into pedagogy and/or research in his definition. Along similar lines, the department chair defines support as primarily the job of entities outside of the department. He lists, for instance, "a variety of sources on campus" as well as "a variety of [university] classrooms that are fully usable and fully wired." These classrooms are "fully wired" for the instructor only. There is a podium with a variety of equipment, including a computer with Internet access and VHS and DVD players connected to a projector. However, networked classrooms in which students are able to engage in production work do not exist, although the department has purchased a "portable wireless laboratory, in which twenty to twenty-five or thirty laptops will be on a cart that we can provide to students." Within the department, the chair says that "graduate students have an area called the workroom, which has a half a dozen computers in it so they can do their email and those sorts of things," and "we do have a departmental web designer that, if you want to put something up, you can put it up on the web."

Though he does recognize and comment on the importance of proper facilities (both spaces and equipment) for supporting digital media teaching and research, his comments indicate that those aspects of support need to be shared by the department and university, with most of the burden shouldered by the university. Furthermore, he stresses support for digital management above other types of digital work—"email and those sorts of things"—for which half a dozen computers is considered sufficient to serve more than 100 PhD students. Pedagogical support—workshops to help faculty and graduate students bring digital media into the classroom, for instance—are not a part of his definition of support.

There is no visible sustainable community of support for those who choose to teach with and/or do research about digital media, though there is a culture of individualized (self-selected) mentoring. Benjamin says that there is a teacher-training seminar and, within it, consultants (more advanced graduate students), "many of [whom] are interested in technology and would be available to help people integrate it." However, he notes that "it's on an individual basis, so there's no real structure in place." He adds that "in terms of the department, it's difficult, in terms of using technology in the classroom; there's no real support, but there's not a lack of support either. It's a tool that we can use." Digital media (all technologies, in fact) are nothing more than tools used for purely instrumental purposes. There is little encouragement to think of work in and with digital media as a valuable process (similar to writing) that might serve to transform pedagogy, methodology, disciplinarity, or professional identity. In this department, the culture is marked by a definition of support as mainly technical and handled by the university (or other outside entities). A by-product of this approach is that issues involving digital media that might be thought of in another department as pedagogical or methodological questions that could generate new knowledge and practices are treated as technical problems to be solved by university technical support.

One of the reasons that the department chair links support with the university rather than with the department is likely financial; material technologies are expensive, technology specialists are expensive, and technologically advanced spaces and classrooms are expensive. On a certain level, it makes sense to outsource some of the purely technological issues to centralized university entities. However, such a linkage—coupled with an absence of department-based, disciplinary-focused pedagogical/research support—encourages a purely functional/skills-based definition of technology that ignores many of the disciplinary questions, both pedagogical and scholarly, raised so far in this book. Furthermore, it makes a discussion of the ways that digital media might productively transform our work impossible. If "learning digital media" means only learning technical skills, and the university already supplies that education, then there is almost no chance for a department-sponsored consideration of how to create a culture of support for digital media professionalization that is informed by disciplinary values.

The Integrated Literacies Department

The integrated literacies department provides opportunities for individuals to learn about integrating digital media into academic work, and the department attempts to incorporate these opportunities throughout the graduate program. In addition, the department provides some basic technical support. According to the department chair, the department has a technical coordinator, a tenured faculty member with a course release who, in addition to teaching and doing research in his field, is "the first line of the department's emphasis on the importance of technology and responding to problems that faculty are having with their technology or upgrading their systems." Although in some cases faculty members still must rely upon the college to provide technical support, the fact that the department invests in a faculty technology coordinator indicates a programmatic commitment to department-provided, discipline-specific support for digital media teaching and research.

The investment in a faculty technology coordinator whose tenure home is in the department, rather than a technology coordinator who is a technical specialist and not a teacher and scholar, also indicates an awareness of the role that disciplinary knowledge plays in providing support in academic environments. Adele, a first-year PhD student with interests in the culture of technology and postcolonial rhetorics, has firsthand experience regarding the importance of such disciplinary knowledge to her own digital media work. She says, "Going to another department where people aren't necessarily familiar with what we do in rhetoric and composition can be tough. I had that situation at [another university], because they don't understand what we want on our web pages, why we would want something structured a certain way, that kind of thing." Further evidence of the department's commitment to sustained programmatic support for digital media work includes (1) an invited speaker series, which provides opportunities to explore the potentials of teaching and research with digital media, and (2) a series of workshops on topics such as the university's online grading system, Photoshop, and teaching writing with technology, which provide opportunities to learn technical skills as well as pedagogical strategies.

Such a commitment to digital media comes out of the history and context of the programs associated with this department, particularly the graduate program. At the time of my interviews, the interdisciplinary graduate program was brand-new, ending its first year of graduate course offerings. There were five students enrolled in the doctoral program, and most of the participating faculty were from the integrated literacies department. From the beginning, conversations about the graduate program have been focused on how to combine digital media with the fields of rhetoric and writing in order to reshape those fields, with a particular emphasis on reshaping research and teaching in those fields through digital media integration.

Consequently, digital media are at the heart of the graduate program. Indeed, the graduate director insists all graduate students attain a certain level of skill: "Digital media is not an option. You just have to do it. It may not be your research focus, and it may not be your principal identity, but there's sort of a certain level of competency and skill and ability that you have to have. And that includes teaching in computer-based environments." The graduate director focuses on the importance of basic digital literacy: everybody has to reach a certain competency level technically. However, he also stresses that digital media pedagogy is important. Even if graduate students do not produce digital media research, they all still have to have basic digital literacy and learn how to teach in a digital environment. Digital media is the business of the program, and curricula are being set up to sustain and support that. Consequently, as part of the degree requirements, the curriculum for graduate students provides opportunities to learn about teaching and doing research with digital media and to put that learning into practice. Moreover, the department is actively engaging questions about professionalization in digital media.

The Parallel Cultures Department

In the parallel cultures department, opportunities for exploring digital media exist primarily through the Center for Digital Media Studies, which provides learning opportunities—such as professional development workshops and one-on-one consultations—to those who seek them out. In this department, digital media work is another thing individuals are able to do and sometimes encouraged to do but rarely (if ever) required to do. According to the director of the CDMS, "There's a real commitment among the current administration to make sure that there are different types of technologies available to faculty and graduate students." In addition to making sure that faculty and graduate students have access to computers in their offices, he says the current administration

> has a philosophy that they would like to centrally locate higher-end technology rather than spread mediocre-level technology widely. So, we have what's called the [Center for Digital Media Studies], which is a teaching and research resource center in the department, and the current administration is funneling a great deal of funding to this program, as a way of making sure that there's a resource center with high-end equipment for everybody involved.

In addition, the CDMS has relationships with two university-level offices that provide technical support for the CDMS's networked classrooms and faculty and staff office computers. The funding of the CDMS indicates a departmental commitment to providing both faculty and graduate students opportunities to learn about digital media work and to integrate it into their professional activities.

That departmental commitment has, in fact, been increasing. According to the department chair, "I would like to think that it has been playing an increasingly greater role in the department, and of course one of the symbols of that shift is the change of the name from [a name involving the word 'computers'] to [a name involving the phrase 'digital media']." She claims that this name shift is "very important" because it signifies the department's desire to take the study of digital media to "a more complex level." It is also an important shift because it recognizes digital media pedagogy and research as a field of study and places it on par with other fields of study in the department. So the shift was partially disciplinary, recognizing the changing shape of English studies. However, the shift was partially motivated by university forces, too. According to the CDMS director, "Digital media obviously has buzzword status right now, and it also has become one of the key initiatives at the university, to improve education through technology and through technological literacy. And so the fact that it's happening in the English department is a way of keeping us competitive."

The department, however, has not simply jumped on the technology bandwagon. It has been invested in exploring the relationship of technology and English studies for over twenty years. According to historical program documents, the "Center for Digital Media Studies"[2] (which has changed its name twice since its inception) "began in 1986 when Apple Computer's Higher Education Donation Program sought innovative proposals involving the use of computers in university settings." The parallel cultures department "applied for and received a grant to equip three classroom labs to be used for teaching first-year writing." In the two decades that followed, the program received multiple grants from different university and outside sources that allowed it to add two new labs and to repeatedly upgrade the labs. Gradually, classes other than first-year writing were added to the schedule, although writing classes still form the backbone of courses that are offered in the five networked classrooms maintained by the CDMS. According to the director, each term the CDMS offers "40 sections of computer-supported writing, literature, folklore, whatever the subject matter is," which "are full at 20 students," so they serve "approximately 800 students" per term. Most of these courses are taught by graduate students, so "for the most part, if graduate students choose to teach them, they get to teach them, and they're rarely booted out of there." Faculty actually have a more difficult time getting scheduled to teach in the networked classrooms because most of the courses that faculty teach are capped at forty students, so it becomes a budgetary issue, and faculty have to get special permission to lower the enrollment cap. However, the CDMS director says that the administration is "*more* than supportive of that, and if faculty members make that request, they seriously consider the request in terms of its pedagogical value, in terms of its PR value for the department, and also in terms of its budgetary weight . . . and make the decision based on that." Consequently, because the CDMS was originally funded as a teaching lab and a place for experimental pedagogy, it has developed a strong mission for pedagogical professional development, particularly for graduate students, though faculty have also been involved and invited to participate.

Since its inception, the CDMS has placed a high value on pedagogical experimentation with digital media and classroom-based research investigating those pedagogical experimentations, beginning in 1986 with word processing and continuing today with digital media production in programs like Flash and iMovie, among many others. The CDMS director notes that he thinks everybody involved with the CDMS is experimental because "we're not completely locked in to a rigid curriculum" and "we have an idea of what [a] class is going to do, but we pay attention to the possibilities of the technology and the opportunities that the technology affords us." Furthermore, he says, "I think we all pay attention to our students so that when we have something going on in class and a student says, 'Well, look at how you could do it with this technology,' we pay attention to that and we're willing to experiment a little bit with that." This experimental attitude is fostered by the director and his view of the CDMS as "as much a teaching lab as anything else." The model of teaching in the CDMS, however, is not a training model but rather a model of community sharing and mentoring.

Such community building begins by educating incoming graduate students about the CDMS and its services. Although the director has worked with the first-year writing program to provide some training for graduate students in the required pedagogy workshop, that training is becoming increasingly less formal. Under previous directors, the CDMS's training tended to be very formal. There were rules about who could request a networked class, as well as a formal orientation in which people learned to use specific software packages and talked about networked classroom pedagogy. The current CDMS director says that the year he came on board, he and the staff decided to incorporate that training throughout the first-year writing program's new GTA pedagogy course, but it failed because it was not well integrated and they were teaching software rather than pedagogy. He describes the new approach that has developed in response to the feedback from GTAs, which is still a part of the new GTA-training course but is focused less on formal skills training:

> This last year, then, what we've tried to do is keep the integration much more pedagogically focused and much more theoretically focused. We didn't teach many software applications at all in that workshop. What we've done is . . . provided that support for anyone to come down to the [CDMS] who would like to teach a C-class.[3] And I think that we've had two or three people who wanted to teach a C-class right away. . . . Most people will want to get comfortable with the curriculum first and then they'll ask if they can teach a C-class.

Rather than formalizing training, the CDMS is trying to cultivate a community of teachers who mentor each other in more informal ways. The director says:

> I try to give as many spiels as I can. New graduate student orientation, I attend those kinds of things. I try to get more new graduate students involved in becoming part of the staff in the [CDMS]. And I think that we were pretty successful this year. We have five staff members. I would say of those five, two are really pretty technically oriented, and the other three were a little surprised that I hired them. I knew that they didn't have a lot of technology background, but they do now, just in working here. And I think that they will become great advocates in talking to the other graduate students about the potentials for technology.

Instead of putting together a list of people who are "trained" to teach in a networked class because they attended a certain number of workshops, the director instead fosters a community of mentorship for experimental pedagogy. The CDMS staff provides continuity and a support structure for this type of community—including informal "brown bag" discussions, more formal workshops, individual consultations, and peer mentoring—as well as some technical support.

That community culture is also being promoted by the department chair, who makes a point of using digital media when she gives presentations, including images and sometimes audio and video clips in her PowerPoint slides. She says, "I think that doing these public presentations have helped more of our faculty get on board because one of the things that I've done, whenever we've done a big public presentation, [is that] I've taken that same presentation and shown it at a faculty meeting, so that the faculty can see that, well, we *all* are making use of technology." The fact that she has to stress to the faculty that "we *all*" use technology indicates that perhaps not all in the department use technology or value its use in pedagogy or as a research subject, reinforcing its "niche" status, but the comment nonetheless illustrates her commitment to the development of a strong foothold for digital media studies in the department and shows that she is a strong advocate for digital media studies in the department, even though it is not her field identity.[4] Moreover, like the integrated literacies department, this department is actively engaging questions about professionalization in digital media and has created a sustainable technological ecology centered in the space of the CDMS.

***

Individuals in these three departments have varying opportunities for professionalization in digital media pedagogy and scholarship because of the cultures of support that exist and because of each department's willingness to be intentional in nurturing its technological ecology in ways that foster such professionalization. Graupner, Nickoson-Massey, and Blair, drawing upon Journet, describe a range of spaces that functioned for them as "rough spaces" where they, as faculty and graduate students, were able to develop technological ecologies that furthered professional development in digital media teaching and research. One of their conclusions is that reciprocal mentoring, particularly involving both graduate students and faculty, can help to foster professionalization.

These kinds of rough spaces and mentoring relationships are evidenced in all three departments included in this study. The print-centric department has perhaps the roughest of rough spaces, with very little intentional nurturing of a technological ecology through official departmental channels and a lack of material resources. However, interested graduate students seek each other out and become mentors to each other for integrating digital media into pedagogy. In the parallel cultures department, the idea of "rough space" is nurtured and even celebrated in the CDMS, which not only provides material support but also supports graduate students and faculty in pedagogical experimentation and the kinds of learning-by-doing activities that Journet says have helped her learn how to integrate technology into her classes. The CDMS also offers a convenient communal space in which mentoring relationships can flourish. The rough spaces in the integrated literacies department are more focused on research—whereas in the other two departments, there is more focus on teaching—and tend to grow out of coursework.

In the integrated literacies department and the parallel cultures department, the existence of these rough spaces suggests that the departments have created space for a consideration of many of the questions in table 4.2. For instance, because the CDMS is the center of support for digital-media-enhanced teaching, it is poised to consider questions of support and sustainability, particularly regarding the role of the department in providing support compared to the role of other university or college entities and ways to make that support sustainable, such as through informal mentoring networks or formal integration into coursework. Additionally, it is ready to consider questions about curriculum, including in which classes it is most appropriate to incorporate alternative texts, and to help faculty and graduate students share best practices. All department members could enter into such conversations through the professional development opportunities the CDMS provides. Likewise, faculty and graduate students are invited—because of those professional development opportunities—to think about their own practices and reflectively integrate digital media into their professional identities as teachers and scholars. Through a consideration of individual cases, the next two sections examine the ways these different technological ecologies influence what faculty and graduate students can do, how they can become professionalized in digital pedagogy and/or scholarship, how they use these "rough spaces" to their advantage, and how they create reciprocal mentoring relationships within and outside of official departmental structures.

Becoming Teachers: Learning and Practicing Digital Media Pedagogies

Both Journet and Graupner, Nickoson-Massey, and Blair advocate different types of learning spaces for fostering digital literacy acquisition and considering questions relating to digital media pedagogies. Journet's concept of "rough space" emphasizes risk taking in the classroom and the development of reciprocal mentoring relationships to help with continuing development of both technical skill and theoretically sound integration of digital media into the undergraduate classroom. Along similar lines, Graupner, Nickoson-Massey, and Blair advocate "a range of face-to-face and virtual spaces within graduate programs for both students and the faculty who work with them to foster multiliteracy acquisition . . . in ways that span the curriculum, not to mention the classroom" (14). Within these spaces, they assert, graduate students in particular can safely experiment with digital teaching. Furthermore, reciprocal mentoring relationships can be created as students and faculty become co-learners or, in Journet's terms, reciprocal mentors.

It is this type of knowledge-making process that is conspicuously absent from Michael's pedagogical process in *The Class*. Although his

Table 4.3. Questions about pedagogical development

Organizing questions	How do we define what counts as a text?	How do we approach reading texts?	How do we approach the production of texts?
Reframed questions	How do we introduce grad students and faculty to new types of texts/genres?	How do we prepare grad students and faculty to read and teach students to read different types of texts/genres?	How do we prepare grad students and faculty to produce and teach students to produce different types of texts/genres?
Questions for individuals	What do you know about alternative texts/genres in your field? In other fields?	How did you learn or are you learning to read alternative and digital texts in your field? In other fields?	Have you produced alternative texts for your teaching?
	What support structures did you utilize to gain this knowledge?	What support structures did you utilize to learn to read these texts?	What support structures did you utilize to produce these texts?
	How can you share/are you sharing this knowledge with others in your field/department?	How can you share/are you sharing this knowledge with others in your field/department?	How can you share/are you sharing your expertise with others in your field/department?
	How have you applied this knowledge in your pedagogical practice?	How have you applied this knowledge in your pedagogical practice?	Have you had students produce alternative texts as assignments in your classes?
	What support do you need to begin/continue to learn and apply knowledge about alternative genres and texts in your teaching?	What support do you need to begin/continue to learn and apply knowledge about reading these texts in your teaching?	What support structures did students utilize to produce these texts? What support structures did you utilize to integrate composing into your class(es)?
	Why is/isn't exposure to alternative texts/genres important to your teaching?	Why is/isn't learning to read different types of texts/genres important to your teaching?	Why is/isn't producing different types of texts/genres important to your teaching?

TA does serve as a kind of mentor, spurring him to use digital media in the class, he does not seek out theoretical or practical discussions with her or with other teachers about best practices for teaching with technology. These concepts of safe or rough spaces and mentoring are essential to professional development in digital media pedagogy, and this section explores the ways that departments make possible such spaces and mentoring. Table 4.3 suggests a set of questions about pedagogical development that individuals can consider in order to help develop their professional teaching identities and reflect on how digital media are or could be a part of those identities. This section also considers the extent to which the technological ecology created by a department encourages students and faculty to reflect on the issues raised by these questions.

Mentoring/Being Mentored in Digital Media Pedagogy: Cosmo's Story

Cosmo has been able to engage in professional development in all of the areas (or columns) represented in table 4.3, and this process has been a longitudinal one that began with an early graduate seminar. Before enrolling in graduate school in the parallel cultures department, Cosmo had little experience composing with new media. He explains: "Before I arrived here, I really was kind of a Luddite. I was on the web, I did my email, I surfed around to websites, but I didn't really do much." He was introduced to website composing and online discussions in the Introduction to Teaching course he took. The final assignment was an electronic portfolio, which he "got really into" because he had "never built a website before." Although he was proud of the site at the time, he says, "I'm glad I didn't permit [the professor] to put it up on her site because on some level I knew then that I was proud of it but I would not be proud of it soon, and that is the case." Although his early attempt at web composing did not stand the test of time, he found the task "really interesting and engaging. I also used WebCT there in discussions, and I also found that to be quite interesting, too."

Because of his experiences with that assignment and the online discussions, the first time he requested and was assigned a composition class that met in a networked classroom, he decided to incorporate both of those activities: "When I got into teaching and was signed up for a C-class, I thought, I'm gonna have my students do a web project and I'm gonna do [online] discussions." Just as Cosmo had enjoyed the tasks in his seminar, "the web project towards the end got a really great response from the students. I got some pretty interesting materials." He adds, "And really I think that what drove me very strongly was the fact that I'd done it myself and then tried it with my students and got a great level of engagement, in that case for a cultural critique of advertising, turning that into a web-based format." What the professor did in the pedagogy class with technology not only served to introduce Cosmo to different technologies as composing tools but also modeled for him how he might incorporate those technologies into his own courses. Although she didn't mentor him individually, her modeling served as a guide to his own pedagogical experimentation. Because it was a TA training seminar, pedagogy was foregrounded, and the use of digital media as a pedagogical tool was modeled in the design and implementation of the class.

The next "major moment" in Cosmo's work with digital media involved another mentor, the director of the Center for Digital Media Studies. Cosmo took two classes with the CDMS director: Teaching College English, a mentorship class, and a graduate seminar on composition pedagogy and theory that focused on digital media. He says that Teaching College English helped extend his thinking about digital media and pedagogy because he got to see an "upper-level English studio course on documentary and Flash production in action and got to learn the technologies along with the students and help them out a little bit." He served as an apprentice of sorts to the CDMS director in an upper-level undergraduate seminar focused on digital media and English studies. In that class, Cosmo says, "I kind of stayed a week ahead of where [the students] were. Hah! Occasionally a week behind." He was able, therefore, not only to learn to compose in a new medium but also to think about creating digital media assignments for students and scaffolding them through the composing process, grading those assignments, and helping students see the rhetorical connections between composing in digital media and composing in print. As was the case with the TA training seminar, this class was a required, pedagogically focused course. Its purpose was to help TAs learn to teach sophomore-level classes; although the professor taught the bulk of the class, Cosmo was expected to share in the planning and execution of the course and to reflect upon the experience. Technology integration was not a programmatic requirement for the course, but Cosmo sought it out because of personal interest.

The composition seminar Cosmo took with the CDMS director also encouraged his professionalization by allowing him to reflect on the work he was doing from a theoretical standpoint. He said it helped him because "we continued that kind of work at the grad level and filled in some of the more theoretical background." The seminar focused on a "paradigm shift" in writing studies that is rewriting the field of "computers and composition" as "digital media studies." In addition to discussing what this change means to teaching and research in the field of composition, students also composed in digital media (Dreamweaver, Photoshop, and Flash), creating "digital media self-, teaching-, and research-portraits." After Teaching College English and the composition seminar focused on digital pedagogy, Cosmo remembers, "I said, 'Oh, well, now I know how to do Flash movies. This seems pretty cool, so now I'm going to do a Flash project.' And I kind of ran off and did a Flash project." Again, observing another teacher and learning new composing technologies spurred Cosmo on to experiment more with his multimodal pedagogy and to create new kinds of composing assignments for students in his writing classes. Mentoring has clearly been a touchstone for Cosmo's integration of digital media into his teaching. However, this mentoring is self-selected on both ends: Cosmo sought it out and was lucky enough to find faculty who integrated digital media into their seminars and were willing to mentor him in digital media pedagogy.

The community of teachers Cosmo has found in the CDMS helps him to shape his pedagogy at least as much as the more formalized learning experiences he has had in coursework. Because he is a technology-pedagogy consultant in the CDMS, he says, "I'm actually not teaching this year, but I'm working a lot with teachers, and I'm learning some new technologies, and I'm sure whatever I do next year is going to look different [because of] that [interaction and learning]." Additionally, he says what got him started with teaching with digital media was "basically a combination of experiences, opportunities I've been given as a graduate student to use technologies and to talk about them in relation to pedagogy and then throw them into class and see what happens and run." Furthermore, the ability to actually experiment with technology during class has contributed to the types of activities he includes in his classes, such as Flash movies, websites, and similar digital media production activities.

Cosmo's learning of pedagogical practices that incorporate digital media has been made possible by the facilities the department has provided and by other graduate students—in other words, by spaces, mentors (both faculty and other graduate students), available technologies, and a culture of sharing. These facilities enable Cosmo's learning through informal talking and experimentation. Although Cosmo is in a department that highly values print, the current administration values digital media work and invests in it. But curricularly, digital media still represent the fringe, not the center, of the department's interests.

Physically, there is an investment in spaces and resources that provide learning opportunities (particularly experimental teaching in networked classrooms) and facilitate a community of teacher-learners who offer ongoing support to each other. But that community is fringe/niche, not central, to the department's ideas of what constitutes good teaching. Although the first-year writing program incorporates formal training into its pedagogy seminar, since Cosmo went through training things have changed and the focus is no longer on website production (which combined digital management, analysis of digital texts, and digital production) but on how to teach online research skills. Thus, while digital media are discussed as an important part of teaching, discussions of technology-enhanced pedagogy in the required introductory course are limited to digital management. As a result, the full range of digital media pedagogy is not promoted in official programmatic channels. The CDMS is well funded and provides many opportunities for individuals to learn about and experiment with digital media pedagogy on their own time and their own terms. Cosmo thus has a safe space in which to experiment in the CDMS. He can, in his own words, "hide out" and do his own thing.

Through his coursework and work in the CDMS, Cosmo has been able to learn about alternative texts/genres and reflect on their usefulness to his teaching; he has been able, because of the "rough spaces" of his graduate seminars on pedagogy and the community mentoring in the CDMS, to experiment with digitally enhanced teaching and to build a theoretically informed pedagogy that incorporates both critical reading/analysis of digital texts and digital production. He department's technological ecology has fostered such professionalization by enabling his "digital literacy acquisition as a longitudinal process, beginning in a single course and extending throughout the program," which Graupner, Nickoson-Massey, and Blair argue is a must for graduate programs (17).

In other words, because the process has been longitudinal and some of his experiences were part of coursework, Cosmo has been able to reflect on many of the questions in tables 4.2 and 4.3, particularly questions about applying disciplinary knowledge about reading and producing alternative texts and genres into his teaching. His department has set the stage to allow these questions to be addressed by providing him the opportunity to take courses and teach in networked classrooms and work in the CDMS. As a result, Cosmo can reflect on his practice from both the level of personal experience and a pedagogical level informed by current research and best practices.

Curricular Identity and Digital Media Pedagogy: Adele's Story

Adele's professionalization in digital media has also been a longitudinal process, allowing her time to reflect on the role of digital texts and digital production in her teaching. Adele began learning about pedagogical applications of digital media during her master's program, before she came to the integrated literacies department. She "worked with a lot of English education faculty who were using it in the classes" she was taking and who were "teaching us about how important it was." In those classes, she developed collaboratively composed websites compiling information on books, including "a page or two pages on the author and the book, resources, and assignment ideas for teachers, that kind of thing." Through these activities, she "saw that [web composing] was useful and productive for me and wanted my students to experience the same thing. And I want them, when they get on the job market or [in] upper-level courses, maybe where that's an option or is required, to have some familiarity with that." In the integrated literacies department, she says, "the majority of classes that I've taken have involved some type of electronic component, from working on an online course management program, or creating a website, or submitting things electronically."

Digital media work is a core aspect of the integrated literacies department, which offers an MA in digital rhetoric and a PhD concentration in digital rhetoric, and curricula are being set up to sustain and support that. In fact, the graduate director notes that there are "digital expectations" in all of the seminars, especially regarding course management tools. He says all of the graduate faculty use the course management tool "for file distribution, for email, and for discussion boards, and so on. So that's just built in to, I think, all the courses." Additionally, there are often digital assignments: "Students have to do a homepage in the Research Colloquium," a course required of all PhD students. Adele adds, "I think we're encouraged as instructors, too, to have our students be doing web page portfolios, web essays, that kind of thing, and not just having them work from print media all the time." Because of the programmatic focus on integration of digital media throughout the curriculum, every graduate student, regardless of research focus, gets some formalized instruction in digital media pedagogy; such instruction includes online discussion and submission of assignments through the course management tool, as well as web page composing. Thus, these activities are modeled in seminars, and Adele interprets this modeling as encouragement to use them in her own teaching.

The curriculum for graduate students provides opportunities to learn about teaching and doing research with digital media and to put that learning into practice by working with digital media in seminars, and Adele positions herself as a newcomer to digital media, a learner. She says, "I think the longer I have been at [this university], the more I see that it is something really necessary, but it can be frustrating too, 'cause you have the learning curve for people like me. I'm not an html code writer or a website designer, so I have to learn how to use these software programs and things." It is interesting that Adele says that working with digital media can be tough for "people like me." Though digital rhetoric is at the center of the MA program, it is one of three possible concentrations in the PhD program in rhetoric and writing, so not all PhD students place digital media at the center of their work. For instance, Adele's research focuses on community literacy, whereas the research of her colleague Alan, another PhD student in the program, focuses on digital media. Although Adele had experience with web composing before she entered the PhD program, Alan came to the program with significantly more experience with digital media pedagogy, allowing him to experiment more and develop his digital media pedagogy alongside his digital media research.

This difference between Alan and Adele points to a subtle difference in the department between those who came to the department already knowing about digital media and teaching with it (Ava, Alan, the graduate director, graduate students whose interests are centered on digital media, some professors in writing studies) and those who didn't (Adele, some other graduate students whose interests are not centered on digital media, many of the visiting assistant professors, some professors in cultural studies). The former are intensely involved with digital media in all of their professional activities and express enthusiasm for the program and department, naming few, if any, departmental barriers to their work. The latter temper that enthusiasm with concerns that they are not receiving the amount of support and direction that they need in order to successfully and confidently incorporate digital media into their pedagogies.

When I interviewed Adele, the PhD program was small—five students, two of whom were focused on digital media. In addition to taking classes with these students, Adele was also in classes with MA students claiming digital rhetoric as their primary scholarly identity. Being surrounded by so many others with more experience with and interest in digital media likely contributes to Adele's identifying herself as someone at the bottom of the digital media learning curve, thus leading her to emphasize her lack of skills rather than what she does know and can do with digital media. Because of this self-identification, she has not begun incorporating many composing technologies into her classes. One example is the university's course management system, which she has had experience with as a student. She says, "I don't feel that I know that program well enough to orchestrate that in my class. Over the summer I hope to take some kind of workshop on it and learn a little bit more about it and how I can use it as a course management tool." Although she has experience using the program as a student, she claims to not be able to use the tool from a teacher's standpoint and thus incorporate it into her teaching; she also feels the need to take a formal workshop in order to learn how to use the program, rather than informally ask one of her colleagues for help.

Her apparent need for formalized training could be related to the program's focus on integrating learning about digital media into formal coursework by encouraging students to expect formal training. However, Adele says that, for graduate students, learning to integrate digital media into their teaching is "generally something that's above and beyond what we're already doing, or something that we have to seek out outside of our coursework, and for a lot of us, we just don't have the time to do it. . . . The people who have really engaged with that are the people who were actually in the area before they got here." It makes sense that a department trying to distinguish itself in digital media studies would attract students with interests in that area and that those students might already have experience teaching in a digital environment. But Adele's comments suggest that the department overestimates graduate students' knowledge and experience with digital pedagogy at the same time as they cultivate interest. To combat this problem and help students who are interested in teaching with technology but don't have a background in it, she recommends that the department "offer workshops and things maybe in the summer or that would be for credit that would work to help not only with professional development using technology but also pedagogically, how to do more of that in your classrooms." Her request for formal training is consistent with the department's stance that digital media are integrated into the curriculum and that students should begin learning about the potentials of digital media through their coursework.

Her request for a pedagogy workshop also reveals that training in digital media pedagogy is not part of the teacher training workshop required of all entering graduate students, whereas digital media are integrated into the required research colloquium. According to the graduate director, TAs take a training workshop concurrently with teaching their first course: "That consists of maybe twenty hours of workshopping the week before the semester begins and then a two-hour session every week of the semester. And that's focused on giving the students the parameters for the first-year curriculum and then helping them develop their own versions of the curriculum for their courses." Digital media are "not formally required as part of the training, but," he adds, "several of the students chose to do their courses in computer classrooms." In every case, the graduate students who chose to do their courses in networked classrooms had previous experience doing so. Although "it isn't formally part of the training, we did do a faculty-graduate student workshop last summer. . . . [Ava] did a workshop on teaching faculty to use technology in writing classes. And we'd like to offer that again, but we don't have any plans to do that right now." This creates something of an imbalance: there are more structured learning opportunities focused on digital media research and scholarship than on digital media pedagogy (whereas the opposite is true in the parallel cultures department).

Adding to the imbalance, there is no visible ongoing conversation about digital media and teaching. Ava, an assistant professor in the department, laments this absence:

> We teach hundreds of sections of first-year writing. We never talk about teaching. Never. So there are pockets of us who are hungry to talk about methods and approaches, and things are changing so dramatically now with grad students. So we're having more conversations about teaching, but not as much as I would like, and not as much on teaching with technology or teaching about technology.

Casual conversations with graduate students revealed that they spent time informally talking with each other and sometimes with faculty about using digital media in their teaching. So while there are small numbers who are talking to each other informally, there is no facility (like the CDMS in the parallel cultures department) that exists to nurture or make visible such interactions. As a result, the departmental stance on formalized learning of technology creates categories of "learners" and "teachers" (or perhaps "experts"). It also raises questions about the framing of digital media work in classes. Digital media pedagogy was modeled for Cosmo in *pedagogy* seminars, which led to his professional pedagogical development; Adele, while she has taken seminars that incorporate digital media, does not interpret that as pedagogical modeling, perhaps because the classes were not focused on discussions of pedagogy but on discussions of research. So the framing of digital media in seminar work is an important issue when it comes to the pedagogical development of graduate students.

Although she positions herself as an inexperienced learner of digital media and is not able to teach regularly in a computer classroom, Adele makes analysis of technology and critical framing of the Internet a regular part of her classes. For instance, she recently began using a "code exercise," which teaches students to analyze the positioning of websites by finding out "who sponsors the site, what servers the site uses, how long it's been established, who runs it." Her goal is to help students "develop a sense of the placement of the website, that it does indeed have a name and a space and a sponsoring organization somewhere; it doesn't just exist somewhere autonomously on the web." In addition, she wants "to get [students] looking at texts as having power." Though this activity is not digital production, it does incorporate some of the philosophies that Adele has learned in graduate seminars about digital media pedagogy and digital rhetoric. For instance, it invites students to consider the rhetorical nature and materiality of digital texts by considering who wrote something, how and why that individual posted it, what technologies he or she had access to in order to create the text, who reads the text, what technologies are needed in order to read the text, and how the text affects those who read it.

Adele teaches the university's introductory writing course. She says that the course director arranged for all of the graduate students' sections of the course to meet at the same time and for a computer lab to be available throughout the semester at that time. So, although her course meets in a traditional classroom, she and her students get some time in a computer lab, "usually once maybe every other week." They do web searches and word processing, as well as collaborative writing that they submit online, "so they can be composing it together as a group in the class and then send it to me electronically." She has also given students the option of doing either a traditional research essay or a web folio as their final project. She says many of the students are interested in the web folio because they "think it's cool and fun and it's different than typing a five-page research essay," but "I think if I do that again, it needs to be more at the center of the curriculum, where part of their assignment is learning how to compose web documents." Consequently, a visit to the university's writing center—housed in the same college as the department in which Adele teaches and the interdisciplinary graduate program in which she is enrolled—is necessary. The students are on their own to learn web designing, but the writing center offers help for them. In addition, the writing center offers help for teachers. "That's the cool thing about the writing center," she says. "They do have workshops you can do on document design and on web page design too."

Even though Adele is incorporating some digital applications into her class, she has trouble fully integrating multimodal composing with digital media into her introductory writing course because it is difficult for her to schedule lab time. The class meets in a classroom that is in a dormitory, and the students "balk" at having to go anywhere else for class (such as the library or a computer lab) because most of them—about 80 percent—live in the dorm where the class meets. Space is at a premium at the university, affecting the department's ability to provide digitally equipped classroom spaces to its students. According to Ava, the college is considering wireless access as an alternative; with laptops, then, any classroom could become digitally mediated. "Then once we get [to the lab]," Adele says, "there's eighteen machines and I have twenty-seven students. So they usually have to double up or I have them do group work on the computers. And it's hot in there, and some of the machines are older." Furthermore, the computers don't all always work, and there aren't enough chairs: "It's those logistics, you know, the uses of space which really affect people's willingness to be there in the first place." Her graduate student identity and her self-image as "not up to speed digitally" magnify these difficulties because she is not at the top of the list for a networked classroom. The department owns only one networked classroom. Because a focus on digital media is at the center of the master's program, those classes have access, as do undergraduate upper-level writing classes that emphasize digital rhetoric. First-year writing is not specifically and programmatically linked with digital media, even though the master's and PhD students (whose programs are linked with digital media) teach first-year writing. This creates an ironic tension: graduate students are expected to learn how to integrate digital media into their teaching; but because of the programmatic focus on digital media, there are more classes that need networked classrooms than there are networked classrooms to go around. As a result, graduate students end up having few opportunities to actually teach in networked environments, even though they are encouraged to think about developing digital media pedagogies and to think about digital media in transformative terms.

Adele has internalized this transformative message and says her pedagogy would change if she were in a computer classroom. She explains that she would "do a lot more on PowerPoint and have a lot more activities like WebQuest where I'd prepare a list of sites for them to go through and look at all those and do an activity surrounding that." Because of the current logistics—having "to finish the work out of class," requesting "a technology cart to be dropped off" in her regular classroom, finding "a laptop with an Ethernet connection"—Adele says that digital media pedagogy right now for her "just gets to be cumbersome. I still work a lot from paper when I'm not in the computer classroom." This reflection about how her pedagogy would change in a computer classroom shows that she is thinking about her pedagogy in regards to digital media and networked classroom teaching even though her opportunities to actually teach in that kind of space are limited. It also shows that she is integrating digital media into her pedagogy theoretically, as her seminars have encouraged her to do and as the stance of the department (that rhetoric is becoming digital rhetoric) has encouraged her to do, even though she can't fully put it into practice yet. Furthermore, it shows that the material conditions of access affect Adele's pedagogy as much as the philosophies of digital rhetoric she has internalized from the seminars she has taken.

Interestingly, Adele finds it necessary to justify her continuing use of print media in courses, and she does this not by refuting the relevance or importance of digital rhetoric but by blaming the logistical realities, further demonstrating her internalization of the program's stance on digital rhetoric. Despite the logistical difficulties, she nonetheless sees the potential for a digital-media-saturated pedagogy:

> I also think that it's really useful and eye opening to have [students] be able to compose something on the web and it be something that's used by real audiences. If we were to create a course website on a novel that we're reading or something where other teachers or other students who might read that same book . . . go to that site and look at things that they've done, that's really useful. It makes them feel like what they're doing isn't for naught and they're just writing for one audience of the teacher. But I feel like I want to be more knowledgeable and savvy than I am with composing software and whatnot to be able to teach that.

Adele is clearly trying to cultivate in her students a critical and rhetorical stance toward technology, as her graduate training has prompted her to do. She is also teaching her students about the materiality of texts, encouraging students to view all texts, digital or not, as material objects and to understand the power that texts have in the lives of people who use them, lessons consistent with her field identity and research interests in cultural rhetorics.

Her department's technological ecology has fostered her learning about new texts/genres and reflecting on their usefulness for her teaching. Although material constraints keep her from being able to always practice a digital pedagogy, the department's culture has enabled her professionalization in digital media and helped her think of digital media in transformative ways. Even though there is a tension between material conditions of access and the kinds of digital media teaching Adele is encouraged to do, she has nonetheless been able to reflect on many of the questions in tables 4.2 and 4.3, particularly questions about applying disciplinary knowledge about reading and composing alternative texts to her teaching and questions about support structures and sustainability.

***

These departments position themselves in very different ways on the questions presented in table 4.2, particularly questions about how to introduce graduate students and faculty to new types of texts/genres and how to support the continued development of digital media pedagogies and scholarship. The print-centric department relies upon a somewhat "underground" network for introducing graduate students to new types of texts and genres and helping them learn to teach those texts. Benjamin, for instance, discusses how the graduate students who want to incorporate more technology into their teaching help each other out on a purely informal level. They don't have the same kinds of resources that the parallel cultures department has, yet these informal networks are still springing up on their own.

Networking and getting help for digital pedagogy is much easier in the parallel cultures department, where there is a combination of informal mentoring and formal instruction. The department chair has provided funding for the CDMS, which allows individuals like Cosmo to engage in experimentation and build new pedagogies that are informed by scholarship in their fields and by research in digital media pedagogy. The CDMS also systematically introduces graduate students to alternative texts/genres, digital media pedagogies, and digital media scholarly practices because of its close connection with the first-year writing program and GTA training. Because of the informal mentoring model of the CDMS, though, graduate students and faculty are supported in learning about and developing new media pedagogies and scholarship only if they so choose. At the same time, because there are faculty in the department who have scholarly interests in digital pedagogy, the department is able to offer graduate seminars introducing students to the big issues in the field, which gives those who seek them out some formal education in digital pedagogy.

This formal education in digital media is at the core of the graduate curriculum in the integrated literacies department; however, there is less of a focus on digital pedagogy than on digital scholarship. Still, graduate students are systematically introduced to digital pedagogy, and because many of their courses meet in the department's computer classroom, they see digital pedagogies modeled for them. They are not able to experiment with digital media pedagogy to the extent that graduate students in the parallel cultures department are, though, because the program has not created a space like the CDMS, which serves as a teaching lab. But because of the seminar focus on the production of digital texts, they gain more formal education in producing different types of texts than do graduate students in the other departments.

Individuals in these three departments thus have different choices available to them against a backdrop of departmental material conditions. These choices are not only practical in nature (what kinds of assignments are viable given the classroom technologies available, for instance) but also theoretical/philosophical (what kinds of assignments are appropriate given the central values of the field, for instance). Not only do the departments' technological ecologies influence the day-to-day support of actual digital media work, but they also encourage graduate students and faculty to see their fields and the discipline in particular ways, adjust their practice (or not) accordingly, and identify themselves (professionally speaking) in particular terms. In her account of how she came to incorporate digital media into her teaching, Journet, referencing David Bartholomae's "Inventing the University," describes inventing herself as a teacher of multimodal writing, the latest of several "reinventions" of herself as a teacher. Cosmo's and Adele's stories demonstrate the ways their departments have encouraged them to invent themselves as teachers with digital media pedagogies. Although these cases focus on PhD students, as Journet demonstrates, faculty also have to continuously reinvent themselves as teachers. This can be a struggle, especially in regard to digital media, because of the additional issues of material access to technologies. Faculty as well as graduate students need a technological ecology that supports their reflecting on the questions suggested in tables 4.2 and 4.3, gives them access to the material technologies and mentors they need, and encourages experimentation in "rough spaces."

Becoming Scholars: Studying and Practicing Digital Scholarship

Not only do Graupner, Nickoson-Massey, and Blair assert that digital media remediates our teaching identities, but they also argue that it remediates our research/scholarly identities. Consequently, they contend that it is important for graduate students to develop multimodal literacies in nontechnical knowledge-making spaces, such as the research seminar: "Just as it is true that to teach writing . . . is to teach digital writing, so too is it to say that to conduct or teach research . . . is to encounter research as a multi-dimensional, technologically mediated enterprise" (15). In their account of incorporating multimodal activities into a research seminar, they note that the multimodal experiences students had "provided a dynamic arena for both analysis *and* practice—a space for informal, collaborative inquiry within the 'safe' space of the classroom" (19). According to Douglas Eyman, Stephanie Sheffield, and Dànielle Nicole DeVoss, it is crucial for graduate programs to facilitate the development of research networks that give graduate students and faculty the opportunity to engage in such collaborative inquiry, which they argue "is often a key component of our work, whether it is explicit or tacit" (50). Based on their experiences, they suggest that a sustainable research network needs a sense of community or a community of practice, a willingness to engage critically with digital media and with the research process, and a willingness to engage in practical application (for example, production) as a rhetorical practice.

These concepts of safe spaces for collaborative multimodal inquiry, communities of practice, critical engagement, and production as a rhetorical practice are key elements of developing technological ecologies that foster professionalization in digital media scholarship, and this section explores the ways that two departments—the integrated literacies department and the parallel cultures department—make space for or foster these ideas, whether through formal, programmatic structures or through informal mentoring relationships. While an "underground" culture exists in the print-centric department for digitally mediated teaching, there is little evidence that the department fosters a culture of support for digital scholarship. Table 4.4 suggests a set of questions about scholarly development that individuals can consider in order to help develop their professional scholarly identities and reflect on how digital media is or could be a part of those identities. While the questions are similar (and in some cases identical) to the questions from table 4.3, focusing on pedagogy, they focus on scholarship and are therefore inflected and/or worded slightly differently because of that focus. This

Table 4.4. Questions about digital media and professional scholarly identities

Organizing Questions	How do we define what counts as a text?	How do we approach reading texts?	How do we approach the production of texts?
Reframed Questions	How do we introduce grad students and faculty to new types of texts/genres?	How do we prepare grad students and faculty to read and teach students to read different types of texts/genres?	How do we prepare grad students and faculty to produce and teach students to produce different types of texts/genres?
Questions for individuals	What do you know about alternative texts/genres in your field? In other fields?	How did you learn or are you learning to read alternative and digital texts in your field? In other fields?	Have you produced alternative texts as scholarship?
	What support structures did you utilize to gain this knowledge?	What support structures did you utilize to learn to read these texts?	What support structures did you utilize to produce these texts?
	How can you share/are you sharing this knowledge with others in your field/department?	How can you share/are you sharing this knowledge with others in your field/department?	How can you share/are you sharing your expertise with others in your field/department?
	How have you applied this knowledge in your scholarly practice?	How have you applied this knowledge in your scholarly practice?	
	What support do you need to begin/continue to learn and apply knowledge about alternative genres and texts in your scholarship?	What support do you need to begin/continue to learn and apply knowledge about reading these texts in your scholarship?	What support do you need to begin/continue to produce alternative scholarly texts/objects?
	Why is/isn't exposure to alternative texts/genres important to your scholarship?	Why is/isn't learning to read different types of texts/genres important to your scholarship?	Why is/isn't producing different types of texts/genres important to your scholarship?

section also considers the extent to which the technological ecology created by a department encourages students and faculty to reflect on the issues raised by these questions.

Integrated Literacies Department

Just as the integrated literacies department creates a technological ecology that allows graduate students the opportunity for longitudinal professionalization in digital media pedagogy, so too does it offer similar opportunities for the development of digital media as part of their scholarly identities. The primary mechanisms for this are coursework and a research center. When the graduate director was negotiating support for the graduate program, he argued that in order "to create a really top-notch graduate program, you've got to have a research center affiliated with it." He says he "was not interested in doing the typical humanities type of program that didn't have research centers. And I kind of made it a point of negotiation that we had to have one." He lists several reasons that he fought so strongly for a research center:

- Revenue generation: "Graduate programs can't rely on the largesse of the institution's general fund or the state legislature's willingness to support education."
- Respect and support across the university:

  It's a mark of distinction. It is amazing what having the center does in terms of people's willingness to talk to us and listen to us in terms of what we have to say. . . . In the sciences and some of the social sciences areas . . . you're just not worth talking to if you're not coming out of a research center. And that shouldn't be the case, but it is the case. So it's given us a lot of entry into discussions that we didn't have before. . . . The medical school's virtual practice group has just invited us to join them, and that's because we have a research center. Pure and simple. It's not 'cause we're nice people or because we know rhetoric and writing or science writing or anything like that. It's because, "Oh, they have a research center, then they're worth talking to."
- Opportunity for graduate student involvement with research projects: "They're heavily involved" in "digital development work" such as building a server and serving as go-to digital technology persons for faculty projects.
- Funding for faculty to work on digital projects: That funding includes but is not limited to course release, summer money, and paying the faculty member to work in the center.

Besides the local issue of funding, the graduate director's comments point out some of the external issues that influence the kinds of work that happen in local programs. Visibility, both within the university and within the discipline, is something that the research center can bring to the program, which in turn can bring more funding and more opportunities for research.

The graduate director is also codirector of the research center, in its first of three years of funding by "a private foundation affiliated with the university." The center's purpose "is to support research on writing in digital environments." According to the graduate director, the center is funding two types of faculty projects:

> One is building innovative digital products related to teaching writing or doing writing online. And that could be software, CDs. We've got several different kinds of projects now, and people are basically building products that we think will either be innovative and interesting and attract attention that way, or they'll generate intellectual property. Preferably both. . . . And then the other sort of work is corporate and community work. We would like to do digital projects for companies and for community organizations. . . . We don't want to do just contract or consulting work. We want to do work that could generate models or products that could be replicable elsewhere, that we could take on the road and use as models. So we're basically looking for digital products, digital models that solve issues, questions, problems that people have with digital writing. But it is primarily a research center [for] faculty research.

This research center is evidence of the department's stance of integrating digital media into the department and curriculum, particularly into the research agenda of the department. It is a programmatic center to support faculty research projects having to do with digital media and, as such, is integrated into the program, further cementing the centrality of digital media in the program. The center supports faculty members' digital projects and considers those projects under the umbrella of research, even though those projects are digital productions rather than more traditionally styled research (typically appearing in print) analyzing digital texts. Though the research center does not directly support graduate students by funding their projects, the center's existence benefits them by supporting faculty projects that deal with writing in digital environments; such projects are likely, eventually, to influence graduate students' professional development when they take courses or teach a course utilizing a digital project developed with support from the research center. Furthermore, the center's existence and support of faculty projects are likely to draw top scholars in digital media fields to the department and, as a result, attract graduate students interested in working with those faculty and doing similar types of projects. The center is also poised to encourage reflection and departmental discussions on questions in the third column of tables 4.2 and 4.4, those dealing with issues surrounding the production of alternative texts, genres, and products of scholarship.

Although the center does not fund graduate student projects, PhD students are offered opportunities to learn about incorporating digital media into their research as well as into their professional identities as scholars. These opportunities come in the form of coursework. According to the graduate director, "It's tied in with the digital rhetoric MA program. Half their courses are in computer classrooms. It's the sea they swim in; it's what they have to do. In the PhD program it's strongly encouraged. A lot of those students are doing the digital rhetoric courses." In the required research colloquium, students must create a website. Additionally, PhD students face a portfolio requirement, which can be fulfilled digitally. Adele, for instance, says, "I maintain an electronic folder on [the university's course management system] that has all of my research so far for this year contained in it, which is for the research colloquium course that we're taking. And then we also respond electronically through threaded discussion to one another's work." This portfolio requirement is unique because students are allowed to fulfill it with any medium. Cosmo, in the parallel cultures department, says, "I'd like to see a valuing of digital composition as a way of doing a candidacy exam or as a way of doing a program of study, doing a dissertation." In other words, he wishes his department would recognize and value digital media as a way of approaching and completing major degree requirements, and this department does: it recognizes digitally produced work as a possible alternative to a printed portfolio. Though Adele uses it more as a container and thus more for digital management, the potential exists for digital production. Additionally, Adele says, "Most of the audience forum analysis that I've done for situating my research in the field is all done on PowerPoint. I'm always creating maps and images and things like that to infuse into text in Microsoft Word. I'm always on the computer. It doesn't seem like I can really get away from that." This use of digital media represents her use of digital production to facilitate analysis. The "maps and images and things like that" she creates help her during the invention stage to complete her scholarly analysis; they then become "infused into" her final, primarily alphabetic, text. Additionally, she is able to easily share her work with committee members and other students for feedback. The integration of digital media work into the required research seminar provides a platform for students to consider questions from the second and third columns of tables 4.2 and 4.4, questions about not only reading/interpreting alternative texts but also producing alternative scholarly objects, regardless of field.

Besides the departmental stance that digital media must be integrated into faculty and graduate students' scholarly identities, the department also seeks to integrate digital media into the study of rhetoric. Not surprisingly, then, an important criterion the graduate director mentions for evaluating colloquium students' websites is "just a general rhetorical one":

> Is the site or . . . the document . . . [or] the discourse appropriate for its intended audience and purpose, whatever that is? We talk about that in our class, too. You're not going on the job market yet, so why would you have a website? That's two or three years down the road. So what's the point of a website now? Well, there's a couple of good answers to that. One is that we have a portfolio requirement in the program. So, the website is in a sense an ongoing portfolio. So they use it in a sense as an archive for their own work and as a way to distribute their work to their committee members for reviewing it. And then the second one is sort of field networking. People in the field find out who you are by checking your website, and people establish research connections.

The graduate director links basic rhetorical principles of composition to professional identity: the website (or any kind of scholarly discourse) represents the graduate student as a professional and is a valuable job market resource. In addition, he stresses the connection between digital management and production: the digital productions the students create (in this case, websites) have the potential to be read and used by other scholars. The graduate director and Adele thus demonstrate that digital media in this department are seen as an integral part of scholarly identity as well as scholarly work. That vision is enacted, in part, through formal programmatic means: a funded research center focused solely on digital projects and digital coursework requirements.

Alan, also a PhD student in the integrated literacies department, is doing unique work that blends digital management, analysis of digital texts, and digital production. One project he is working on involves research on how online citations are being used in print publications.

For that project, he says that he and his co-researchers are "looking at developing methodologies for seeing where these things were when they were originally cited. So I'm using a lot of the Wayback Machine and a lot of stuff on the web to do that, that kind of technology." This involves digital management, using online tools to trace the evolution of web-based publications and the length of time they remain live on the web before disappearing. It also involves analysis of digital texts and studying digital citation, publication, and archiving patterns. In addition, he says, "We've developed a database to put the data into and then get information out of it based on the queries we give it. So I've been working a lot on developing the web interface of the database, structuring the database and getting that to work, which is kind of new stuff for me but interesting. Could be really functional in a lot of different ways for research." This database development involves digital production because Alan is designing and coding a database that enacts both analytical and managerial tasks and might eventually be useful to other researchers. But, as suggested by the "MLA Evaluation Wiki," building the database is also an analytical, not just a technical, challenge because it is "an implementation of potential method" that requires Alan to develop a method of citation analysis, think critically about it, explore its potential consequences, and present that theory in a form that will be easily used by others for inquiry.

There are several support structures that encourage Alan's work. First and foremost are the faculty, whom he calls "fabulous" and "totally supportive." He says, "They are very good at giving feedback and just encouraging me to do work in the areas that I want to do work in." In addition, he says, "the resources that have been made available to me are stunning. I mean, I'm not even teaching this semester, and, look, I've got an office with a brand-spankin'-new computer. When I got here they said, 'What kind of computer do you want? We'll order it.' And I had looked at a lot of grad schools. . . . It's a nice setup." Although he imagines that the reason he has such resources at his disposal is "because there are only five students right now," he hopes "that they'll be able to continue that kind of level of support." Even without the stellar resources at his personal disposal in his office, however, the department's other resources help support Alan's work. As a graduate student employed as an assistant by the research center, he notes that "having access to the stuff we're doing at the [research] center" is also helpful because "I can have servers and do really interesting work in interesting ways." As previously mentioned, although the research center does not fund graduate student projects, its existence encourages and thus helps to create a culture of support for digital media production; in other words, digital media production has a place in the department, and that attitude allows Alan to feel comfortable building real digital media scholarship in his seminars. The fact that graduate students are encouraged and sometimes required to practice digital media production as scholarship in seminars also contributes to this culture of support.

The department's technological ecology enables opportunities for students like Adele and Alan to develop multimodal literacy in nontechnical knowledge-making spaces, as Graupner, Nickoson-Massey, and Blair advocate. The technological ecology fosters reflection on many of the questions about professional identity from tables 4.2 and 4.4, particularly questions about the role of digital media in scholarly processes. In the research seminar, for instance, Adele was able to analyze as well as practice multimodal scholarship, enhancing the process of professionalization. Furthermore, the use of the course management system enables the opportunity for participation in informal, collaborative research networks, which Eyman, Sheffield, and DeVoss advocate, and encourages students to approach digital media production through a rhetorical lens. These opportunities also prompt students to reflect on digital media's role in their scholarship—both the processes and the products of their scholarship—as well as, more generally, on the ways that digital media might influence scholarly processes and products in their fields, encouraging them to think of themselves as players in the digital media transition in the discipline that Jerome McGann discusses in the 2011 issue of *Profession*. He argues, "In the near future, digital technology will supplant print-based technology as the medium of scholarly publication. This is not only a fact, it is a very good thing for scholarship and education, however awkward and painful the transition we are experiencing" (184). Students in the integrated literacies department will be well positioned to thrive in that scholarly landscape, even if their work does not focus on digital media per se.

Parallel Cultures Department

Integrating digital media into his scholarly professional identity has been a trickier enterprise for Cosmo, a PhD student in the parallel cultures department. The department generously funds the Center for Digital Media Studies, and although it is a teaching *and* research center, it has been viewed (and used) more as a resource center for digital teaching than for digital scholarship. Cosmo notes that this perception is beginning to change, as the CDMS director and the department chair are beginning to promote the CDMS differently; however, the CDMS's role as a center for support of digital pedagogy is still stressed. Though the CDMS has the potential to function as a research center for the parallel cultures department, at the time of my interviews it had not yet begun to fulfill that potential. Cosmo also notes the lack of seminars in which digital media are central. He says he would like to see "graduate courses taught in computer labs, well, taught in computer labs where the computers are actually used." He adds, "Even the [pedagogy class] that got me started wasn't really taught in a computer lab all the time because of its great size that year. So I really only had one class that was taught intensively in a computer lab environment where production was central." This reality—that no graduate seminar is required to include a digital production component—is evidence of the department's stance toward digital media in the program/curriculum: those professors who want to include digital media are certainly supported, but their courses are not a requirement in the way that the integrated literacies department's research colloquium with its focus on website production is a requirement.

Cosmo also touches on another related issue: the in-class structure supporting digital media production. He says he has had professors who have been open to students' doing alternative, digital projects in place of a final research paper, "but in some ways it's a project that is just in place of a print project and not integrated into the course. I've done that once or twice, but it's not nearly as powerful as taking a class that really centrally used the computers." Typically, students do digital media projects in courses specifically focused on digital media studies as a field. While professors in other fields might allow individuals to compose digital media projects in place of a seminar paper, they typically don't explore, as a class, the influence of digital media on that area of study or the potentials for it; thus, the project seems like an add-on rather than a fully integrated part of the class, and the reflection that Graupner, Nickoson-Massey, and Blair and Eyman, Sheffield, and DeVoss suggest should accompany digital production is absent. He notes, in addition, that graduate coursework is the perfect place "to build scholarly work that is maybe just a draft and just an experiment," which he sees as part of the goal of graduate coursework, "which is where you're supposed to create fake scholarly work, for the purposes of learning rather than for publication." Furthermore, he says that he doesn't have many models for this kind of scholarly work in digital media: "I mean, I definitely read *Kairos*, so I have some models, but I think that, within the department . . . I've just been trained very much to think of the print article, and it's a challenge to move beyond that. I want to, and I think I will, but I think I'm still in the moment of figuring that out."

Cosmo's graduate work has, not surprisingly, focused almost exclusively on analysis of digital texts from a variety of perspectives, which is common and encouraged in the department. But the production of scholarship—even scholarship focused on digital media—is by and large expected to be alphabetic and printed. The requirements for candidacy exams, dissertations, and the like discussed earlier reinforce this tension between essayistic analysis of digital texts and analytical digital production. This tension is played out not only in terms of research but also in teaching. In the parallel cultures department, teaching digital production is encouraged (and undergraduates are encouraged to create digital products that present critical analysis in alternative forms), and the CDMS supports teachers choosing to do it. It is likely, in the future, that such encouragement will ultimately extend to digital scholarly production by graduate students, and it is likely that the department's recent hires have the potential to increase graduate course offerings in digital media studies.

This tension between analysis and production is deeply entrenched in both scholarly and programmatic conversations, which tend to subordinate production to analysis. In scholarship in Cosmo's field of rhetoric and composition, analysis of digital texts typically has printed products as its outcome, and digital management also typically supports the production of traditional products. Even Adele notes that, often, digital media are seen as an enhancement: "Most people who have mentored me have pointed to the necessity of having that be one of the components of what I do and using it to enhance the things that I do." This "enhancement" attitude indicates that digital management and analysis of digital texts often support production in print, rather than lead to the production of scholarly texts in multiple media.

Part of the reason for the lack of formal programmatic integration in the parallel cultures department is the lack of faculty who integrate digital media into their own professional identities, which also influences informal mentoring in the department. According to the CDMS director, the support for digital media is in place. However, he adds, "we are unfortunately a little short-handed in terms of being able to mentor." He ties this to the larger departmental culture, saying, "I think it's a bigger-picture issue. We're a traditional department. Our reputation is that we're a traditional department." Because of that reputation, he says that the graduate students who apply and enroll do so "because they know of that traditional focus of the department." Consequently, "we're not getting many applicants, necessarily, who are interested in doing digital media studies." But the graduate student culture is directly related to the faculty culture. According to the CDMS director, of nearly 100 faculty members in the department, only 2 are invested in digital media research, "and one of those now is an administrator and isn't in the department very much at all and [is] very difficult to find time to work with." As a result, he says,

> you've got this bigger picture, where the department is very committed yet only has one faculty member doing research in digital media. That sends a message to the graduate students, then, who want to do work in digital media, [making them] probably a little apprehensive to want to come [here] to do that. So there are lots of opportunities to do that kind of work, but it can be difficult just because the size of the program right now is pretty small.

This state of affairs indicates the importance of informal mentoring from faculty to the professional development of PhDs, particularly when it comes to incorporating digital media into their professional identities.[5] This situation also reinforces the point that Graupner, Nickoson-Massey, and Blair make that integrating digital media into the curriculum should be the job of all faculty in a program, not "the role of the lone technology specialist in the doctoral program to prepare future faculty to teach and research in technological environments" (20). It also underscores their point that graduate students need exposure to digital media across their studies, not just here and there in specifically technically focused classes, if we are to enact a transformational model of digital media as opposed to seeing digital media as an add-on to traditional studies.

Luckily, the CDMS is set up so that graduate students become mentors for their peers as well as for their professors. (The pedagogical mentoring that the CDMS has established was described previously.) All three PhD students in the parallel cultures department who participated in this study—Cosmo, Chester, and Roxie—have worked in the CDMS, and they all attest to its importance in their pedagogical development. They don't locate scholarly mentoring there; however, Cosmo notes that his appointment in the CDMS "has definitely provided me a space to do even more multimodal composition that approaches something like research." While the CDMS has ventured into research—it has provided support and facilities for a summer colloquium for scholars in digital media studies, helped other programs in the department develop digital research materials, and hosted a panel presentation of research done by CDMS staff members, for instance—its reputation in the department is primarily that of a center for pedagogical support. Programmatic and informal mentoring are two sides of the same coin in the department when it comes to pedagogical professional development. And for students working in traditional areas and producing printed texts as scholarship, the department provides programmatic training through coursework and fellowship competitions as well as traditional mentoring structures such as exam and dissertation committees to encourage scholarly professional development. However, for students interested in producing digital media texts as scholarship, the department is still struggling to offer both programmatic and informal mentoring in digital media scholarship. The CDMS provides a structure in which both formal programmatic training and informal mentoring in digital media scholarship might be located and flourish, based upon the model of pedagogical training and mentoring that currently thrives there.

Cosmo is in a field—rhetoric and composition—in which pedagogical mentoring, with digital media or without, is a given and teaching methods and philosophies are constant subjects of conversation. It is not surprising that two composition professors, one whose research area is digital media and one whose research area is not digital media, were his pedagogical mentors. Because he works in the same field of study as the CDMS director and has had the experience of working in the CDMS, he also has received mentoring for doing digital media research in a way that is unlike the experience of most of the graduate students in the department. The CDMS director explains that "a lot of our graduate students come here to engage in some very traditional academic study programs," and if they don't see their mentors, "those faculty members they obviously came here to work with," being "really engaged in technology, it's not that nobody's necessarily discouraging them, but nobody's also encouraging them at the same time." He tries to invite students in all fields as much as he can to come to the CDMS and find out about the potential for digital media in pedagogy and research, but it can be difficult for some students to overcome the barrier of having few role models in their scholarly areas who engage in digital media scholarship.

Related to the centralization of peer mentors in the CDMS is the centralization of physical resources there, as well. The CDMS director notes that graduate students do not have access to good equipment in their offices and consequently are not encouraged enough to do innovative work with digital media:

> Unfortunately, the graduate students, in their offices, are provided
> with some of our most outdated technology. So, right off the bat

they're being sent a signal that I'm not really comfortable with and that is that because they're teaching freshman composition or second-year writing and because they're graduate students, then they are not worthy of good computer equipment, which certainly sets their attitude about why they should want to use technology in their research right now. Again, I think it's one of those issues that in this department, they're not seeing a lot of people who are doing that work in research with technology, and so they're just not aware of what the possibilities are at this point.

The centralization of computer equipment in the CDMS, then, while it fosters a community of teachers and scholars interested in digital media, also maintains the digital media community as a niche, located in a particular place. Those in the CDMS community argue that digital media is transformative, but because the CDMS is something of an add-on to the department, graduate students as a whole are encouraged to see digital media as, ultimately, an add-on or a tool that they can choose to use or not and the CDMS as a place they can choose to visit or not.

Although digital media are not being integrated into nontechnological courses in the parallel cultures department as much as they are in the integrated literacies department, the technological ecology of the parallel cultures department nonetheless enables safe spaces for collaborative digital media inquiry, through the CDMS. While digital media praxis (production with reflection) might be possible only in certain technologically focused courses, the CDMS is a sustainable community of practice that fosters both critical engagement and a rhetorical view of digital media production. Furthermore, it promotes reflection on many of the questions listed in tables 4.2 and 4.4 about the role of digital media in scholarship in all fields of English studies and encourages graduate students to consider ways that digital media might productively transform scholarship in the discipline.

Conclusion: Transforming Graduate Education/ Transforming English Studies

A point of tension in departments is the extent to which digital media production should be something that gets added to traditional pedagogies and scholarship or something that transforms such work. While some individuals in the print-centric department are adding digital media into their work, the department's technological ecology does not foster a culture of critical engagement with technology, nor does it encourage viewing digital media production as a rhetorical rather than an instrumental skill. Conversely, in the integrated literacies department, digital media are viewed as transformative; however, because of material constraints, it is difficult for individuals, especially graduate students, to put that philosophy fully into practice. Faculty and graduate students in the parallel cultures department are able to more fully transform their pedagogies because of the support offered by the CDMS and the investment in material technologies and spaces to encourage experimentation and the scholarship of teaching. Other types of digital media scholarship, however, are more difficult to engage in, primarily because the department as a whole is working from an additive model of digital media. Digital media studies has become an important field in the department, but it has simply been added into the mix of a department with many fields. Individually, the only field to approach digital media as transformative to the field is composition, evidenced by the graduate courses Cosmo has taken that specifically focus on digital media's role in the field, from both a scholarly and a pedagogical perspective.

That composition is the field approaching digital media as transformative is not surprising. This is the field that has been talking about multimodal composing in various forms now for several decades. And recently, the scholarly conversation has turned to the refashioning of MA and PhD programs in the field with digital media at the core. Graupner, Nickoson-Massey, and Blair, for example, argue that "in response to the need for professionalizing graduate students who are likely to work in a range of spaces, including digital environments, it is only fitting that programs take a multimodal approach to teaching and research" (13). They discuss the importance of both formal and informal "collaborative knowledge-making spaces" to the professional development of both graduate students and existing faculty and also stress the importance of specialists and nonspecialists working together toward the goal of professional development. The CDMS is a wonderful example of an entity that fosters such spaces.

In considering how to create a conscious culture of support for digital media, departments must face a range of tough questions about the role of digital media in their fields, specifically, and in the profession, generally. The questions introduced throughout this chapter in tables 4.1–4.4 are designed to facilitate discussions about the formal and informal structures necessary for sustaining a culture of support for digital media that is appropriate for the local context. These questions encourage faculty *and* graduate students, who must be a part of these discussions, to interrogate the support structures that helped them learn about digital media and continue to support their professional development in this area. These questions also prompt faculty and graduate students to articulate the role that digital media should play in their ongoing professional development (through curricular or other formalized structures or informal mentoring)—in other words, what the department's responsibility is and should be in actively supporting and encouraging professional development in digital media pedagogy and digital media research/scholarship. The core question underpinning all the others is whether digital media should be its own field, added into the mix of English studies, or if it should be integrated throughout the curriculum and throughout fields, transforming the profession.

This question is yet another manifestation of Ellen Cushman's concept of the hierarchy of signs and again indicates the importance of engaging in an open discussion about the transformative potential of digital media, not only to teaching and scholarship in the discipline but also to the structure of graduate programs themselves. When Cosmo says he would like to be able to safely experiment with digital media production in a class, thereby learning how to do digital scholarship without the pressure of publication interfering with his learning process, he hints at a broader discussion in the discipline about the role of graduate students' writing, particularly the dissertation. Sidonie Smith, former president of the MLA, asserts that despite the primary arguments for the current form of the dissertation, most dissertations are far from being a draft of a publishable book. Instead, they represent "a demonstration of expertise" and the habits of mind that characterize a sustained inquiry into a topic ("Agenda" 2). However, she argues forcefully for reconceptualizing the dissertation's form because of "the failure to attract diverse cohorts of students, the changes wrought by the digital revolution, the acknowledged limitations of overspecialization, and the imperative to rethink knowledge production in the context of our networked, globalized world," which increasingly calls for collaborative and public scholarship that she suggests the current model does not prepare students for ("Beyond" 2). She specifically suggests that the discipline consider new forms, asking, "Why should the dissertation remain inflexibly wedded to traditional book-culture formats?" ("Beyond" 2), and arguing that rather than focus on the form of the dissertation, we should focus on the scholarship enacted in it and the habits of mind it develops.

Scholarly habits of mind are intertwined with pedagogical habits of mind, and both must respond to the new literacy landscape. Smith writes:

> We will better prepare our graduate students to navigate a scholarly environment in which the modes of production are increasingly collaborative, the vehicles of scholarly dissemination increasingly interactive, the circulation of knowledge more openly accessible, and the audiences for which we compose purposefully varied. We will also better prepare them to develop supple and sophisticated pedagogies for teaching undergraduates whose habits of mind and attention, modes of learning, and repertoire of literacies are changing before us. ("Agenda" 2)

Such a transformation in the dissertation model (and by extension graduate education) goes hand in hand with transformations in teaching and scholarship necessitated by changes in the context of education and literacy brought about, in part, by digital media. If departments are to enact new models of graduate education and encourage new forms of knowledge making, they need to be intentional in creating technological ecologies that not only foster opportunities for professional development of graduate students and faculty in digital media but also make room for new forms of teaching and scholarship. The matrices of questions introduced throughout the last three chapters must thus be considered in concert with each other, and the next chapter draws connections among the three big questions that have organized this study across the three realms of work discussed—teaching, scholarship, and professional development—and provides models of practice that can illuminate a robust discussion of these issues.

Conclusion: The Future of Digital Media and/in English Studies—Models of Practice

> Peer review and other academic processes, such as promotion and tenure reviews, increasingly do not reflect the ways scholarship actually is conducted. In a climate in which the established methods of peer review are grounded in print-based publications, acknowledging and verifying scholarly contributions in unusual formats can be quite difficult. Where standards are not clearly defined, it is a challenge indeed to estimate the academic significance of digital works. This affects tenure, promotion, selection of new faculty, and other academic processes, as well.
> —*Horizon Report*

The 2006 *Horizon Report*, a collaboration between the New Media Consortium and the EDUCAUSE Learning Initiative, was published the same year as the "Report of the MLA Task Force on Evaluating Scholarship for Tenure and Promotion." It "describes the continuing work of the NMC's Horizon Project, a research oriented effort that seeks to identify and describe emerging technologies likely to have a large impact on teaching, learning, or creative expression within higher education" (3). In addition to describing the technological trends that will affect colleges and universities (for example, social computing and personal broadcasting), the report also "for the first time this year . . . explicitly identified and considered many challenges facing higher education" over the next five years (4). The report presents five challenges listed in "rank order," the first of which is peer review and other academic processes. Other challenges include pedagogical issues (for example, teaching information literacy) and problems that are not specific to the academy but affect academic discourse (for example, intellectual property concerns) (4).

The report does not specifically describe how the emerging technologies listed might impact peer review and other academic processes but instead focuses on their "relevance for teaching, learning, and creative expression," speculating about the potential applications of each technology in the classroom and in research/scholarship.

The fact that the report does not consider the specific impact on promotion and tenure or hiring processes is not surprising because those academic processes are so dependent, as the preceding chapters have demonstrated, upon local context. Furthermore, as the preceding chapters have argued, those processes are complicated by individuals' departmental and disciplinary locations, identifications, and affiliations. In addition to professional identifications and affiliations, part of the difficulty affecting the evaluation of digital media work is finding models of what that work looks like and how that work could be evaluated. As the *Horizon Report* notes, standards are often not clearly defined; however, it is difficult to define new standards in the absence of a test case. It is these two questions—What might new models of scholarship look like? Who is doing such work now?—that can help the discipline understand the implications for revising tenure and promotion policy, training teachers to use digital media in their classes, and generally supporting all kinds of digital media work in a variety of fields. Through a series of case studies, this book has sought to describe some of the work that is being done and what some new models of scholarship and teaching might look like.

Furthermore, digital media have revealed some of the ways that scholarship, teaching, and service overlap, bringing into full relief the issues that Ernest Boyer raised in 1997 about the narrow and inflexible definition of scholarship and the problem of evaluating a range of intellectual work (work that is often not easily categorized under current tenure and promotion paradigms). Toby's website for training professional writing TAs is a great example of a "problematic" project, problematic not primarily because it involves digital media production but because it crosses the categories of "teaching" and "service" (at least as the print-centric department defines those categories). However, it also fits into Boyer's categories of the scholarship of integration and the scholarship of teaching. Under the print-centric department's definition of scholarship (which most closely resembles Boyer's category of the scholarship of discovery), though, it simply does not fit.

Boyer further asserts that higher education is stuck in a rhetorical battle between the "competing goals" of teaching and research and argues that our restricted view of the nature of scholarship needs to be broadened, helping us to break out of the teaching versus research debate and view scholarship as composed of a variety of functions and activities. Digital media scholars are also caught in the middle of two sets of competing goals in their departments and disciplines: innovation and replication. Faculty are always seeking to innovate in their fields, but the conservative nature of tenure and promotion combined with the slow rate of institutional change ensures that departmental and disciplinary values are replicated. These innovations and replications happen differently in the three departments in this study and point to the ways in which they have responded to the three "big questions" that digital media work has forced the discipline to (re)consider: what counts as a text, how should we approach the reading of texts, and how should we approach the production of texts?

Departmental responses to these questions, though rarely explicit, can be read in the ways they position themselves in the discipline and in how individuals within each department position themselves in both their department and their field. The stances departments take can be understood through multiple elements:

- *Official policy.* One example of how departments create official policies on digital media is through their tenure and promotion policies that are laid out in print. Both the parallel cultures department and integrated literacies department have written guidelines about publication expectations for tenure and promotion that explicitly reference medium of publication. These policies thus foster an environment that encourages particular types of publication and inquiry at the expense of others, at least until individuals are tenured. Both departments have begun discussing ways to make their policies more "friendly" to digital media scholarship, but their examples show that it is a complicated process involving local considerations of scholarly and disciplinary values.
- *The chair's leadership.* Though I don't mean to claim that the department chair "speaks for" all members of the department, he or she does set a tone for the manner in which digital media are or can be discussed or approached. In the parallel cultures department, for instance, the chair is open about her digital media use and promotes the Center for Digital Media Studies in the department and in the university and thus sets the tone that digital media work is something not only appropriate to English studies but an integral part of it. In contrast, the chair of the

print-centric department focuses on the question of the appropriateness of digital texts as objects of analysis, which occludes considerations of questions about reading/scholarly methods and textual production.

- *Other digital media leaders.* Individuals who also influence the environment or culture in a department regarding digital media are faculty who are digital media leaders, such as the integrated literacies department's graduate director (a tenured member of the faculty and recognized scholar in his field) and the parallel cultures department's CDMS director (also tenured and a recognized scholar in his field, as well as in an administrative leadership position). These individuals can help shape not only faculty perceptions but also the chair's discourse on digital media by making digital media scholarship and teaching visible and by being technological activists within a department.

- *Public forums for digital scholarship and teaching.* Lectures, symposia, workshops, regular visiting scholars programs, and the like focusing on digital media contribute to creating an open environment for the discussion of pedagogical approaches and challenges relating to digital media and teaching, as well as for local sharing of new scholarly forms and practices.

- *Curricula and course requirements.* The way a department institutionalizes digital media studies as a field through its curricula also says a lot about how it sees digital media fitting into the larger discipline. The integrated literacies department, for instance, is trying to integrate digital media coursework throughout the curriculum by not only having courses focused primarily on digital media but also by integrating discussions of digital media into its core graduate curriculum, such as its required pedagogy and methodology courses. On the other hand, the print-centric department's curriculum is set up to make studying digital media through coursework difficult, if not impossible, sending a message that digital media scholarship and teaching are fringe elements of English studies.

- *Facilities and opportunities.* Physical technologies and technological support are, of course, important. But often more important (and more lacking) are spaces and moments in which to talk about best practices for using those tools. Ava, for instance, laments that in the integrated literacies department, they "never talk about teaching." For her, it's about more than just learning or teaching people how to use a specific technology. The model of the CDMS in the parallel cultures department demonstrates that having the space to share ideas and experiment is crucial to sustaining ongoing conversations about the place of digital media within the department and to thinking through the role of digital media in the larger discipline.

- *Mentoring.* Mentoring can be one way to create opportunities for such talk. It can be formalized through coursework and workshops, as in the integrated literacies department, or it can be a combination of informal and formal, as in the parallel cultures department, where the CDMS encourages and sustains various types of mentoring.

The different positions that these departments take (whether explicit and intentional or not) demonstrate the complexity of local culture on questions about digital media, and it follows that the "big questions" referenced above need to be answered within these overlapping communities of field/discipline and department, paying attention not only to local institutional contexts but also to wider scholarly and pedagogical concerns.

To this end, I have introduced a matrix of questions and argued for the intentional creation of technological ecologies, or at the very least conversations about these issues so that English departments can respond to the paradigm shift the *Horizon Report* describes and can recognize a wider variety of work in a wider variety of media as part of our discipline while maintaining shared values. In other words, departments need to seriously consider how to define core terms, such as scholarship, in ways that are relevant to the current literacy and media landscape that is the backdrop for our work.

An important aspect of this landscape is the economic viability/ sustainability (or lack thereof) of the traditional model of academic publishing. Stanford University president John L. Hennessy notes that we have "backed ourselves into" a model of publishing that relies on publishing houses, "which are limited in their ability to publish something because of the number of dollars they can afford to lose per publication." He further argues that relying on the publishers "for the way we look at the quality of our colleagues' work doesn't make any sense. . . . We have to think outside the box here" (qtd. in "Cost Death of Academic Publishing" n. pag.). The "Report of the MLA Task Force on Evaluating Scholarship for Tenure and Promotion" makes a similar call, noting that "the MLA survey further documents that the demands placed on candidates for tenure, especially demands for publication, have been expanding in kind and increasing in quantity," even as publishing outlets have been shrinking and "universities have lowered or eliminated subsidies for scholarly presses and libraries have dramatically reduced their purchases of books in the humanities." Furthermore, the report notes that "despite a worsening climate for book publication, the monograph has become increasingly important in comparison with other forms of publication" (10). The report offers several recommendations to deal with the situation, among which is the well-known and often-repeated call for the profession to "develop a more capacious conception of scholarship by rethinking the dominance of the monograph, promoting the scholarly essay, establishing multiple pathways to tenure, and using scholarly portfolios" (11). A related recommendation charges the profession with recognizing and creating standards for evaluating digital scholarship.

The MLA's call for a flexible, "more capacious" definition of scholarship has implications not just for promotion and tenure procedures and for scholarly communication but also for graduate and undergraduate education. As Sidonie Smith's remarks about rethinking the dissertation suggest, these areas are all interconnected. Scholarship in the discipline influences what graduate students are taught and the genres of writing they are expected to produce (for example, the dissertation monograph). Likewise, scholarly findings, particularly in pedagogy, often influence the way that undergraduate programs are structured. Such interconnectedness underpins recent comments by Ohio State University president E. Gordon Gee and provost Joseph Alutto about broadening the criteria for promotion to full professor. They argue that there should be different paths to promotion, or as Gee famously puts it, "multiple paths to salvation." Alutto states that faculty often "contribute to their disciplines and the university in unique and powerful ways other than—or in addition to—traditional research" ("Different Paths" n. pag.). Consequently, universities need to find ways to fairly value multiple contributions of faculty.

Models for evaluating broadened notions of professional contributions already exist. As mentioned previously, Boyer promotes a redefinition of scholarship to include four overlapping functions—discovery, integration, application, and teaching—which he argues better represent the scope of work faculty do and create space for valuing a greater variety of work and different types of contributions. When it comes to broadening the definition of scholarship to include digital media work, James P. Purdy and Joyce R. Walker offer a way of thinking about the scholarly activities that texts enact, which can be applied to a range of professional texts. Likewise, John Unsworth provides a heuristic for analyzing and evaluating the work that goes into digital media projects: the "scholarly primitives" of discovering, annotating, comparing, referring, sampling, illustrating, and representing. All of these models can help departments conceive of evaluation criteria that focus not only on published texts but also on other kinds of texts/objects and bodies of work, including digital media work.

Rethinking needs to happen at the department level. Not everybody in an English department needs to do digital media scholarship or teach digital media in his or her classes, but everybody has to engage with the issues in order to create cultures of support or technological ecologies that value and create space/opportunities for such work. The matrix of questions I propose can help frame discussions in local contexts about scholarship as well as about other areas to develop technological ecologies that make sense for local contexts. Examples of practice can help illuminate and spark discussion of the issues raised by the matrix of questions. Throughout the book I have provided examples from the data I have collected. However, in this chapter I present a variety of examples drawn from published scholarship and provide screen captures of some of the work to help those who are not very familiar with digital media scholarship and teaching better visualize the kind of work that is happening now. As Cheryl E. Ball notes, there is a distinction between scholarship that utilizes mainly printed forms (use of primarily alphabetic text, linear text, and argumentation) and what she terms digital media scholarship (and others term multimodal scholarship), which is scholarship that uses multiple modes and is not linear in nature ("Show, Not Tell"). In the following sections, I am chiefly concerned with this multimodal/digital media scholarship, rather than with more traditional scholarship that just happens to be disseminated online.

Models of Scholarly Practice

Peer-Reviewed Digital Publication

There are numerous examples of scholarship that utilize new media to make arguments multimodally or to disseminate scholarly arguments more quickly than is possible with print. Several online and open-access, peer-reviewed journals, in particular, have emerged to publish multimodal scholarship, and outlets are beginning to emerge for digital projects that have the intellectual equivalent of a book. The Computers and Composition Digital Press, for instance, is a venue for publishing digital books with multimedia components. It is an online, open-access, peer-reviewed imprint of Utah State University Press. According to its mission statement, the press

> is committed to publishing innovative, multimodal digital projects. The Press will also publish e-books (print texts in electronic form available for reading online or for downloading); however, we are particularly interested in digital projects that cannot be printed on paper, but that have the same intellectual heft as a book. The goal of the Press is to honor the traditional academic values of rigorous peer review and intellectual excellence, but also to combine such work with a commitment to innovative digital scholarship and expression. (n. pag.)

Several projects have been released, including *Technological Ecologies and Sustainability* (edited by Dànielle Nicole DeVoss, Heidi A. McKee, and Richard Selfe) in 2009 and *Generaciones' Narratives* (by John Scenters-Zapico) in 2010. *Technological Ecologies and Sustainability* is a collection of essays about creating sustainable technological ecologies for digital media teaching and research. *Generaciones' Narratives* is a single-authored study of literacy practices of people living on the US-Mexico border. Both are available as PDFs. Because of the PDF format, authors are able to include multimedia elements, such as sound, video (for example, interviews), and full-color images that are either prohibitively expensive or impossible in print formats (fig. 5.1).

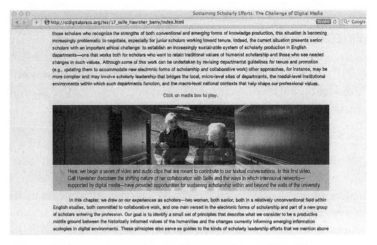

Figure 5.1. Screen capture from Selfe, Hawisher, and Berry's "Sustaining Scholarly Efforts," the final chapter of *Technological Ecologies and Sustainability* (ed. DeVoss, McKee, and Selfe), which utilizes multimedia elements, such as the video pictured here, that contribute to and reinforce the textual arguments

The press might raise eyebrows when viewed from a traditional paradigm because of its commitment to digital projects and open access. This might be partly because, as previously mentioned, digital projects, particularly ones that utilize multimodal elements in addition to or in place of words to make arguments, are often misunderstood. Additionally, it might be difficult for some to determine if a digital project has the equivalent intellectual "heft" of a book. However, CCDP's goal is to use familiar structures from traditional publishing, such as peer review, an editorial board, and a university imprint, to help ensure that the scholarship is sound. Furthermore, in an audio editorial statement, Lewis Ulman and Dickie Selfe explain that two of the larger goals of the press are to "create a tool that suggests a new paradigm for scholarly publishing" and to "change the economics of distribution while maintaining peer review." As others have pointed out, because of dwindling university support for their presses, often market concerns outweigh scholarly concerns in the consideration of book manuscripts. The CCDP provides an "outside the box" (but not *too* outside the box) model of the sort Hennessy calls for. Furthermore, it models a way for the discipline to resee the paradigm of scholarly publishing, addressing many of the questions raised in chapter 3 about the scholarly publishing of digital media scholarship, particularly the issue of peer review.

In addition to "book-heft" projects, much multimodal scholarship published online is comparable in scope to a scholarly essay in a peer-reviewed journal. An online, peer-reviewed journal that has established a strong reputation for publishing multimodal scholarship, particularly in the field of rhetoric and composition, is *Kairos: A Journal of Rhetoric, Technology, and Pedagogy*. It is difficult to represent the texts published in *Kairos* appropriately in the static black-and-white medium of the page, and I encourage readers to explore the journal online to get a feel for the ways different authors use multimedia to help make their arguments. However, I have included several screen captures to show a range of ways that individual scholars are using digital media in the production of scholarship.

Figure 5.2 shows a screen capture from a portion of Susan Delagrange's "*Wunderkammer*, Cornell, and the Visual Canon of Arrangement," which takes advantage of the multimedia aspects of online publication. The navigation in the text is represented by different colored boxes across the top of the screen, and the reader is able to navigate linearly or nonlinearly through the text. Below the navigation element, on the right-hand side, is a scrollable box of text analyzing the video element on the left. In a text about the making of this webtext, Delagrange argues that "the *Wunderkammer* serves as an ideal trope for the process of intellectual inquiry.

And interactive electronic media constitute an ideal environment in which to design both the structure and activity of a digital *Wunderkammer*" ("When Revision is Redesign" n. pag.). She further explains that she wanted the text itself to operate as a *Wunderkammer*, or cabinet of curiosities, "which would function as a thought engine in which the manipulation and arrangement of its contents by both collector/designer and visitor/viewer animates the process of inquiry and insight" ("When Revision is Redesign" n. pag.). Moreover, she asserts that she wanted the experience of the reader to be like that of exploring a *Wunderkammer*, and the design of the text certainly creates that experience for readers.

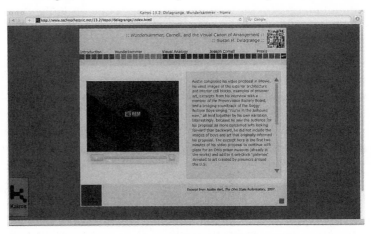

Figure 5.2. Screen capture from Delagrange's "*Wunderkammer*, Cornell, and the Visual Canon of Arrangement"

Delagrange also addresses the theory-techné connection that often characterizes digital media scholarship. As Ellen Cushman and Robert Scholes have both noted, theory and techné—or the productive arts—are often split in English departments. Similarly, much traditional scholarship focuses on the theory side of the binary, but much digital media scholarship involves engaging in both. Delagrange reflects on this connection in her own work:

> As the writer/designer of this webtext, which reflects on the redesign of "*Wunderkammer*, Cornell, and the Visual Canon of Arrangement," I am my own first audience, and from my perspective, this reflection enriches both my practice and understanding of composing digital scholarship. *Techné* is a making, and involves knowledge in the hand and knowledge in the head. Knowledge in the hand comes from practice and experience, knowledge in the

head from reflection on causes and effects; shaping this webtext helps me become a better, more aware practitioner of my visual/ verbal/interactive art. While treated separately here, the categories I've discussed are always in play together in a productive oscillation of thinking and doing, making and remaking. It is also important to keep in mind that *techné* is neither intuitive nor innate. Because it encompasses the why as well as the how, it can be taught, and composing this reflective webtext helps me become a better teacher. ("When Revision Is Redesign" n. pag.)

Her reflection helps us remember that there is a theory-techné connection/split not only in scholarship, as well as in English studies, but also in teaching. Many of the examples in this chapter, as well as throughout the book, help to demonstrate that digital media work is a site of reconciliation of these two terms. This blending of scholarship and teaching must be recognized in order for the full force of digital media work to be appreciated.

Anthony Ellertson's "Some Notes on Simulacra Machines, Flash in FYC & Tactics in Spaces of Interruption" looks completely different from Delagrange's text and incredibly different from any printed text. Figure 5.3 shows a screen capture of the main page of Ellertson's text, which employs many moving and interactive parts. In the middle of the screen is a scrollable box of text explaining the exigency of the piece. All of the other "pages" have similar boxes of text (sometimes one, sometimes two) that use words to advance Ellertson's arguments. At the top left is a little vertical rectangle that, when clicked, causes a movie to become visible. The same icon is on some other pages and, when clicked, reveals different movies that add pieces of Ellertson's argument. Near the bottom are two scrolling bars, one scrolling from left to right and one scrolling from right to left, that offer provocative statements that relate to his arguments. Finally, at the bottom, are two navigational elements: left and right arrows to move linearly through the "pages" and a pop-up, filmstrip-like menu that allows for nonlinear browsing.

A third example of digital media scholarship is Joyce Walker's "Hyper. Activity." Her text takes the trifold brochure as its jumping-off point in terms of visual design, and it refashions each panel as a fully scrollable and changeable space, taking advantage of the affordances of the online medium (fig. 5.4). Through its content, her text advances an argument about the process of composing a new media text versus composing a printed text. Additionally, though, through its design, her text also points out that new media challenge our thinking about what constitutes a scholarly form or genre.

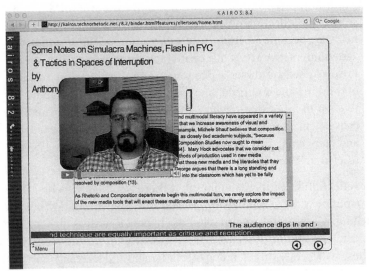

Figure 5.3. Screen capture from Ellertson's "Some Notes on Simulacra Machines, Flash in FYC & Tactics in Spaces of Interruption"

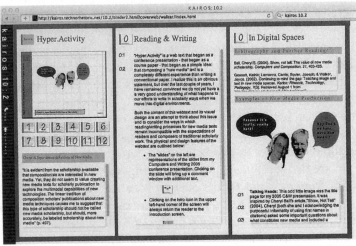

Figure 5.4. Screen capture from Walker's "Hyper.Activity"

Examples of digital media scholarship in literary studies are more difficult to find. A great deal of literary scholarship that appears online is styled much like printed text, often presented as a long, scrolling page of text or as a PDF file. Some of the texts do include some multimedia elements, such as images that can be enlarged for examination or links to primary and other texts archived online. For the most part, however, literary scholarship published in online, peer-reviewed journals does not experiment with form in the way the other texts discussed here do. Some online journals in literary fields point to the future of literary scholarship in digital media and state that they will accept born-digital scholarship (such as *Poetess Archive Journal*); however, as of this writing, I am aware of no such scholarship having been published. What some of the journals do offer, however, is an online space in which scholars can access and discuss essays appearing in the journal. *Victorians Institute Journal*, for instance, maintains a "Digital Annex" that allows registered users to discuss articles and digital supplements to the printed journal, offering a robust model for postpublication, crowd-sourced peer reviewing of academic work by scholars in the field.

As these few examples demonstrate, digital media scholarship is not all the same, even in the same field; it can look and function differently from piece to piece, which can raise questions for evaluators, who are accustomed to scholarship that "looks" a particular way. However, the models for reading/evaluating the digital media work cited above can help us to resee scholarship and read the ways that such texts enact scholarship. They can also help us imagine new models of scholarly communication and peer review of our research, moving toward a model of a digital commons.

Besides a lack of understanding of how to read digital scholarship, some argue that colleagues outside of digital fields have difficulty understanding the physical work put into digital media scholarship. Helen J. Burgess and Jeanne Hamming argue that

> while traditional ideas of what "counts" as scholarship continue to privilege content over form, intellectual labor over physical labor, and print over digital media, new media's functional (and in some cases even biological) difference from old media contributes to a double erasure, for scholars working in multimedia, of both their intellectual contributions and their material labor. (n. pag.)

Furthermore, they argue that "scholarly media restructure intellectual work" and have the potential to take radical, performative, physically embodied forms. They conclude, "The multimedia scholar, by taking seriously the materiality of knowledge production, embodies an intellectual identity that is dispersed over material, rhetorical, and technical networks—a crucial transformation that must be acknowledged when assessing 'what counts' as scholarly activity in the academy" (n. pag.).

There are ways to address this "erasure" or lack of understanding. Delagrange's essay about her redesign process in the "*Wunderkammer*" text provides a model for scholars to reflect on and address questions about their rhetorical choices and to make visible the work—both intellectual and material—put into their scholarship. In addition to theorizing the practice of redesign through her experience, Delagrange engages in the kind of reflection I suggest in the section of the matrix that proposes questions for individuals. Such reflection is important not just for digital media scholarship but for all scholarship. It should be just as important to understand why a scholar chooses the print format as it is to understand why a scholar chooses a digital/multimodal form or a performance, and space should be created for scholars to engage in this reflection, whether in published forms or other ways, such as in tenure and promotion dossiers.

These examples focus on publishing in the field of rhetoric and composition primarily because there are few outlets for scholars creating digital scholarship in literary fields. *Digital Humanities Quarterly* claims to publish "a wide range of peer-reviewed materials," including "experiments in interactive media." However, as of this writing, no such experiments had been published, and most of the texts were print-styled essays. This is not to say *DHQ* will not publish such texts in the future; and it is hard to say if none have been published because nobody has created them or for some other reason. But *Kairos* and the CCDP can serve as models for other fields to create sustainable venues for digital media scholarship.

Digital Scholarly Projects

In addition to multimodal texts, much digital scholarship exists in the form of scholarly projects, which are not as explicitly analytical in nature as the works in the previous section; however, as "curating" or textual editing projects, they are just as valuable scholarly endeavors and should be considered scholarship. As explored in chapter 3, digital media offer the potential for creating scholarly projects that are not published in the traditional sense through an established peer-reviewed venue but are distributed online. One such project is the Digital Library of Illuminated Manuscripts (fig. 5.5). The library is hosted by Lehigh University's digital library and allows other libraries to digitize their collections and submit them, enabling "institutions that may have only one or a few of these documents to participate in a digital project without the need for them to develop the technology or expertise to support such an effort. Through the power of the Internet these locally known resources will be made accessible to an international audience" ("About the Project" n. pag.). Visitors can browse collections or search across works by manuscript type, country of origin, century, and type of decoration. Finally, the Digital Library of Illuminated Manuscripts provides an example course assignment that utilizes the collections.

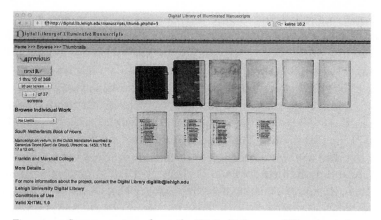

Figure 5.5. Screen capture from the Digital Library of Illuminated Manuscripts

A similar project in the field of literacy studies is the Digital Archive of Literacy Narratives (fig. 5.6). According to its website, the DALN "is a publicly available archive of personal literacy narratives in a variety of formats (text, video, audio) that together provide a historical record of the literacy practices and values of contributors, as those practices and values change" (n. pag.). This project is, in Jay David Bolter and Richard Grusin's terms, "remediating" literacy research and creating the conditions for nonacademics to become a part of the research process. It is also a tool that other academic researchers can use to explore questions about literacy.

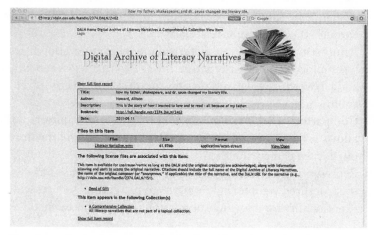

Figure 5.6. Screen capture from the Digital Archive of Literacy Narratives

Some might be tempted to view these two projects as merely a problem of coding or design and not as research or scholarship. They don't involve the production of a linear critical analysis of a set of texts, for instance, which is instantly recognizable in English studies as scholarship (though they certainly can be used by scholars as data for such a project). But if we separate our notion of scholarly activity from scholarly products, we can analyze the character of the work involved in creating something like the DALN or the Digital Archive of Illuminated Manuscripts and see the scholarliness of that work. Unsworth posits the idea of scholarly "primitives," referring to "basic functions common to scholarly activity across disciplines, over time, and independent of theoretical orientation," which "form the basis for higher-level scholarly projects, arguments, statements, and interpretations." His list, as noted above, includes discovering, annotating, comparing, referring, sampling, illustrating, and representing. He argues that "these activities are basic to scholarship across eras and across media," and he uses them to analyze the scholarliness of a digital literary archive (n. pag.). In other words, Unsworth, like Purdy and Walker, focuses on the activities a scholar engages in to create a piece of scholarship (scholarly composing processes, if you will), as opposed to the mediated outcome of that work alone.

In the example of the DALN, which is in many ways like a scholarly electronic edition, the builders of the site, the "editorial board," would need to engage in several (if not all) of the scholarly primitives (which overlap somewhat with Boyer's activity categories):

- Discovering—creating the conditions for academic and non-academic researchers to engage in the scholarship of discovery through the design of its database
- Annotating—building a theoretical model of annotation that can be employed consistently across the site so that users can either add keywords to their submissions or use keywords to search submissions
- Comparing—building a model of searching and an interface that allows scholars to find texts that are similar to each other for the purpose of comparing them
- Representing—creating both structured (collections) and unstructured ways for submissions to be represented; creating functionality for allowing submissions in multiple formats

All of these activities have both theoretical and technical sides to them. In the case of representation, for instance, displaying the structure visually through the web browser is a technical problem, but designing the structure to be displayed is a scholarly question that must take into account the type of data that is being collected and the potential research questions to be asked of that data, which is intimately connected not only to a knowledge of the history of the field of literacy studies but also of the methods valued by that field and of a sense of where the field is headed. Likewise, for the Digital Library of Illuminated Manuscripts to be a useful resource for researchers, its editors would have to contend with similar questions. As it stands now, the library is more of a resource for teaching and a collection of interesting texts than it is a scholarly tool because of its small size (only nine manuscripts and only octavo size or smaller are accepted) and the lack of a robust searching and annotation model that is informed by scholarly work in the field, as the DALN has. However, looking at the DALN as a model, one can certainly imagine the possibilities.

One of the problems associated with such projects is, of course, the issue of peer review. Because these types of projects usually do not (and because of their very nature, cannot) go through traditional publication channels, it is often difficult for them to be appropriately evaluated by tenure and promotion committees used to the stamp-of-approval peer-review offers. However, scholars in several fields are working to create alternative models of peer review to ameliorate this situation. NINES (Networked Infrastructure for Nineteenth-Century Electronic Scholarship), for instance, "is a scholarly organization devoted to forging links between the material archive of the nineteenth century and the digital research environment of the twenty-first" (n. pag.). One of its goals is "to serve as a peer-reviewing body for digital work in the long 19th century (1770–1920), British and American" (n. pag.). In addition, it develops "software tools for new and traditional forms of research and critical analysis" (n. pag.). Not only does NINES collect, make available, and peer review work existing on the web, but it also provides an authoring space and research tools to support best practices in the field.

As Susan Schreibman, Laura Mandell, and Stephen Olsen note, many digital projects, particularly the development of software programs or archives that enable certain types of research, are often considered and evaluated as service, but in fact they are scholarship, and organizations like NINES can help to make visible (through careful peer review) the ways these projects engage in interpretation and advance literary (or rhetorical) scholarship. They argue, furthermore, that such work "is essential to literary study in the digital age" (125), adding that

> our discipline needs to draw more subtle distinctions between what
> counts as research and what counts as service. Indeed, if we do not
> come to terms with these new forms of scholarship we risk discour-
> aging junior scholars from digital pursuits and ghettoizing or even
> losing new talent and knowledge that the profession needs for the
> future.... To put this in less dramatic terms, the digital revolution
> requires us as a profession to make conscious the motivations and
> the values inhering in material practices, from putting a manuscript
> in the mail to a publisher to requiring for tenure "a book between
> covers." We must transfer the values informing these activities and
> practices onto new modes of activity, so that we understand, value,
> and evaluate theoretical decisions about database modeling, algo-
> rithms, and information flows to best support new research and
> reading practices. (126)

One of the methods the authors suggest for helping the field understand
the scholarliness of digital projects is for individuals to experience creating them. In a workshop, they made the discouraging discovery that
"evaluators who were not themselves creators of digital scholarship found
it extremely challenging to see how technical decisions are theoretically
informed and constitute research-supported argumentation" (128).

Besides engaging in digital artifact creation, the theory-techné connection could be explored using models such as Unsworth's to help us
discuss systematically such works and understand the academic/scholarly
processes that go into creating various forms of scholarship, aiding us in
focusing less on the form of final products and more on the intellectual
work that goes into producing them. Unsworth's work provides a new way
of understanding scholarship that concentrates on characterizing scholarly *activity*, which should be the focus of any assessment of scholarship.
Such a focus allows departments to value multiple methods and multiple
forms without sacrificing scholarly excellence or any quality indicators
that departments set up. The matrix of questions I have proposed about
scholarly textuality can be used by departments to determine the shared
values and quality indicators for scholarship that make sense in their local
contexts. Because these projects are also teaching tools, not just research
tools, they bring into relief issues about the categorization of professional
work that Boyer raises and reinforce the need to measure the "impact" of
work in broader terms, as Gee and Alutto propose. As Boyer specifically
advocates and Gee and Alutto's comments suggest, in some cases teaching
and service activities should be evaluated as scholarship. Developing effective digital pedagogies based on the most up-to-date research about best

practices involves a great deal of scholarly activity and often the creation of sophisticated digital texts for students' use, which requires a strong technological ecology to support instructors in doing such work.

A Model of Pedagogical Practice for Literature Classes

Without a strong technological ecology, it can be difficult for instructors to resee their teaching in a way that allows them to incorporate digital media effectively. This can be especially true for faculty in literary studies, where examples of digital media pedagogies are still emerging. Most of the examples presented in previous chapters have focused on teaching writing, but there are some examples of new media pedagogies in literature classes. For instance, Lis Lindeman and Gregory O. Smith have published a multimedia piece arguing for the importance of incorporating digital media into literature classes and describing the ways they use digital illumination in their classes. They argue that, instead of making obsolete the study of the printed text, "the book that 'becomes' digital or takes advantage of new media can be restored, with expanded relevance, to a worldwide audience, including today's literature students" (n. pag.). A screen capture from their webtext shows an image of a traditional illumination from the Book of Kells next to a hypertext illumination of T. S. Eliot's *The Waste Land* (fig. 5.7). They explain that the hypertext illumination "utilizes a separate window to gloss the text and provide supplemental information based on the links the reader selects. This kind of project, like the genealogy, guides the reader by revealing aspects of the text previously obscured or unknown" (n. pag.).

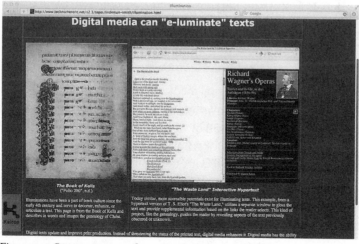

Figure 5.7. Screen capture from Lindeman and Smith's "Literature and Digital Illumination"

This type of project might raise eyebrows for traditionalists because hypertext coding is not seen as reading or writing in the traditional literary senses of analyzing and interpreting a text and communicating that interpretation through the written word. However, such work is interpretive and analytical, as well as productive (in the sense of producing a text). Lindeman and Smith explain:

> Digital texts update and improve print production. Instead of threatening the status of the printed text, digital media enhances it. Digital media has the ability to turn a two-dimensional work into a multidimensional one. Readers can easily move back and forth between the primary source and the historical, philosophical, and aesthetic backgrounds that inform it. Digital "e-lumination," therefore, provides a rich textual layering that students would normally overlook because of difficulty in locating all the materials. This type of work encourages students to use the resources on the Internet to gain a better understanding of the background of the text, the allusions therein, and the work's later relevance and influence. "E-lumination" requires students to make choices about the most important aspects of the texts to explore, along with the best way to do so. Digital media allows students to enhance their readings and think critically through the examination of others' illuminated texts and the creation of their own. (n. pag.)

Such projects clearly connect to the goals of literary study even though they utilize new methods and media. Furthermore, Lindeman and Smith argue persuasively that such projects have the potential to increase student engagement with literature.

Models of Practice for Sustainable Professional Development in Digital Media

In addition to examples of digital media pedagogies and spaces/forums in which to talk with others about developing such pedagogies, faculty need ongoing professional development opportunities to support their continuing pedagogical growth, as technologies and best practices change. Though the *Horizon Report* discusses the future of technologies for teaching and learning, it does not mention how teachers are supposed to learn how to teach with these technologies. Teaching teachers to teach with digital media is important and complicated, but models of practice for professional development with digital media are often not visible outside of local departments; in addition, this work is typically not recognized as having a broad, let alone scholarly, impact. However, one example of such a program that has had such impact is the Ohio State University English department's Digital Media and Composition (DMAC) Institute. DMAC is a two-week-long intensive institute in which participants learn about best practices in digital media pedagogy for composition classes and have the opportunity to create media-rich projects, such as audio and video compositions and webtexts. According to the DMAC website, "The goal of DMAC is to suggest and encourage innovative rhetorically-based approaches to composing that students and faculty can use as they employ digital media in support of their own educational and professional goals, in light of the specific context at their home institutions and within their varied personal experiences" (n. pag.). Most departments won't be able to host something like DMAC; however, they can incorporate some of DMAC's elements into their technological ecologies: providing funds for faculty/graduate students to attend DMAC or other digital media retreats, hosting visiting speakers, offering small workshops or one-day retreats for faculty, having regular discussions about digital media pedagogy and/or research, and presenting showcases of digital media work.

The integrated literacies and parallel cultures departments provide two different models for offering professional development opportunities focused on digital media for teachers at all levels, not only TAs. Both programs recognize that it takes time and ongoing support not only to learn to use digital media but also to learn how to incorporate such work into teaching; they structure that time and support in different ways, however. The integrated literacies department provides training integrated into coursework, whereas the parallel cultures department offers a community-based peer support model.

The two department models and DMAC suggest a list of elements that are necessary for fostering the professional development of teachers comfortable with digital media pedagogy:

- A fully integrated pedagogy class for incoming TAs. This offers a space to imagine the possibilities for digital pedagogy.
- A second pedagogy/teaching methods class that could be integrated with digital media if the graduate student were interested. This would require faculty who regularly teach undergraduate classes in computer classrooms. It offers a space to learn hands-on about digital pedagogy and to see it modeled.
- The ability for teachers at all ranks (MA, PhD, lecturer, tenure track, tenured) to teach in computer classrooms. This requires computer classrooms and technological infrastructure. It offers a space to experiment with digital pedagogy.

- Support people to consult about pedagogy and to call upon for classroom assistance. A centralized location for this kind of interaction, such as in the CDMS, helps create a community that can provide ongoing support and encouragement. Such consultants need to be knowledgeable about hardware/software issues (for example, which buttons to press) as well as about theoretical/methodological issues so that the technology never precedes the pedagogy.
- Up-to-date computer technology in both graduate student and faculty offices with the highest-end computer technology centrally available to all. This provides spaces to learn, practice, and experiment with specific applications either alone or in groups without overburdening the budget by "duplicating" the most expensive technologies or restricting access to them.
- Regular workshops and ongoing professional development activities such as discussion groups, reading/writing groups, or research colloquia that could carry credit (for graduate students) or release time (for faculty). This provides spaces to learn, practice, and experiment with applications and to develop digital pedagogies and scholarly works/agendas. It also provides space and time for learning communities to develop.
- Special awards for digital media innovation in teaching and release time (or fellowships) for the development of digital media pedagogies.

Not all of these elements exist at either location, but they provide a vision for an approach to providing professional development in digital media pedagogy that takes into account four key ingredients—technological infrastructure, mentors, skills training, and ongoing pedagogical support—that combine to create a culture in which digital media pedagogy and scholarship can flourish.

An issue that was not discussed in depth in the preceding chapters but has been raised by scholars in the field of computers and composition is the lack of reward for orchestrating digital media support and professional development opportunities, such as DMAC. This work, much like WPA work, typically counts as "service," even though it is a major teaching endeavor and often involves scholarly activity. Using Boyer's framework "as a springboard" (9), Barry Maid suggests a fifth scholarship, the scholarship of administration. Citing position statements by the Council of Writing Program Administrators, he argues that "programmatic administrative duties," such as those necessary for supporting digital media work in departments, are "intellectual work" that is "best done by trained professionals using their professional expertise" (12). This work often does not count much at all for tenure or promotion, even though it is a major scholarly and pedagogical contribution to the department and sometimes, as in the case of orchestrating something like DMAC, to the profession. This work is the kind of activity that is undervalued by traditional criteria and that Boyer and Gee and Alutto seek to value. Maid's scholarship of administration opens the door for "relevant administrative documents that call on [administrators'] rhetorical skills as well as their professional knowledge and expertise," such as "the integration of technology into the first-year composition curriculum and pedagogical guides to online or other distance-learning journals," to count as scholarly contributions for tenure and promotion (15). When departments discuss issues associated with creating technological ecologies for professional development with digital media, they must be sure to address this issue of evaluating and rewarding the "administrative" work as a kind of scholarship of administration and to recognize the contribution such work makes to the department and to the discipline.

Programmatic Revision

Throughout the book, I have been encouraging departments to discuss issues that digital media have raised for the discipline about textuality and to consider how their curricula, scholarly evaluation criteria, and departmental cultures might change to better support and cultivate digital media work. These conversations might lead to small incremental changes. Or, in some places, they might lead to major programmatic revisions. Some programs, in fact, are redesigning themselves to respond to the emergence of digital media and new knowledge-making structures. Kathleen Blake Yancey, for instance, describes the redesign of Florida State's rhetoric and composition program around the concept of "remix." She and her colleagues found themselves in the unique position of being able to reimagine the graduate program from the ground up, although they built upon many of the elements that were already existing, including several established courses and a visiting speaker series. She says that "in thinking about all this—about making a new, coherent program both from fragments of the old program and from new programmatic pieces—the concept that seemed to express best our program design was that of the *remix*" ("Re-designing" 5). She recognizes that remixing has a long history as "both a practice and a set of material practices," citing Shakespeare's remixing of classical sources and contemporary Italian works, children's scrapbooking as a site of literacy learning during the Georgian era, and the Renaissance practice of creating commonplace books. However, "seen through a wider lens, . . . remix—the combining of ideas, narratives, sources—is a *classical means of invention*, even (or perhaps especially) for canonical writers" (5).

In stressing remix as a process of building upon prior work, Yancey emphasizes that while it is often thought of as a technical concept, it is not necessarily inherently digital in nature. However, she and her colleagues did want the "remixed program to be informed by digital technologies in intentional and systematic ways" but to avoid "naturalizing" digital technologies ("Re-designing" 7). She says their goal was to integrate digital media in order that such media would be used "both critically and rhetorically," so they were building on theoretical scholarship about the systematic and pedagogical integration of digital media by scholars such as Cynthia Selfe and Stuart Selber (7). In addition to redesigning the program with digital technologies at its core, they also created a space (their "Digital Studio") for technological collaboration, experimentation, and professional development activities such as "workshops offered by faculty and TAs . . . and a new set of smaller symposia" (9). She argues that the reason they were able to develop the new program was because of "the set of practices and spaces *already* in place, practices and spaces permitting and encouraging re-design and remix" (10). However, she also asserts that such remixing needs to be built into their model, suggesting that ongoing reflection and conversations about the program will be necessary to its continued relevance and vitality.

I present this example not as a model for what all English graduate programs should do or even to suggest that the concept of "remix" should be at the center of English studies per se. I present it instead as an example of what is possible when a local community working from shared values collaborates to create a program responsive to our twenty-first-century literacy/media landscape while not sacrificing the rhetorical tradition or the field's shared values. What is English studies? Is it the study of a particular canon of literary works, or is it, as Scholes argues, the study of textuality, broadly understood? If it is the latter, digital media are an integral part of that and programs need to be refashioned, as Scholes suggests, around the study of textuality with digital media purposefully integrated. To accomplish this refashioning, departments need to have discussions locally about the issues of textuality raised in the previous chapters with a particular emphasis on the matrix of questions I have proposed throughout the book and a particular focus on how digital media fit with other aspects of textuality that are already a central part of the discipline.

Questions for the Future

The two questions I raised at the beginning of this chapter—What might new models of digital work look like? Who is doing such work now?— shed light on the implications for revising tenure and promotion policy, training teachers to use digital media in their classes, and generally supporting all kinds of digital media work. In order for change to occur, the following questions need to be considered within both departmental and disciplinary contexts:

- How can we evaluate work that pushes at the boundaries of academic genres without privileging any particular medium? The fault line between analysis and production needs to be seriously contemplated as we consider this question. Perhaps we can look to art or performance for models, such as curation, of how to value both digital analytical and production work.
- How can we build flexibility into graduate education while maintaining "standards"? Discussions about balancing standards with flexibility when evaluating scholarship will likely help as we consider how to create such a balance in graduate requirements. Cosmo's ideas for a multimedia candidacy exam suggest future possibilities, as do Sidonie Smith's suggestions about rethinking (and perhaps remixing) the dissertation; perhaps everybody's work doesn't have to be composed in the same medium in order to fulfill requirements.
- How can we support and encourage digital media production in any class? The analysis/production split is still alive among composition teachers, not to mention among teachers of other subjects; providing proper professional development for digital pedagogy is likely to make digital production in any class, but particularly in literature classes, more attractive and increasingly accepted.
- How can we support the time it takes to learn technology? Currently, time spent in an archive is seen as a valuable part of the process of scholarship, and scholars are often given fellowships and release time to do this; perhaps learning digital media skills could be seen as a parallel activity for scholars whose work is heavily dependent upon the use of digital media.

As we consider these questions, we should keep in mind the experiences of the individuals in this study. Ava, Alan, Benjamin, Toby, Cosmo, and

Roxie can teach us about the potentials of digital media scholarship. Their projects reveal the variety of ways that digital media could be and are being used for research and scholarly production. The tenure track faculty in this study—Ava, Toby, and Emily—can teach us about the assumptions about scholarship and medium that underwrite tenure and promotion policy. Their experiences reveal the underlying assumptions that govern how we define and conduct scholarship. Moreover, their negotiations of their professional identities reveal the role of departments and disciplines in shaping choices about digital media research and in shaping the ways that digital media are addressed in tenure and promotion policies. The PhD students in this study—Adele, Alan, Benjamin, Chester, Roxie, and Cosmo—can teach us about helping teachers learn to teach with digital media. Their attempts to come to terms with using digital media as teachers reveal the role of departments and disciplines in shaping choices about digital media teaching and in providing learning experiences focused on digital media pedagogy. As untenured faculty and PhD students, these individuals represent the future of the profession. Their negotiations of their professional identities in disciplinary and departmental contexts give us a glimpse into what the future might hold for digital media in English studies.

Notes
Bibliography
Index

Notes

Introduction: Institutional Frameworks and "the Risky Thing" of Digital Scholarship and Teaching

1. At this time, attempting to publish a traditional printed book might be at least as risky as composing a digital project. If they are not going under, university presses are publishing fewer and fewer books, especially in the humanities. English departments are going to have to seriously rethink the monograph requirement, or they risk losing a great many talented scholars because of market factors that have nothing to do with the scholarly worth of those faculty members' work. Conversations about digital media works can help lead departments to think about and discuss the underlying issue of scholarly values in ways that can help us imagine a definition of scholarship that is not bound to a single, no longer sustainable form.

1. Cultivating Digital Media Work in English Studies: Negotiating Disciplinary Questions

1. See Selfe; Tyner; Wysocki; Wysocki, Johnson-Eilola, Selfe, and Sirc; Yagelski; and Yancey, "Made Not Only in Words."

2. Ethnography is a method that involves a researcher's spending time in "the field," observing a community or culture, and gathering artifacts and interviews in order to understand how the community or culture understands itself. I say my approach is semi-ethnographic because, although I spent time observing individuals' classes and interviewing them, I did not observe faculty and graduate students in the departments I visited interacting with each other. My main goal, however, was to see these departments as communities/cultures and to study how members of these departments understand the inner workings of their departments.

3. For this terminology, I am grateful to the graduate program and policy committee of the English department at the Ohio State University, who referred to English as a "set of inter-disciplines" in an internal document.

4. Disciplinary identities can be multiple, depending on the rhetorical situation. For instance, a faculty member in rhetoric and composition, with a specialty in computers and composition, who works in an English department might identify primarily as an English professor at university functions but as a compositionist at certain conferences and as a digital media specialist in another context.

5. Of course, these are not the only realms of academic work, and in actual practice these realms overlap. However, categorizing academic work in this way not only helps to make sense of the data but also corresponds well (though not completely) to the classification system most American colleges and universities use to evaluate academic work for tenure and promotion.

2. Situating Digital Media Teaching: Challenging the "Hierarchy of Signs"

1. The university requires all undergraduate students to complete two writing courses—a first-year writing class and a second-year writing class. The first-year writing program is administered by the parallel cultures department and has a TA training course associated with it, as well as an official curriculum. The second-level writing program is a Writing Across the Curriculum initiative, and many departments across the university offer variations. The required common theme is "the American experience," and the WAC program (a college-level administrative unit) sponsors nonrequired professional development opportunities for instructors, most of whom are graduate students.

2. See Steven Heller, "Designing Hate," *Texts on Type: Critical Writings on Typography*, ed. Steven Heller and Philip B. Meggs (New York: Allworth Press, 2001), 42–44.

3. Although literature faculty are not located in the integrated literacies department, that department does include faculty in fields like cultural studies, who are as concerned with reading and texts as Scholes argues literature faculty are.

3. Scholarship through a New Lens: Digital Production and New Models of Evaluation

1. *Kairos: A Journal of Rhetoric, Technology, and Pedagogy* is one of the premier online journals in Cosmo's field. *Computers and Composition* is one of the leading print journals in Cosmo's field.

2. I have omitted the brief rationale that accompanies each question in the "MLA Evaluation Wiki."

3. The department's policy was still in draft form when I gathered my data; however, the department chair and Ava were confident that the draft would be ratified by the department with few, if any, changes.

4. The Wayback Machine, now called the Internet Archive (http://web.archive.org), began archiving web pages in 1996 and provides a way for users to find copies of websites that have become defunct.

4. Professional Development in/with Digital Media: Sustaining a Technological Ecology

1. Unfortunately, because the video used the actual theme song from *The Office*, NBC has blocked it on YouTube, alleging copyright infringement. It was previously available here: http://www.youtube.com/watch?v=6svk_r_rVhA.

2. This is a pseudonym for the center's current actual name.

3. "C-class" is the term used in this department to refer to a class that meets in a networked classroom with a computer station for each student.

4. In fact, since my interviews were conducted, the parallel cultures department has hired four faculty members with research interests in digital media studies, three at the assistant professor rank and one at the rank of professor. These hires will no doubt change the extent of mentoring in digital research, the role of the CDMS in the department, the profile of the graduate student body, and the national reputation of the department within the field of digital media studies. The importance of the department chair's leadership on these hires, especially the full professor hire, cannot be underestimated.

5. Although the number of faculty in rhetoric and composition in this department who do work with digital media has increased since my interviews (because of the return to the department of the faculty member whom the CDMS director mentions and because of hiring), there is still a dearth of faculty in fields other than rhetoric and composition who make analysis of digital texts or digital production part of their scholarly agendas.

Bibliography

"About the Project." *Digital Library of Illuminated Manuscripts*, n.d. Web. 23 June 2012. http://digital.lib.lehigh.edu/manuscripts/about.html.

Anderson, Steve, and Tara McPherson. "Engaging Digital Scholarship: Thoughts on Evaluating Multimedia Scholarship." *Profession* 2011, 136–51. Print.

Ball, Cheryl E. "Are you ready to assign multimedia projects? A pedagogical question/naire." *This Is English Studies! Classes Taught by Dr. Cheryl E. Ball*, 29 Jan. 2009. Web. 24 Feb. 2010. http://www.ceball.com/classes/.

———. "Show, Not Tell: The Value of New Media Scholarship." *Computers and Composition* 21 (2009): 403–25. Print.

Barndollar, David. "A Rationale for Teaching Hypertext Authoring in Literature Courses." *Computer Writing and Research Lab White Paper Series.* U of Texas at Austin, 22 Aug. 2003. Web. Jan. 2005. http://www.cwrl.utexas.edu/research/rationale-teaching-hypertext-authoring-literature-courses.

Bolter, Jay David. *Writing Space: Computers, Hypertext, and the Remediation of Print.* 2nd ed. Mahwah, NJ: Lawrence Erlbaum, 2001. Print.

Bolter, Jay David, and Richard Grusin. *Remediation: Understanding New Media.* Cambridge: MIT, 2000. Print.

Boyer, Ernest L. *Scholarship Reconsidered: Priorities of the Professorate.* San Francisco: Jossey-Bass, 1997. Print.

Brantley, Peter. "Storm Clouds in Academic Publishing." *Publishers Weekly* 25 May 2012. Web. 15 June 2012. http://blogs.publishersweekly.com/blogs/PWxyz/2012/05/25/storm-clouds-in-academic-publishing/.

Braun, Catherine C. "'I'm really not a technology person': Digital Media and the Discipline of English." Diss. Ohio State U, Columbus, 2006. Web. 9 Dec. 2009.

Braun, Catherine C., and Kenneth L. Gilbert. "This Is Scholarship." *Kairos: A Journal of Rhetoric, Technology, and Pedagogy* 12.3 (May 2008): n. pag. Web. June 2011. http://kairos.technorhetoric.net/12.3/binder.html?topoi/braun_gilbert/index.html.

Burgess, Helen J., and Jeanne Hamming. "New Media in the Academy: Labor and the Production of Knowledge in Scholarly Multimedia." *Digital Humanities Quarterly* 5.3 (Summer 2011): n. pag. Web. 1 Sept. 2011. http://digitalhumanities.org/dhq/vol/5/3/000102/000102.html.

Burke, Kenneth. *Language as Symbolic Action: Essays on Life, Literature, and Method.* Berkeley: U of California P, 1966. Print.

Cecire, Natalia. "It's Not 'the Job Market'; It's the Profession (and It's Your Problem Too)." *Works Cited* 25 Sept. 2011. Web. 15 June 2012. http://nataliacecire.blogspot.com/2011/09/its-not-job-market-its-profession-and.html.

Cohen, Dan, Stephen Ramsay, and Kathleen Fitzpatrick. "Open Access and Scholarly Values: A Conversation." *Hacking the Academy.* Ed. Dan Cohen and Tom Scheinfeldt. Ann Arbor: U of Michigan P and MPublishing, 2011. Web. 10 Sept. 2011. http://www.digitalculture.org/hacking-the-academy/.

Cohen, Dan, and Tom Scheinfeldt, eds. *Hacking the Academy.* Ann Arbor: U of Michigan P and MPublishing, 2011. Web. http://www.digitalculture.org /hacking-the-academy/.

———. "Preface." *Hacking the Academy.* Ed. Dan Cohen and Tom Scheinfeldt. Ann Arbor: U of Michigan P and MPublishing, 2011. Web. 10 Sept. 2011. http://www.digitalculture.org/hacking-the-academy/.

Computers and Composition Digital Press. Utah State UP, n.d. Web. 23 June 2012. http://ccdigitalpress.org/.

Conference on College Composition and Communication. "CCCC's Promotion and Tenure Guidelines for Work with Technology." *NCTE* 1998. Web. Sept. 2004. http://www.ncte.org/cccc/resources/positions/promotionandtenure.

"Cost Death of Academic Publishing." *ReMix: News from the Stanford Libraries* 35 (9 Dec. 2010). Web. 10 Sept. 2011. http://hosted.verticalresponse.com /260487/e651672620/

Cushman, Ellen. "New Media Scholarship and Teaching: Challenging the Hierarchy of Signs." *Pedagogy* 11.1 (2010): 63–79. Print.

Daley, Elizabeth. "Expanding the Concept of Literacy." *EDUCAUSE Review* March/ April 2003: 32–40. Web. April 2003.

Davidson, Cathy N. "Humanities 2.0: Promise, Perils, Predictions." *PMLA* 123.3 (2008): 707–17. Print.

Delagrange, Susan. "When Revision Is Redesign: Key Questions for Digital Scholarship." *Kairos: A Journal of Rhetoric, Technology, and Pedagogy* 14.1 (Fall 2009): n. pag. Web. 15 Sept. 2011.

———. "*Wunderkammer,* Cornell, and the Visual Canon of Arrangement." *Kairos: A Journal of Rhetoric, Technology, and Pedagogy* 13.2 (Spring 2009): n. pag. Web. 20 July 2011.

"Different Paths to Full Professor." *Inside Higher Ed* 5 March 2010, n. pag. Web. 15 Sept. 2011. http://umassmsp.org/different_paths_to_full_professor_ %28inside_higher_ed%29.

Digital Archive of Literacy Narratives. Web. 23 June 2012. http://daln.osu.edu/.

Digital Commons@USU. Utah State UP, n.d. Web. 23 June 2012. http://digitalcommons .usu.edu/.

Digital Humanities Quarterly. Web. 23 June 2012. http://www.digitalhumanities .org/dhq/.

Digital Media and Composing Institute (DMAC) at the Ohio State University. Web. 23 June 2012. http://dmp.osu.edu/dmac/.

Donoghue, Frank. "The Closing of University Presses, Part 2." *Innovations: Insights and Commentary on Higher Education* 4 June 2012. Web. 15 June 2012. http://chronicle.com/blogs/innovations/the-closing-of-university -presses-part-2/32681.

———. "The Consequences of Closing University Presses." *Innovations: Insights and Commentary on Higher Education* 30 May 2012. Web. 15 June 2012. http://chronicle.com/blogs/innovations/the-consequences-of-closing -university-presses/32639.

Elbow, Peter. *What Is English?* New York: MLA, 1990. Print.

Eligon, John. "Missouri Rewrites Plot, Rehiring Editor in Chief of the University Press." *New York Times* 5 Oct. 2012. Web. 14 January 2013. http://www.nytimes.com/2012/10/06/us/missouri-rewrites-plot-rehiring-editor-in-chief-of-the-university-press.html?_r=0.

Ellertson, Anthony. "Some Notes on Simulacra Machines, Flash in FYC & Tactics in Spaces of Interruption." *Kairos: A Journal of Rhetoric, Technology, and Pedagogy* 8.2 (Fall 2003): n. pag. Web. 30 Jan. 2004. http://english.ttu.edu/kairos/8.2/index.html.

Eyman, Douglas, Stephanie Sheffield, and Dànielle Nicole DeVoss. "Developing Sustainable Research Networks in Graduate Education." *Computers and Composition* 26 (2009): 49–57. Print.

Feenberg, Andrew. *Questioning Technology.* New York: Routledge, 1999. Print.

Fitzpatrick, Kathleen. "Do 'the Risky Thing' in Digital Humanities." *Chronicle of Higher Education* 5 Sept. 2011. Web. 28 Sept. 2011. http://chronicle.com/article/Do-the-Risky-Thing-in/129132/.

———. "Obsolescence." *PMLA* 123.3 (2008): 718–22. Print.

———. "On the Future of Academic Publishing, Peer Review, and Tenure Requirements." *The Valve, A Literary Organ* (6 Jan. 2006): n. pag. Web. Feb. 2006. http://www.thevalve.org/go/valve/article/on_the_future_of_academic_publishing_peer_review_and_tenure_requirements_or/.

———. "Open Access Publishing." *Hacking the Academy.* Ann Arbor: U of Michigan P and MPublishing, 2011. Web. 10 Sept. 2011. http://www.digitalculture.org/hacking-the-academy/.

———. *Planned Obsolescence: Publishing, Technology, and the Future of the Academy.* New York: NYUP, 2009. MediaCommons Press. Web. 10 Aug. 2011. http://mediacommons.futureofthebook.org/mcpress/plannedobsolescence/.

Galarza, Alex. "Graduate Training and the Digital Humanities." *gradhacker* 30 Sept. 2011. Web. 15 June 2012. http://www.gradhacker.org/2011/09/30/graduate-training-and-the-digital-humanities/.

Graupner, Meredith, Lee Nickoson-Massey, and Kristine Blair. "Remediating Knowledge-Making Spaces in the Graduate Curriculum: Developing and Sustaining Multimodal Teaching and Research." *Computers and Composition* 26 (2009): 13–23. Print.

Horizon Report. Austin, TX: The New Media Consortium, 2006. Web. 1 Feb 2006. http://www.nmc.org/pdf/2006_Horizon_Report.pdf.

Howard, Jennifer. "Planned Shutdown of U. of Missouri Press Underscores Shift in Traditional Publishing." *Chronicle of Higher Education* 25 May 2011. Web. 15 June 2012. http://chronicle.com/article/Planned-Shutdown-of-U-of/132026/.

Journet, Debra. "Inventing Myself in Multimodality: Encouraging Senior Faculty to Use Digital Media." *Computers and Composition* 24 (2007): 107–20. Print.

"The Kairos Editorial Review Process." *Kairos: A Journal of Rhetoric, Technology, and Pedagogy,* n.d. Web. Sept. 2011. http://kairos.technorhetoric.net/board.html.

Kelly, Mills. "Making Scholarship Count." *Hacking the Academy.* Ann Arbor: U of Michigan P and MPublishing, 2011. Web. 10 Sept. 2011. http://www.digitalculture.org/hacking-the-academy/.

Killoran, John B. "@ home among the .coms: Virtual Rhetoric in the Agora of the Web." *Alternative Rhetorics: Challenges to the Rhetorical Tradition.* Ed. Laura Gray-Rosendale and Sibylle Gruber. Albany: SUNY, 2001. 127–47. Print.

Kress, Gunther. "'English' at the Crossroads: Rethinking Curricula of Communication in the Context of the Turn to the Visual." *Passions, Pedagogies, and 21st Century Technologies.* Ed. Gail E. Hawisher and Cynthia L. Selfe. Logan: Utah State UP, 1999. Print.

———. *Literacy in the New Media Age.* New York: Routledge, 2003. Print.

———. "Multimodality, Multimedia, and Genre." *Visual Rhetoric in a Digital World: A Critical Sourcebook.* Ed. Carolyn Handa. Boston: Bedford/St. Martin's, 2004. 38–54. Print.

Kress, Gunther, and Theo Van Leeuwen. *Multimodal Discourse: The Modes and Media of Contemporary Communication.* New York: Oxford UP, 2001. Print.

Lanham, Robert. "Internet-Age Writing Syllabus and Course Overview." *McSweeney's Internet Tendency* (April 2009): n. pag. Web. May 2009. http://www.mcsweeneys.net/2009/4/20lanham.html.

Lee, Valerie, and Cynthia L. Selfe. "Our Capacious Caper: Exposing Print-Culture Bias in Departmental Tenure Documents." *ADE Bulletin* (Spring 2008): 51–58. Print.

Lindeman, Lis, and Gregory O. Smith. "Literature and Digital Illumination." *Kairos: A Journal of Rhetoric, Technology, and Pedagogy* 12.3 (2008): n. pag. Web. 20 July 2011.

Lunsford, Andrea, and Lisa Ede. *Singular Texts/Plural Authors: Perspectives on Collaborative Writing.* Carbondale: Southern Illinois UP, 1990. Print.

Maid, Barry. "Yes, a Technorhetorician Can Get Tenure." *Computers and Composition* 17 (2000): 9–18. Print.

McGann, Jerome. "On Creating a Usable Future." *Profession* 2011, 182–95. Print.

MLA. "Guidelines for Evaluating Work with Digital Media in the Modern Languages." *MLA*, 2000: n. pag. Web. http://www.mla.org/guidelines_evaluation_digital.

"MLA Evaluation Wiki." *Modern Language Association.* MLA, n.d. Web. Sept. 2011. http://wiki.mla.org/index.php/Evaluation_Wiki.

MLA Task Force on Evaluating Scholarship for Tenure and Promotion. "Report of the MLA Task Force on Evaluating Scholarship for Tenure and Promotion." *Modern Language Association* (2006) and *Profession* (2007). Web. Jan. 2007. http://www.mla.org/tenure_promotion.

Monaghan, Peter. "Clair Willcox Is Rehired as Editor in Chief at U. of Missouri Press." *PageView: News and Notes on Scholarly Publishing* 6 Oct. 2012. Web. 14 Jan. 2013. http://chronicle.com/blogs/pageview/clair-willcox-rehired-as-editor-in-chief-at-u-of-missouri-press/30938.

———. "Critics Attack Closing of U. of Missouri Press." *PageView: News and Notes on Scholarly Publishing* 7 June 2012. Web. 15 June 2012.

Nardi, Bonnie A., and Vicki L. O'Day. *Information Ecologies: Using Technology with Heart.* Cambridge: MIT, 1999. Print.

NINES: Nineteenth-Century Scholarship Online. N.p., n.d. Web. 1 Dec. 2011. http://www.nines.org.

Nowviskie, Bethany. "Where Credit Is Due: Preconditions for the Evaluation of Collaborative Digital Scholarship." *Profession* 2011, 169–81. Print.

Poetess Archive Journal. Web. 23 June 2012. http://paj.muohio.edu.

Purdy, James P., and Joyce R. Walker. "Scholarship on the Move: A Rhetorical Analysis of Scholarly Activity in Digital Spaces." *The New Work of Composing.* Ed. Debra Journet, Cheryl E. Ball, and Ryan Trauman. Logan: Computers and Composition Digital Press and Utah State UP, 2012. Web. http://ccdigitalpress.org/nwc.

———. "Valuing Digital Scholarship: Exploring the Changing Realities of Intellectual Work." *Profession* 2010, 177–95. Print.

Rickly, Rebecca. "The Tenure of the Oppressed: Ambivalent Reflections from a Critical Optimist." *Computers and Composition* 17 (2000): 19–30. Print.

Rockwell, Geoffrey. "On the Evaluation of Digital Media as Scholarship." *Profession* 2011, 152–68. Print.

Scholes, Robert. *The Rise and Fall of English.* New Haven: Yale UP, 1998. Print.

Schreibman, Susan, Laura Mandell, and Stephen Olsen. "Introduction." *Profession* 2011, 123–35. Print.

Selber, Stuart A. *Multiliteracies for a Digital Age.* Carbondale: Southern Illinois UP, 2004. Print.

Selfe, Cynthia L. *Technology and Literacy in the Twenty-First Century: The Importance of Paying Attention.* Carbondale: Southern Illinois UP, 1999. Print.

Selfe, Cynthia L., and Gail E. Hawisher. *Literate Lives in the Information Age: Narratives of Literacy from the United States.* Mahwah, NJ: Lawrence Erlbaum, 2004. Print.

Selfe, Cynthia L, Gail E. Hawisher, and Patrick W. Berry. "Sustaining Scholarly Efforts: The Challenge of Digital Media." *Technological Ecologies and Sustainability.* Ed. Dànielle Nicole DeVoss, Heidi A. McKee, and Richard (Dickie) Selfe. Logan: Computers and Composition Digital Press and Utah State UP, 2009. *Computers and Composition Digital Press.* Web. 23 Sept. 2011. http://ccdigitalpress.org/ebooks-and-projects/tes.

Selfe, Cynthia L., and Richard J. Selfe, Jr. "The Politics of the Interface: Power and Its Exercise in Electronic Contact Zones." *College Composition and Communication* 45.5 (Dec. 1994): 480–504. Print.

Selfe, Dickie, Dànielle Nicole DeVoss, and Heidi A. McKee. "Collectives, Common Worlds, and the Idea of Sustainability: An Introduction." *Technological Ecologies and Sustainability.* Ed. Dànielle Nicole DeVoss, Heidi A. McKee, and Richard (Dickie) Selfe. Logan: Computers and Composition Digital Press and Utah State UP, 2009. *Computers and Composition Digital Press.* Web. 23 Sept. 2011. http://ccdigitalpress.org/ebooks-and-projects/tes.

Selfe, Richard. *Sustainable Computer Environments: Cultures of Support in English Studies and Language Arts.* Cresskill, NJ: Hampton, 2004. Print.

———. "Technological Activism: Understanding and Shaping Environments for Technology-Rich Communication." In *Resources in Technical Communication: Outcomes and Approaches.* Ed. Cynthia L. Selfe. Norwood, NJ: Baywood Publishing, 2007. 145–60. Print.

"Shakespeare Quarterly Open Review: 'Shakespeare and New Media.'" MediaCommons Press. Web. 10 August 2011.

Sheppard, Jennifer. "The Rhetorical Work of Multimedia Production Practices: It's More Than Just Technical Skill." *Computers and Composition* 26 (2009): 122–31. Print.

Silver, Naomi. "Sweetland, U-M Press, and MPublishing Launch Digital Rhetoric Collaborative Website and Book Series." *Record Update*, Office of the Vice President for Communications, University of Michigan, 19 June 2012. Web. 23 June 2012. http://www.ur.umich.edu/update/archives/120619/sweetland.

Silvey, Janese. "University Rehires Former UM Press Editor-in-Chief." *Columbia Daily Tribune* 5 Oct. 2012. Web. 14 January 2013. http://www.columbiatribune .com/news/education/university-rehires-former-um-press-editor-in-chief /article_86c8c7cb-01b8–5194-a90a-278e547aaa07.html.

Smith, Sidonie. "An Agenda for the New Dissertation." *MLA Newsletter* 42.2 (2010): 2–3. Print.

———. "Beyond the Dissertation Monograph." *MLA Newsletter* 42.1 (2010): 2–3. Print.

Takayoshi, Pamela, and Brian Huot. *Teaching Writing with Computers*. Boston: Houghton Mifflin, 2003. Print.

Thaiss, Chris, and Terry Myers Zawacki. *Engaged Writers Dynamic Disciplines: Research on the Academic Writing Life*. Portsmouth, NH: Boynton/Cook, Heinemann, 2006. Print.

Tyner, Kathleen. *Literacy in a Digital World: Teaching and Learning in the Age of Information*. Mahwah, NJ: Lawrence Erlbaum, 1998. Print.

"UM System to Continue to Focus on Strategic Priorities." *Inside UM System*. The Curators of the University of Missouri, 24 May 2012. Web. 14 June 2012. http://www.umsystem.edu/ums/news/news_releases/052412_news.

Unsworth, John. "Scholarly Primitives: What Methods Do Humanities Researchers Have in Common, and How Might Our Tools Reflect This?" Symposium on Humanities Computing: Formal Methods, Experimental Practice. King's College, London, 13 May 2000. Web. January 2005. http://www3 .isrl.illinois.edu/~unsworth/Kings.5–00/primitives.html.

Walker, Joyce. "Hyper.Activity." *Kairos: A Journal of Rhetoric, Technology, and Pedagogy* 10.1 (Spring 2006): n. pag. Web. Jan. 2007. http://kairos.technorhetoric .net/10.2/binder2.html?coverweb/walker/index.html.

Wysocki, Anne Frances. "Opening New Media to Writing: Openings and Justifications." *Writing New Media: Theory and Applications for Expanding the Teaching of Composition*. Ed. Anne Frances Wysocki, Johndan Johnson-Eilola, Cynthia L. Selfe, and Geoffrey Sirc. Logan: Utah State UP, 2004. 1–41. Print.

———. "With Eyes That Think, and Compose, and Think: On Visual Rhetoric." *Teaching Writing with Computers*. Ed. Pamela Takayoshi and Brian Huot. Boston: Houghton Mifflin, 2003. 182–201. Print.

Wysocki, Anne Frances, Johndan Johnson-Eilola, Cynthia L. Selfe, and Geoffrey Sirc. *Writing New Media: Theory and Applications for Expanding the Teaching of Composition*. Logan: Utah State UP, 2004. Print.

Yagelski, Robert. *Literacy Matters: Writing and Reading the Social Self*. New York: Teachers College, 2000. Print.

Yancey, Kathleen Blake. "Made Not Only in Words: Composition in a New Key." *College Composition and Communication* 56.2 (2004): 297–328. Print.

———. "Re-designing Graduate Education in Composition and Rhetoric: The Use of Remix as Concept, Material, and Method." *Computers and Composition* 26 (2009): 4–12. Print.

Index

Page numbers in italics refer to tables and figures.

Catherine C. Braun is an associate professor of English at the Ohio State University at Marion, where she teaches courses in digital media, professional writing, composition, and film studies. Her scholarly interests include digital pedagogy, professional writing, basic writing, and professional issues, and she has published both traditional and digital/multimodal texts on these topics in venues such as *Computers and Composition Online* and *Kairos: A Journal of Rhetoric, Technology, and Pedagogy.*